D0055533

LANGUAGE

Edward Sapir was born in Pomerania, Germany, in 1884, and came to this country at the age of five. He first made his reputation as an expert on languages of the American Indian. He taught at the University of Chicago and later at Yale, and was one of the first to explore the relations between language studies and anthropology. He died in 1939. *Language,* first published in 1921, is his only full-length book for a general audience. He published a great many articles and some verse in periodicals.

LANGUAGE

An Introduction to the Study of Speech

BY EDWARD SAPIR

1368

A HARVEST BOOK

Harcourt, Brace and Company · New York

PREFACE

This little book aims to give a certain perspective on the subject of language rather than to assemble facts about it. It has little to say of the ultimate psychological basis of speech and gives only enough of the actual descriptive or historical facts of particular languages to illustrate principles. Its main purpose is to show what I conceive language to be, what is its variability in place and time, and what are its relations to other fundamental human interests—the problem of thought, the nature of the historical process, race, culture, art.

The perspective thus gained will be useful, I hope, both to linguistic students and to the outside public that is half inclined to dismiss linguistic notions as the private pedantries of essentially idle minds. Knowledge of the wider relations of their science is essential to professional students of language if they are to be saved from a sterile and purely technical attitude. Among contemporary writers of influence on liberal thought Croce is one of the very few who have gained an understanding of the fundamental significance of language. He has pointed out its close relation to the problem of art. I am deeply indebted to him for this insight. Quite aside from their intrinsic interest, linguistic forms and historical processes have the greatest possible diagnostic value for the understanding of some of the more difficult and elusive problems in the psychology of thought and in the strange, cumulative drift in the life of the human spirit that we call history or progress or evolution. This value depends chiefly on the unconscious and unrationalized nature of linguistic structure.

I have avoided most of the technical terms and all of the technical symbols of the linguistic academy. There is not a single diacritical mark in the book. Where possible, the discussion is based on English material. It was necessary, however, for the scheme of the book, which includes a consideration of the protean forms in which human thought has found expression, to quote some exotic instances. For these no apology seems necessary. Owing to limitations of space I have had to leave out many ideas or principles that I should have liked to touch upon. Other points have had to be barely hinted at in a sentence or flying phrase. Nevertheless, I trust that enough has here been brought together to serve as a stimulus for the more fundamental study of a neglected field.

I desire to express my cordial appreciation of the friendly advice and helpful suggestions of a number of friends who have read the work in manuscript, notably Profs. A. L. Kroeber and R. H. Lowie of the University of California, Prof. W. D. Wallis of Reed College, and Prof. J. Zeitlin of the University of Illinois.

EDWARD SAPIR

Ottawa, Ont.
April 8, 1921

CONTENTS

by phonetic laws. New morphological features due to phonetic change.

LANGUAGE

CHAPTER I

Introductory: Language Defined

❍

Speech is so familiar a feature of daily life that we rarely pause to define it. It seems as natural to man as walking, and only less so than breathing. Yet it needs but a moment's reflection to convince us that this naturalness of speech is but an illusory feeling. The process of acquiring speech is, in sober fact, an utterly different sort of thing from the process of learning to walk. In the case of the latter function, culture, in other words, the traditional body of social usage, is not seriously brought into play. The child is individually equipped, by the complex set of factors that we term biological heredity, to make all the needed muscular and nervous adjustments that result in walking. Indeed, the very conformation of these muscles and of the appropriate parts of the nervous system may be said to be primarily adapted to the movements made in walking and in similar activities. In a very real sense the normal human being is predestined to walk, not because his elders will assist him to learn the art, but because his organism is prepared from birth, or even from the moment of conception, to take on all those expenditures of nervous energy and all those muscular adaptations that result in walking. To put it concisely, walking is an inherent, biological function of man.

Not so language. It is of course true that in a certain sense the individual is predestined to talk, but that is due entirely to the circumstance that he is born not merely in nature, but in the lap of a society that is certain, reasonably certain, to lead him to its traditions. Eliminate society and there is every reason to believe that he will learn to walk, if, indeed, he survives at all. But it is just as certain that he will never learn to talk, that is, to communicate ideas according to the traditional system of a particular society. Or, again, remove the new-born individual from the social environment into which he has come and transplant him to an utterly alien one. He will develop the art of walking in his new environment very much as he would have developed it in the old. But his speech will be completely at variance with the speech of his native environment. Walking, then, is a general human activity that varies only within circumscribed limits as we pass from individual to individual. Its variability is involuntary and purposeless. Speech is a human activity that varies without assignable limit as we pass from social group to social group, because it is a purely historical heritage of the group, the product of long-continued social usage. It varies as all creative effort varies—not as consciously, perhaps, but none the less as truly as do the religions, the beliefs, the customs, and the arts of different peoples. Walking is an organic, an instinctive, function (not, of course, itself an instinct); speech is a non-instinctive, acquired, "cultural" function.

There is one fact that has frequently tended to prevent the recognition of language as a merely conventional system of sound symbols, that has seduced the popular mind into attributing to it an instinctive basis that it does not really possess. This is the well-known observation that under the stress of emotion, say of a sudden twinge of pain or of unbridled joy, we do involuntarily give utterance to sounds that the hearer

nterprets as indicative of the emotion itself. But there
s all the difference in the world between such involuntary expression of feeling and the normal type of
communication of ideas that is speech. The former
kind of utterance is indeed instinctive, but it is non-
symbolic; in other words, the sound of pain or the
sound of joy does not, as such, indicate the emotion,
t does not stand aloof, as it were, and announce that
such and such an emotion is being felt. What it does
s to serve as a more or less automatic overflow of the
emotional energy; in a sense, it is part and parcel of
the emotion itself. Moreover, such instinctive cries
hardly constitute communication in any strict sense.
They are not addressed to any one, they are merely
overheard, if heard at all, as the bark of a dog, the
sound of approaching footsteps, or the rustling of
the wind is heard. If they convey certain ideas to the
hearer, it is only in the very general sense in which
any and every sound or even any phenomenon in our
environment may be said to convey an idea to the perceiving mind. If the involuntary cry of pain which is
conventionally represented by "Oh!" be looked upon
as a true speech symbol equivalent to some such idea
as "I am in great pain," it is just as allowable to in-
terpret the appearance of clouds as an equivalent symbol that carries the definite message "It is likely to
rain." A definition of language, however, that is so
extended as to cover every type of inference becomes
utterly meaningless.

The mistake must not be made of identifying our
conventional interjections (our oh! and ah! and sh!)
with the instinctive cries themselves. These interjections are merely conventional fixations of the natural
sounds. They therefore differ widely in various languages in accordance with the specific phonetic genius
of each of these. As such they may be considered an
integral portion of speech, in the properly cultural
sense of the term, being no more identical with the in-

stinctive cries themselves than such words as "cuckoo" and "killdeer" are identical with the cries of the birds they denote or than Rossini's treatment of a storm in the overture to "William Tell" is in fact a storm. In other words, the interjections and sound-imitative words of normal speech are related to their natural prototypes as is art, a purely social or cultural thing, to nature. It may be objected that, though the interjections differ somewhat as we pass from language to language, they do nevertheless offer striking family resemblances and may therefore be looked upon as having grown up out of a common instinctive base. But their case is nowise different from that, say, of the varying national modes of pictorial representation. A Japanese picture of a hill both differs from and resembles a typical modern European painting of the same kind of hill. Both are suggested by and both "imitate" the same natural feature. Neither the one nor the other is the same thing as, or, in any intelligible sense, a direct outgrowth of, this natural feature. The two modes of representation are not identical because they proceed from differing historical traditions, are executed with differing pictorial techniques. The interjections of Japanese and English are, just so, suggested by a common natural prototype, the instinctive cries, and are thus unavoidably suggestive of each other. They differ, now greatly, now but little, because they are builded out of historically diverse materials or techniques, the respective linguistic traditions, phonetic systems, speech habits of the two peoples. Yet the instinctive cries as such are practically identical for all humanity, just as the human skeleton or nervous system is to all intents and purposes a "fixed," that is, an only slightly and "accidentally" variable, feature of man's organism.

Interjections are among the least important of speech elements. Their discussion is valuable mainly because it can be shown that even they, avowedly the nearest of all language sounds to instinctive utterance, are only superficially of an instinctive nature. Were it therefore possible to demonstrate that the whole of language is traceable, in its ultimate historical and psychological foundations, to the interjections, it would still not follow that language is an instinctive activity. But, as a matter of fact, all attempts so to explain the origin of speech have been fruitless. There is no tangible evidence, historical or otherwise, tending to show that the mass of speech elements and speech processes has evolved out of the interjections. These are a very small and functionally insignificant proportion of the vocabulary of language; at no time and in no linguistic province that we have record of do we see a noticeable tendency towards their elaboration into the primary warp and woof of language. They are never more, at best, than a decorative edging to the ample, complex fabric.

What applies to the interjections applies with even greater force to the sound-imitative words. Such words as "whippoorwill," "to mew," "to caw" are in no sense natural sounds that man has instinctively or automatically reproduced. They are just as truly creations of the human mind, flights of the human fancy, as anything else in language. They do not directly grow out of nature, they are suggested by it and play with it. Hence the onomatopoetic theory of the origin of speech, the theory that would explain all speech as a gradual evolution from sounds of an imitative character, really brings us no nearer to the instinctive level than is language as we know it to-day. As to the theory itself, it is scarcely more credible than its interjectional counterpart. It is true that a number of words which we do not now feel to have a sound-imitative value can be shown to have once had a phonetic form that strongly suggests their origin as imitations of natural sounds. Such is the English word "to laugh." For all that, it is quite impossible to show, nor does it seem intrinsically reasonable to suppose, that more than a negligible proportion of the elements of speech or anything at all of its formal apparatus is derivable from an onomatopoetic source. However much we may be disposed on general principles to assign a fundamental importance in the languages of primitive peoples to the imitation of natural sounds, the actual fact of the matter is that these languages show no particular preference for imitative words. Among the most primitive peoples of aboriginal America, the Athabaskan tribes of the Mackenzie River speak languages in which such words seem to be nearly or entirely absent, while they are used freely enough in languages as sophisticated as English and German. Such an instance shows how little the essential nature of speech is concerned with the mere imitation of things.

The way is now cleared for a serviceable definition of language. Language is a purely human and non-instinctive method of communicating ideas, emotions, and desires by means of a system of voluntarily produced symbols. These symbols are, in the first instance, auditory and they are produced by the so-called "organs of speech." There is no discernible instinctive basis in human speech as such, however much instinctive expressions and the natural environment may serve as a stimulus for the development of certain elements of speech, however much instinctive tendencies, motor and other, may give a predetermined range or mold to linguistic expression. Such human or animal communication, if "communication" it may be called, as is brought about by involuntary, instinctive cries is not, in our sense, language at all.

I have just referred to the "organs of speech," and it would seem at first blush that this is tantamount to an admission that speech itself is an instinctive, biologically predetermined activity. We must not be misled by the mere term. There are, properly speaking, no organs of speech; there are only organs that are incidentally useful in the production of speech sounds. The lungs, the larynx, the palate, the nose, the tongue, the teeth, and the lips, are all so utilized, but they are no more to be thought of as primary organs of speech than are the fingers to be considered as essentially organs of piano-playing or the knees as organs of prayer. Speech is not a simple activity that is carried on by one or more organs biologically adapted to the purpose. It is an extremely complex and ever-shifting network of adjustments—in the brain, in the nervous system, and in the articulating and auditory organs— tending towards the desired end of communication. The lungs developed, roughly speaking, in connection with the necessary biological function known as breathing; the nose, as an organ of smell; the teeth, as organs useful in breaking up food before it was ready for digestion. If, then, these and other organs are being constantly utilized in speech, it is only because any organ, once existent and in so far as it is subject to voluntary control, can be utilized by man for secondary purposes. Physiologically, speech is an overlaid function, or, to be more precise, a group of overlaid functions. It gets what service it can out of organs and functions, nervous and muscular, that have come into being and are maintained for very different ends than its own.

It is true that physiological psychologists speak of the localization of speech in the brain. This can only mean that the sounds of speech are localized in the auditory tract of the brain, or in some circumscribed portion of it, precisely as other classes of sounds are localized; and that the motor processes involved in speech (such as the movements of the glottal cords in the larynx, the movements of the tongue required to pronounce the vowels, lip movements required to articulate certain consonants, and numerous others) are localized in the motor tract precisely as are all other impulses to special motor activities. In the same way control is lodged in the visual tract of the brain over all those processes of visual recognition involved in reading. Naturally the particular points or clusters of points of localization in the several tracts that refer to any element of language are connected in the brain by paths of association, so that the outward, or psycho-physical, aspect of language is of a vast network of associated localizations in the brain and lower nervous tracts, the auditory localizations being without doubt the most fundamental of all for speech. However, a speech-sound localized in the brain, even when associated with the particular movements of the "speech organs" that are required to produce it, is very far from being an element of language. It must be further associated with some element or group of elements of experience, say a visual image or a class of visual images or a feeling of relation, before it has even rudimentary linguistic significance. This "element" of experience is the content or "meaning" of the linguistic unit; the associated auditory, motor, and other cerebral processes that lie immediately back of the act of speaking and the act of hearing speech are merely a complicated symbol of or signal for these "meanings," of which more anon. We see therefore at once that language as such is not and cannot be definitely localized, for it consists of a peculiar symbolic relation—physiologically an arbitrary one—between all possible elements of consciousness on the one hand and certain selected elements localized in the auditory, motor, and other cerebral and nervous tracts on the other. If language can be said to be definitely "localized" in the brain, it is only in that general and rather useless sense in which all aspects of consciousness, all human interest and activity, may be said to be "in the brain." Hence, we have no recourse but to accept language as a fully formed functional system within man's psychic or "spiritual" constitution. We cannot define it as an entity in psycho-physical terms alone, however much the psycho-physical basis is essential to its functioning in the individual.

From the physiologist's or psychologist's point of view we may seem to be making an unwarrantable abstraction in desiring to handle the subject of speech without constant and explicit reference to that basis. However, such an abstraction is justifiable. We can profitably discuss the intention, the form, and the history of speech, precisely as we discuss the nature of any other phase of human culture—say art or religion—as an institutional or cultural entity, leaving the organic and psychological mechanisms back of it as something to be taken for granted. Accordingly, it must be clearly understood that this introduction to the study of speech is not concerned with those aspects of physiology and of physiological psychology that underlie speech. Our study of language is not to be one of the genesis and operation of a concrete mechanism; it is, rather, to be an inquiry into the function and form of the arbitrary systems of symbolism that we term languages.

I have already pointed out that the essence of language consists in the assigning of conventional, voluntarily articulated, sounds, or of their equivalents, to the diverse elements of experience. The word "house" is not a linguistic fact if by it is meant merely the acoustic effect produced on the ear by its constituent consonants and vowels, pronounced in a certain order; nor the motor processes and tactile feelings which make up the articulation of the word; nor the visual perception on the part of the hearer of this articulation; nor the visual perception of the word "house" on the written or printed page; nor the motor processes and tactile feelings which enter into the writing of the word; nor the memory of any or all of these experiences. It is only when these, and possibly still other, associated experiences are automatically asso-

ciated with the image of a house that they begin to
take on the nature of a symbol, a word, an element of
language. But the mere fact of such an association is
not enough. One might have heard a particular word
spoken in an individual house under such impressive
circumstances that neither the word nor the image
of the house ever recur in consciousness without the
other becoming present at the same time. This type
of association does not constitute speech. The association must be a purely symbolic one; in other words,
the word must denote, tag off, the image, must have
no other significance than to serve as a counter to
refer to it whenever it is necessary or convenient to
do so. Such an association, voluntary and, in a sense,
arbitrary as it is, demands a considerable exercise of
self-conscious attention. At least to begin with, for
habit soon makes the association nearly as automatic
as any and more rapid than most.

But we have traveled a little too fast. Were the symbol "house"—whether an auditory, motor, or visual
experience or image—attached but to the single image of a particular house once seen, it might perhaps,
by an indulgent criticism, be termed an element of
speech, yet it is obvious at the outset that speech so
constituted would have little or no value for purposes
of communication. The world of our experiences must
be enormously simplified and generalized before it is
possible to make a symbolic inventory of all our experiences of things and relations and this inventory is
imperative before we can convey ideas. The elements
of language, the symbols that ticket off experience,
must therefore be associated with whole groups, delimited classes, of experience rather than with the
single experiences themselves. Only so is communication possible, for the single experience lodges in an
individual consciousness and is, strictly speaking, in-
communicable. To be communicated it needs to be
referred to a class which is tacitly accepted by the

community as an identity. Thus, the single impression which I have had of a particular house must be identified with all my other impressions of it. Further, my generalized memory or my "notion" of this house must be merged with the notions that all other individuals who have seen the house have formed of it. The particular experience that we started with has now been widened so as to embrace all possible impressions or images that sentient beings have formed or may form of the house in question. This first simplification of experience is at the bottom of a large number of elements of speech, the so-called proper nouns or names of single individuals or objects. It is, essentially, the type of simplification which underlies, or forms the crude subject of, history and art. But we cannot be content with this measure of reduction of the infinity of experience. We must cut to the bone of things, we must more or less arbitrarily throw whole masses of experience together as similar enough to warrant their being looked upon—mistakenly, but conveniently—as identical. This house and that house and thousands of other phenomena of like character are thought of as having enough in common, in spite of great and obvious differences of detail, to be classed under the same heading. In other words, the speech element "house" is the symbol, first and foremost, not of a single perception, nor even of the notion of a particular object, but of a "concept," in other words, of a convenient capsule of thought that embraces thousands of distinct experiences and that is ready to take in thousands more. If the single significant elements of speech are the symbols of concepts, the actual flow of speech may be interpreted as a record of the setting of these concepts into mutual relations.

The question has often been raised whether thought is possible without speech; further, if speech and thought be not but two facets of the same psychic process. The question is all the more difficult because it has been hedged about by misunderstandings. In the first place, it is well to observe that whether or not thought necessitates symbolism, that is speech, the flow of language itself is not always indicative of thought. We have seen that the typical linguistic element labels a concept. It does not follow from this that the use to which language is put is always or even mainly conceptual. We are not in ordinary life so much concerned with concepts as such as with concrete particularities and specific relations. When I say, for instance, "I had a good breakfast this morning," it is clear that I am not in the throes of laborious thought, that what I have to transmit is hardly more than a pleasurable memory symbolically rendered in the grooves of habitual expression. Each element in the sentence defines a separate concept or conceptual relation or both combined, but the sentence as a whole has no conceptual significance whatever. It is somewhat as though a dynamo capable of generating enough power to run an elevator were operated almost exclusively to feed an electric doorbell. The parallel is more suggestive than at first sight appears. Language may be looked upon as an instrument capable of running a gamut of psychic uses. Its flow not only parallels that of the inner content of consciousness, but parallels it on different levels, ranging from the state of mind that is dominated by particular images to that in which abstract concepts and their relations are alone at the focus of attention and which is ordinarily termed reasoning. Thus the outward form only of language is constant; its inner meaning, its psychic value or intensity, varies freely with attention or the selective interest of the mind, also, needless to say, with the mind's general development. From the point of view of language, thought may be defined as the highest latent or potential content of speech, the content that is obtained by interpreting each of the elements in the flow of language as possessed of its very fullest conceptual value. From this it follows at once that language and thought are not strictly coterminous. At best language can but be the outward facet of thought on the highest, most generalized, level of symbolic expression. To put our viewpoint somewhat differently, language is primarily a pre-rational function. It humbly works up to the thought that is latent in, that may eventually be read into, its classifications and its forms; it is not, as is generally but naïvely assumed, the final label put upon the finished thought.

Most people, asked if they can think without speech, would probably answer, "Yes, but it is not easy for me to do so. Still I know it can be done." Language is but a garment! But what if language is not so much a garment as a prepared road or groove? It is, indeed, in the highest degree likely that language is an instrument originally put to uses lower than the conceptual plane and that thought arises as a refined interpretation of its content. The product grows, in other words, with the instrument, and thought may be no more conceivable, in its genesis and daily practice, without speech than is mathematical reasoning practicable without the lever of an appropriate mathematical symbolism. No one believes that even the most difficult mathematical proposition is inherently dependent on an arbitrary set of symbols, but it is impossible to suppose that the human mind is capable of arriving at or holding such a proposition without the symbolism. The writer, for one, is strongly of the opinion that the feeling entertained by so many that they can think, or even reason, without language is an illusion. The illusion seems to be due to a number of factors. The simplest of these is the failure to distinguish between imagery and thought. As a matter of fact, no sooner do we try to put an image into conscious relation with another than we find ourselves slipping into a silent flow of words. Thought may be a natural domain apart from the artificial one of speech, but speech would seem to be the only road we know of that leads to it. A still more fruitful source of the illusive feeling that language may be dispensed with in thought is the common failure to realize that language is not identical with its auditory symbolism. The auditory symbolism may be replaced, point for point, by a motor or by a visual symbolism (many people can read, for instance, in a purely visual sense, that is, without the intermediating link of an inner flow of the auditory images that correspond to the printed or written words) or by still other, more subtle and elusive, types of transfer that are not so easy to define. Hence the contention that one thinks without language merely because he is not aware of a coexisting auditory imagery is very far indeed from being a valid one. One may go so far as to suspect that the symbolic expression of thought may in some cases run along outside the fringe of the conscious mind, so that the feeling of a free, non-linguistic stream of thought is for minds of a certain type a relatively, but only a relatively, justified one. Psycho-physically, this would mean that the auditory or equivalent visual or motor centers in the brain, together with the appropriate paths of association, that are the cerebral equivalent of speech, are touched off so lightly during the process of thought as not to rise into consciousness at all. This would be a limiting case—thought riding lightly on the submerged crests of speech, instead of jogging along with it, hand in hand. The modern psychology has shown us how powerfully symbolism is at work in the unconscious mind. It is therefore easier to understand at the present time than it would have been twenty years ago that the most rarefied thought may be but the conscious counterpart of an unconscious linguistic symbolism.

One word more as to the relation between language and thought. The point of view that we have developed does not by any means preclude the possibility of the growth of speech being in a high degree dependent on the development of thought. We may assume that language arose pre-rationally—just how and on what precise level of mental activity we do not know—but we must not imagine that a highly developed system of speech symbols worked itself out before the genesis of distinct concepts and of thinking, the handling of concepts. We must rather imagine that thought processes set in, as a kind of psychic overflow, almost at the beginning of linguistic expression; further, that the concept, once defined, necessarily reacted on the life of its linguistic symbol, encouraging further linguistic growth. We see this complex process of the interaction of language and thought actually taking place under our eyes. The instrument makes possible the product, the product refines the instrument. The birth of a new concept is invariably foreshadowed by a more or less strained or extended use of old linguistic material; the concept does not attain to individual and independent life until it has found a distinctive linguistic embodiment. In most cases the new symbol is but a thing wrought from linguistic material already in existence in ways mapped out by crushingly despotic precedents. As soon as the word is at hand, we instinctively feel, with something of a sigh of relief, that the concept is ours for the handling. Not until we own the symbol do we feel that we hold a key to the immediate knowledge or understanding of the concept. Would we be so ready to die for "liberty," to struggle for "ideals," if the words themselves were not ringing within us? And the word, as we know, is not only a key; it may also be a fetter.

Language is primarily an auditory system of symbols. In so far as it is articulated it is also a motor system, but the motor aspect of speech is clearly secondary to the auditory. In normal individuals the impulse to speech first takes effect in the sphere of auditory imagery and is then transmitted to the motor nerves that control the organs of speech. The motor processes and the accompanying motor feelings are not, however, the end, the final resting point. They are merely a means and a control leading to auditory perception in both speaker and hearer. Communication, which is the very object of speech, is successfully effected only when the hearer's auditory perceptions are translated into the appropriate and intended flow of imagery or thought or both combined. Hence the cycle of speech, in so far as we may look upon it as a purely external instrument, begins and ends in the realm of sounds. The concordance between the initial auditory imagery and the final auditory perceptions is the social seal or warrant of the successful issue of the process. As we have already seen, the typical course of this process may undergo endless modifications or transfers into equivalent systems without thereby losing its essential formal characteristics.

The most important of these modifications is the abbreviation of the speech process involved in thinking. This has doubtless many forms, according to the structural or functional peculiarities of the individual mind. The least modified form is that known as "talking to one's self" or "thinking aloud." Here the speaker and the hearer are identified in a single person, who may be said to communicate with himself. More significant is the still further abbreviated form in which the sounds of speech are not articulated at all. To this belong all the varieties of silent speech and of normal thinking. The auditory centers alone may be excited; or the impulse to linguistic expression may be communicated as well to the motor nerves that communicate with the organs of speech but be inhibited either in the muscles of these organs or at some point in the motor nerves themselves; or, possibly, the auditory centers may be only slightly, if at all, affected, the speech process manifesting itself directly in the motor sphere. There must be still other types of abbreviation. How common is the excitation of the motor nerves in silent speech, in which no audible or visible articulations result, is shown by the frequent experience of fatigue in the speech organs, particularly in the larynx, after unusually stimulating reading or intensive thinking.

All the modifications so far considered are directly patterned on the typical process of normal speech. Of very great interest and importance is the possibility of transferring the whole system of speech symbolism into other terms than those that are involved in the typical process. This process, as we have seen, is a matter of sounds and of movements intended to produce these sounds. The sense of vision is not brought into play. But let us suppose that one not only hears the articulated sounds but sees the articulations themselves as they are being executed by the speaker. Clearly, if one can only gain a sufficiently high degree of adroitness in perceiving these movements of the speech organs, the way is opened for a new type of speech symbolism—that in which the sound is replaced by the visual image of the articulations that correspond to the sound. This sort of system has no great value for most of us because we are already possessed of the auditory-motor system of which it is at best but an imperfect translation, not all the articulations being visible to the eye. However, it is well known what excellent use deaf-mutes can make of "reading from the lips" as a subsidiary method of apprehending speech. The most important of all visual speech symbolisms is, of course, that of the written or printed word, to which, on the motor side, corresponds the system of delicately adjusted movements which result in the writing or typewriting or other graphic method of recording speech. The significant feature for our recognition in these new types of symbolism, apart from the fact that they are no longer a by-product of normal speech itself, is that each element (letter or written word) in the system corresponds to a specific element (sound or sound-group or spoken word) in the primary system. Written language is thus a point-to-point equivalence, to borrow a mathematical phrase, to its spoken counterpart. The written forms are secondary symbols of the spoken ones—symbols of symbols—yet so close is the correspondence that they may, not only in theory but in the actual practice of certain eye-readers and, possibly, in certain types of thinking, be entirely substituted for the spoken ones. Yet the auditory-motor associations are probably always latent at the least, that is, they are unconsciously brought into play. Even those who read and think without the slightest use of sound imagery are, at last analysis, dependent on it. They are merely handling the circulating medium, the money, of visual symbols as a convenient substitute for the economic goods and services of the fundamental auditory symbols.

The possibilities of linguistic transfer are practically unlimited. A familiar example is the Morse telegraph code, in which the letters of written speech are represented by a conventionally fixed sequence of longer or shorter ticks. Here the transfer takes place from the written word rather than directly from the sounds of spoken speech. The letter of the telegraph code is thus a symbol of a symbol of a symbol. It does not, of course, in the least follow that the skilled operator, in order to arrive at an understanding of a telegraphic message, needs to transpose the individual sequence of ticks into a visual image of the word before he experiences its normal auditory image. The precise method of reading off speech from the telegraphic communication undoubtedly varies widely with the individual. It is even conceivable, if not exactly likely, that certain operators may have learned to think directly, so far as the purely conscious part of the process of thought is concerned, in terms of the tick-auditory symbolism or, if they happen to have a strong natural bent toward motor symbolism, in terms of the correlated tactile-motor symbolism developed in the sending of telegraphic messages.

Still another interesting group of transfers are the different gesture languages, developed for the use of deaf-mutes, of Trappist monks vowed to perpetual silence, or of communicating parties that are within seeing distance of each other but are out of earshot. Some of these systems are one-to-one equivalences of the normal system of speech; others, like military gesture-symbolism or the gesture language of the Plains Indians of North America (understood by tribes of mutually unintelligible forms of speech) are imperfect transfers, limiting themselves to the rendering of such grosser speech elements as are an imperative minimum under difficult circumstances. In these latter systems, as in such still more imperfect symbolisms as those used at sea or in the woods, it may be contended that language no longer properly plays a part but that the ideas are directly conveyed by an utterly unrelated symbolic process or by a quasi-instinctive imitative-ness. Such an interpretation would be erroneous. The intelligibility of these vaguer symbolisms can hardly be due to anything but their automatic and silent translation into the terms of a fuller flow of speech.

We shall no doubt conclude that all voluntary communication of ideas, aside from normal speech, is either a transfer, direct or indirect, from the typical symbolism of language as spoken and heard or, at the least, involves the intermediary of truly linguistic symbolism. This is a fact of the highest importance. Auditory imagery and the correlated motor imagery leading to articulation are, by whatever devious ways we follow the process, the historic fountain-head of all speech and of all thinking. One other point is of still greater importance. The ease with which speech symbolism can be transferred from one sense to an-

other, from technique to technique, itself indicate
that the mere sounds of speech are not the essentia
fact of language, which lies rather in the classification
in the formal patterning, and in the relating of con
cepts. Once more, language, as a structure, is on it
inner face the mold of thought. It is this abstractec
language, rather more than the physical facts o
speech, that is to concern us in our inquiry.

There is no more striking general fact abou
language than its universality. One may argue as to
whether a particular tribe engages in activities tha
are worthy of the name of religion or of art, but we
know of no people that is not possessed of a fully de
veloped language. The lowliest South African Bush
man speaks in the forms of a rich symbolic system
that is in essence perfectly comparable to the speec
of the cultivated Frenchman. It goes without saying
that the more abstract concepts are not nearly so
plentifully represented in the language of the savage
nor is there the rich terminology and the finer defini
tion of nuances that reflect the higher culture. Yet the
sort of linguistic development that parallels the his
toric growth of culture and which, in its later stages
we associate with literature is, at best, but a superficia
thing. The fundamental groundwork of language—
the development of a clear-cut phonetic system, th
specific association of speech elements with concepts
and the delicate provision for the formal expression
of all manner of relations—all this meets us rigidl
perfected and systematized in every language known
to us. Many primitive languages have a formal rich
ness, a latent luxuriance of expression, that eclipse
anything known to the languages of modern civiliza
tion. Even in the mere matter of the inventory o
speech the layman must be prepared for strange sur
prises. Popular statements as to the extreme pov
erty of expression to which primitive languages ar
doomed are simply myths. Scarcely less impressiv

than the universality of speech is its almost incredible diversity. Those of us that have studied French or German, or, better yet, Latin or Greek, know in what varied forms a thought may run. The formal divergences between the English plan and the Latin plan, however, are comparatively slight in the perspective of what we know of more exotic linguistic patterns. The universality and the diversity of speech lead to a significant inference. We are forced to believe that language is an immensely ancient heritage of the human race, whether or not all forms of speech are the historical outgrowth of a single pristine form. It is doubtful if any other cultural asset of man, be it the art of drilling for fire or of chipping stone, may lay claim to a greater age. I am inclined to believe that it antedated even the lowliest developments of material culture, that these developments, in fact, were not strictly possible until language, the tool of significant expression, had itself taken shape.

CHAPTER II

The Elements of Speech

੦

We have more than once referred to the "elements of speech," by which we understood, roughly speaking, what are ordinarily called "words." We must now look more closely at these elements and acquaint ourselves with the stuff of language. The very simplest element of speech—and by "speech" we shall henceforth mean the auditory system of speech symbolism, the flow of spoken words—is the individual sound, though, as we shall see later on, the sound is not itself a simple structure but the resultant of a series of independent, yet closely correlated, adjustments in the organs of speech. And yet the individual sound is not, properly considered, an element of speech at all, for speech is a significant function and the sound as such has no significance. It happens occasionally that the single sound is an independently significant element (such as French *a* "has" and *à* "to" or Latin *i* "go!"), but such cases are fortuitous coincidences between individual sound and significant word. The coincidence is apt to be fortuitous not only in theory but in point of actual historic fact; thus, the instances cited are merely reduced forms of originally fuller phonetic groups—Latin *habet* and *ad* and Indo-European *ei* respectively. If language is a structure and if the significant elements of language are the bricks of the structure, then the sounds of speech can only be compared to the unformed and unburnt clay of which the bricks are fashioned. In this chapter we shall have nothing further to do with sounds as sounds.

The true, significant elements of language are generally sequences of sounds that are either words, significant parts of words, or word groupings. What distinguishes each of these elements is that it is the outward sign of a specific idea, whether of a single concept or image or of a number of such concepts or images definitely connected into a whole. The single word may or may not be the simplest significant element we have to deal with. The English words *sing, sings, singing, singer* each conveys a perfectly definite and intelligible idea, though the idea is disconnected and is therefore functionally of no practical value. We recognize immediately that these words are of two sorts. The first word, *sing,* is an indivisible phonetic entity conveying the notion of a certain specific activity. The other words all involve the same fundamental notion but, owing to the addition of other phonetic elements, this notion is given a particular twist that modifies or more closely defines it. They represent, in a sense, compounded concepts that have flowered from the fundamental one. We may, therefore, analyze the words *sings, singing,* and *singer* as binary expressions involving a fundamental concept, a concept of subject matter *(sing)*, and a further concept of more abstract order—one of person, number, time, condition, function, or of several of these combined.

If we symbolize such a term as *sing* by the algebraic formula A, we shall have to symbolize such terms as *sings* and *singer* by the formula $A + b$.[1] The element A may be either a complete and independent word *(sing)* or the fundamental substance, the so-called root or stem[2] or "radical element" *(sing-)* of a word. The

---

[1] We shall reserve capitals for radical elements.

[2] These words are not here used in a narrowly technical sense.

element *b* (-*s*, -*ing*, -*er*) is the indicator of a subsidiar
and, as a rule, a more abstract concept; in the wides
sense of the word "form," it puts upon the funda
mental concept a formal limitation. We may term i
a "grammatical element" or affix. As we shall see late
on, the grammatical element or the grammatical in
crement, as we had better put it, need not be suffixe
to the radical element. It may be a prefixed elemen
(like the *un-* of *unsingable*), it may be inserted int
the very body of the stem (like the *n* of the Latir
vinco "I conquer" as contrasted with its absence i
vici "I have conquered"), it may be the complete o
partial repetition of the stem, or it may consist o
some modification of the inner form of the sten
(change of vowel, as in *sung* and *song;* change of con
sonant as in *dead* and *death;* change of accent; actua
abbreviation). Each and every one of these types o
grammatical element or modification has this peculiar
ity, that it may not, in the vast majority of cases, b
used independently but needs to be somehow attache
to or welded with a radical element in order to conve
an intelligible notion. We had better, therefore, mod
ify our formula, *A* + *b*, to *A* + (*b*), the round bracket
symbolizing the incapacity of an element to stan
alone. The grammatical element, moreover, is no
only non-existent except as associated with a radica
one, it does not even, as a rule, obtain its measure o
significance unless it is associated with a particula
class of radical elements. Thus, the -*s* of English *h*
hits symbolizes an utterly different notion from the -
of *books,* merely because *hit* and *book* are differentl
classified as to function. We must hasten to observe
however, that while the radical element may, on occa
sion, be identical with the word, it does not follow
that it may always, or even customarily, be used as a
word. Thus, the *hort-* "garden" of such Latin form
as *hortus, horti,* and *horto* is as much of an abstrac
tion, though one yielding a more easily apprehende

ignificance, than the *-ing* of *singing*. Neither exists as
an independently intelligible and satisfying element
of speech. Both the radical element, as such, and the
grammatical element, therefore, are reached only by
a process of abstraction. It seemed proper to symbolize *sing-er* as $A + (b)$; *hort-us* must be symbolized
as $(A) + (b)$.

So far, the first speech element that we have found
which we can say actually "exists" is the word. Before defining the word, however, we must look a little
more closely at the type of word that is illustrated by
sing. Are we, after all, justified in identifying it with
a radical element? Does it represent a simple correspondence between concept and linguistic expression?
Is the element *sing-*, that we have abstracted from
sings, singing, and *singer* and to which we may justly
ascribe a general unmodified conceptual value, actually the same linguistic fact as the word *sing?* It would
almost seem absurd to doubt it, yet a little reflection
only is needed to convince us that the doubt is entirely legitimate. The word *sing* cannot, as a matter
of fact, be freely used to refer to its own conceptual
content. The existence of such evidently related forms
as *sang* and *sung* at once shows that it cannot refer to
past time, but that, for at least an important part of
its range of usage, it is limited to the present. On
the other hand, the use of *sing* as an "infinitive" (in
such locutions as *to sing* and *he will sing*) does indicate that there is a fairly strong tendency for the word
sing to represent the full, untrammeled amplitude of
a specific concept. Yet if *sing* were, in any adequate
sense, the fixed expression of the unmodified concept,
there should be no room for such vocalic aberrations
as we find in *sang* and *sung* and *song,* nor should we
find *sing* specifically used to indicate present time for
all persons but one (third person singular *sings*).

The truth of the matter is that *sing* is a kind of twilight word, trembling between the status of a true

radical element and that of a modified word of the
type of *singing*. Though it has no outward sign to
indicate that it conveys more than a generalized idea
we do feel that there hangs about it a variable mist of
added value. The formula A does not seem to represent it so well as $A + (o)$. We might suspect *sing* of
belonging to the $A + (b)$ type, with the reservation
that the (b) had vanished. This report of the "feel"
of the word is far from fanciful, for historical evidence
does, in all earnest, show that *sing* is in origin a number of quite distinct words, of type $A + (b)$, that have
pooled their separate values. The (b) of each of these
has gone as a tangible phonetic element; its force,
however, lingers on in weakened measure. The *sing*
of *I sing* is the correspondent of the Anglo-Saxon
singe; the infinitive *sing,* of *singan;* the imperative
sing of *sing*. Ever since the breakdown of English
forms that set in about the time of the Norman Conquest, our language has been straining towards the
creation of simple concept-words, unalloyed by formal
connotations, but it has not yet succeeded in this,
apart, possibly, from isolated adverbs and other elements of that sort. Were the typical unanalyzable
word of the language truly a pure concept-word (type
A) instead of being of a strangely transitional type
(type $A + [o]$), our *sing* and *work* and *house* and thousands of others would compare with the genuine radical words of numerous other languages.[3] Such a
radical-word, to take a random example, is the
Nootka[4] word *hamot* "bone." Our English correspondent is only superficially comparable. *Hamot*
means "bone" in a quite indefinite sense; to our English word clings the notion of singularity. The Nootka
Indian can convey the idea of plurality, in one of

[3] It is not a question of the general isolating character of such
languages as Chinese (see Chapter VI). Radical-words may and
do occur in languages of all varieties, many of them of a high
degree of complexity.
[4] Spoken by a group of Indian tribes in Vancouver Island.

everal ways, if he so desires, but he does not need
o; *hamot* may do for either singular or plural, should
o interest happen to attach to the distinction. As
oon as we say "bone" (aside from its secondary usage
o indicate material), we not merely specify the nature
f the object but we imply, whether we will or no,
hat there is but one of these objects to be considered.
And this increment of value makes all the difference.

We now know of four distinct formal types of word:
(Nootka *hamot*); $A + (o)$ (*sing,bone*); $A + (b)$ (*sing-
ng*); $(A) + (b)$ (Latin *hortus*). There is but one other
ype that is fundamentally possible: $A + B$, the union
f two (or more) independently occurring radical
lements into a single term. Such a word is the com-
ound *fire-engine* or a Sioux form equivalent to *eat-
and* (i.e., "to eat while standing"). It frequently
appens, however, that one of the radical elements
ecomes functionally so subordinated to the other
hat it takes on the character of a grammatical element. We may symbolize this by $A + b$, a type that
nay gradually, by loss of external connection between
he subordinated element *b* and its independent coun-
erpart *B* merge with the commoner type $A + (b)$. A
ord like *beautiful* is an example of $A + b$, the *-ful*
arely preserving the impress of its lineage. A word
ke *homely,* on the other hand, is clearly of the type
+ (b), for no one but a linguistic student is aware
f the connection between the *-ly* and the independent
ord *like.*

In actual use, of course, these five (or six) fun-
amental types may be indefinitely complicated in a
umber of ways. The (o) may have a multiple value;
n other words, the inherent formal modification of
he basic notion of the word may affect more than
ne category. In such a Latin word as *cor* "heart," for
nstance, not only is a concrete concept conveyed, but
here cling to the form, which is actually shorter than
ts own radical element (*cord-*), the three distinct, yet

intertwined, formal concepts of singularity, gende
classification (neuter), and case (subjective-objective
The complete grammatical formula for *cor* is, ther
$A + (o) + (o) + (o)$, though the merely external, phc
netic formula would be $(A) -$, (A) indicating th
abstracted "stem" *cord-*, the minus sign a loss of ma
terial. The significant thing about such a word as *co*
is that the three conceptual limitations are not merel
expressed by implication as the word sinks into plac
in a sentence; they are tied up, for good and al
within the very vitals of the word and cannot b
eliminated by any possibility of usage.

Other complications result from a manifolding c
parts. In a given word there may be several element
of the order A (we have already symbolized this b
the type $A + B$), of the order (A), of the order b, an
of the order (b). Finally, the various types may b
combined among themselves in endless ways. A con
paratively simple language like English, or even Latir
illustrates but a modest proportion of these theoretica
possibilities. But if we take our examples freely fror
the vast storehouse of language, from languages exoti
as well as from those that we are more familiar with
we shall find that there is hardly a possibility tha
is not realized in actual usage. One example wil
do for thousands, one complex type for hundreds c
possible types. I select it from Paiute, the languag
of the Indians of the arid plateaus of southwester
Utah. The word *wii-to-kuchum-punku-rügani-yugw
va-ntü-m(ü)*[5] is of unusual length even for its ow
language, but it is no psychological monster for al
that. It means "they who are going to sit and cut u|
with a knife a black cow (*or* bull)," or, in the orde
of the Indian elements, "knife-black-buffalo-pet-cu
up-sit(plur.)-future-participle-animate plur." The for

[5] In this and other examples taken from exotic languages I ar
forced by practical considerations to simplify the actual phoneti
forms. This should not matter perceptibly, as we are concerne
with form as such, not with phonetic content.

mula for this word, in accordance with our symbolism,
would be $(F) + (E) + C + d + A + B + (g) + (h) +$
$(i) + (o)$. It is the plural of the future participle of a
compound verb "to sit and cut up"—$A + B$. The elements (g)—which denotes futurity—, (h)—a participial
suffix—, and (i)—indicating the animate plural—are
grammatical elements which convey nothing when de-
tached. The formula (o) is intended to imply that the
finished word conveys, in addition to what is definitely
expressed, a further relational idea, that of subjectivity; in other words, the form can only be used as the
subject of a sentence, not in an objective or other
syntactic relation. The radical element A ("to cut up"),
before entering into combination with the coördinate
element B ("to sit"), is itself compounded with two
nominal elements or element-groups—an instrumen-
tally used stem (F) ("knife"), which may be freely used
as the radical element of noun forms but cannot be
employed as an absolute noun in its given form, and
an objectively used group—$(E) + C + d$ ("black cow
or bull"). This group in turn consists of an adjectival
radical element (E) ("black"), which cannot be independently employed (the absolute notion of "black"
can be rendered only as the participle of a verb:
"black-be-ing"), and the compound noun $C + d$ ("buf-
falo-pet"). The radical element C properly means
"buffalo," but the element d, properly an independently occurring noun meaning "horse" (originally
"dog" or "domesticated animal" in general), is regularly used as a quasi-subordinate element indicating
that the animal denoted by the stem to which it is
affixed is owned by a human being. It will be observed
that the whole complex $(F) + (E) + C + d + A + B$
is functionally no more than a verbal base, corresponding to the *sing-* of an English form like *singing;*
that this complex remains verbal in force on the addition of the temporal element (g)—this (g), by the way,
must not be understood as appended to B alone, but

to the whole basic complex as a unit—; and that the
elements $(h) + (i) + (o)$ transform the verbal expression into a formally well-defined noun.

It is high time that we decided just what is meant
by a word. Our first impulse, no doubt, would have
been to define the word as the symbolic, linguistic
counterpart of a single concept. We now know that
such a definition is impossible. In truth it is impossible to define the word from a functional standpoint
at all, for the word may be anything from the expression of a single concept—concrete or abstract or
purely relational (as in *of* or *by* or *and*)—to the expression of a complete thought (as in Latin *dico* "I
say" or, with greater elaborateness of form, in a
Nootka verb form denoting "I have been accustomed
to eat twenty round objects [e.g., apples] while engaged in [doing so and so]"). In the latter case the
word becomes identical with the sentence. The word
is merely a form, a definitely molded entity that takes
in as much or as little of the conceptual material of
the whole thought as the genius of the language cares
to allow. Thus it is that while the single radical
elements and grammatical elements, the carriers of
isolated concepts, are comparable as we pass from
language to language, the finished words are not.
Radical (or grammatical) element and sentence—these
are the primary *functional* units of speech, the former
as an abstracted minimum, the latter as the esthetically satisfying embodiment of a unified thought. The
actual *formal* units of speech, the words, may on occasion identify themselves with either of the two functional units; more often they mediate between the
two extremes, embodying one or more radical notions
and also one or more subsidiary ones. We may put the
whole matter in a nutshell by saying that the radical
and grammatical elements of language, abstracted as
they are from the realities of speech, respond to the
conceptual world of science, abstracted as it is from

he realities of experience, and that the word, the existent unit of living speech, responds to the unit of actually apprehended experience, of history, of art. The sentence is the logical counterpart of the complete thought only if it be felt as made up of the radical and grammatical elements that lurk in the recesses of its words. It is the psychological counterpart of experience, of art, when it is felt, as indeed it normally is, as the finished play of word with word. As the necessity of defining thought solely and exclusively for its own sake becomes more urgent, the word becomes increasingly irrelevant as a means. We can therefore easily understand why the mathematician and the symbolic logician are driven to discard the word and to build up their thought with the help of symbols which have, each of them, a rigidly unitary value.

But is not the word, one may object, as much of an abstraction as the radical element? Is it not as arbitrarily lifted out of the living sentence as is the minimum conceptual element out of the word? Some students of language have, indeed, looked upon the word as such an abstraction, though with very doubtful warrant, it seems to me. It is true that in particular cases, especially in some of the highly synthetic languages of aboriginal America, it is not always easy to say whether a particular element of language is to be interpreted as an independent word or as part of a larger word. These transitional cases, puzzling as they may be on occasion, do not, however, materially weaken the case for the psychological validity of the word. Linguistic experience, both as expressed in standardized, written form and as tested in daily usage, indicates overwhelmingly that there is not, as a rule, the slightest difficulty in bringing the word to consciousness as a psychological reality. No more convincing test could be desired than this, that the naïve Indian, quite unaccustomed to the concept of the

written word, has nevertheless no serious difficulty i
dictating a text to a linguistic student word by word
he tends, of course, to run his words together as i
actual speech, but if he is called to a halt and is mad
to understand what is desired, he can readily isolat
the words as such, repeating them as units. He regu
larly refuses, on the other hand, to isolate the radica
or grammatical element, on the ground that it "make
no sense." [6] What, then, is the objective criterion o
the word? The speaker and hearer feel the word, le
us grant, but how shall we justify their feeling? I
function is not the ultimate criterion of the word
what is?

It is easier to ask the question than to answer it
The best that we can do is to say that the word i
one of the smallest, completely satisfying bits o
isolated "meaning" into which the sentence resolve
itself. It cannot be cut into without a disturbance o
meaning, one or the other or both of the severed part
remaining as a helpless waif on our hands. In prac
tice this unpretentious criterion does better servic
than might be supposed. In such a sentence as *It i
unthinkable,* it is simply impossible to group th
elements into any other and smaller "words" than th

---

[6] These oral experiences, which I have had time and again a
a field student of American Indian languages, are very neatl
confirmed by personal experiences of another sort. Twice I hav
taught intelligent young Indians to write their own language
according to the phonetic system which I employ. They wer
taught merely how to render accurately the sounds as such. Bot
had some difficulty in learning to break up a word into its con
stituent sounds, but none whatever in determining the words
This they both did with spontaneous and complete accuracy. In
the hundreds of pages of manuscript Nootka text that I have
obtained from one of these young Indians the words, whethe
abstract relational entities like English *that* and *but* or comple
sentence-words like the Nootka example quoted above, are, prac
tically without exception, isolated precisely as I or any othe
student would have isolated them. Such experiences with naïve
speakers and recorders do more to convince one of the definitel
plastic unity of the word than any amount of purely theoretica
argument.

three indicated. *Think* or *thinkable* might be isolated, but as neither *un-* nor *-able* nor *is-un* yields a measurable satisfaction, we are compelled to leave *unthinkable* as an integral whole, a miniature bit of art. Added to the "feel" of the word are frequently, but by no means invariably, certain external phonetic characteristics. Chief of these is accent. In many, perhaps in most, languages the single word is marked by a unifying accent, an emphasis on one of the syllables, to which the rest are subordinated. The particular syllable that is to be so distinguished is dependent, needless to say, on the special genius of the language. The importance of accent as a unifying feature of the word is obvious in such English examples as *unthinkable, characterizing*. The long Paiute word that we have analyzed is marked as a rigid phonetic unit by several features, chief of which are the accent on its second syllable (*wi'-* "knife") and the slurring ("unvoicing," to use the technical phonetic term) of its final vowel (*-mü*, animate plural). Such features as accent, cadence, and the treatment of consonants and vowels within the body of a word are often useful as aids in the external demarcation of the word, but they must by no means be interpreted, as is sometimes done, as themselves responsible for its psychological existence. They at best but strengthen a feeling of unity that is already present on other grounds.

We have already seen that the major functional unit of speech, the sentence, has, like the word, a psychological as well as a merely logical or abstracted existence. Its definition is not difficult. It is the linguistic expression of a proposition. It combines a subject of discourse with a statement in regard to this subject. Subject and "predicate" may be combined in a single word, as in Latin *dico;* each may be expressed independently, as in the English equivalent, *I say;* each or either may be so qualified as to lead to complex propositions of many sorts. No matter how many of

these qualifying elements (words or functional part
of words) are introduced, the sentence does not lose
its feeling of unity so long as each and every one of
them falls in place as contributory to the definition of
either the subject of discourse or the core of the predicate.[7] Such a sentence as *The mayor of New York is
going to deliver a speech of welcome in French* is
readily felt as a unified statement, incapable of reduction by the transfer of certain of its elements, in their
given form, to the preceding or following sentences.
The contributory ideas of *of New York, of welcome,*
and *in French* may be eliminated without hurting
the idiomatic flow of the sentence. *The mayor is
going to deliver a speech* is a perfectly intelligible
proposition. But further than this we cannot go in
the process of reduction. We cannot say, for instance,
Mayor is going to deliver.[8] The reduced sentence re-
solves itself into the subject of discourse—*the mayor*
—and the predicate—*is going to deliver a speech.* It is
customary to say that the true subject of such a sentence is *mayor,* the true predicate *is going* or even *is,*
the other elements being strictly subordinate. Such an
analysis, however, is purely schematic and is without
psychological value. It is much better frankly to recognize the fact that either or both of the two terms of
the sentence-proposition may be incapable of expression in the form of single words. There are languages
that can convey all that is conveyed by *The-mayor
is-going-to-deliver-a-speech* in two words, a subject

---

[7] "Coördinate sentences" like *I shall remain but you may go*
may only doubtfully be considered as truly unified predications,
as true sentences. They are sentences in a stylistic sense rather
than from the strictly formal linguistic standpoint. The orthography *I shall remain. But you may go* is as intrinsically justified
as *I shall remain. Now you may go.* The closer connection in
sentiment between the first two propositions has led to a conventional visual representation that must not deceive the analytic spirit.

[8] Except, possibly, in a newspaper headline. Such headlines,
however, are language only in a derived sense.

word and a predicate word, but English is not so highly synthetic. The point that we are really making here is that underlying the finished sentence is a living sentence type, of fixed formal characteristics. These fixed types or actual sentence-groundworks may be freely overlaid by such additional matter as the speaker or writer cares to put on, but they are themselves as rigidly "given" by tradition as are the radical and grammatical elements abstracted from the finished word. New words may be consciously created from these fundamental elements on the analogy of old ones, but hardly new types of words. In the same way new sentences are being constantly created, but always on strictly traditional lines. The enlarged sentence, however, allows as a rule of considerable freedom in the handling of what may be called "unessential" parts. It is this margin of freedom which gives us the opportunity of individual style.

The habitual association of radical elements, grammatical elements, words, and sentences with concepts or groups of concepts related into wholes is the fact itself of language. It is important to note that there is in all languages a certain randomness of association. Thus, the idea of "hide" may be also expressed by the word "conceal," the notion of "three times" also by "thrice." The multiple expression of a single concept is universally felt as a source of linguistic strength and variety, not as a needless extravagance. More irksome is a random correspondence between idea and linguistic expression in the field of abstract and relational concepts, particularly when the concept is embodied in a grammatical element. Thus, the randomness of the expression of plurality in such words as *books, oxen, sheep,* and *geese* is felt to be rather more, I fancy, an unavoidable and traditional predicament than a welcome luxuriance. It is obvious that a language cannot go beyond a certain point in this randomness. Many languages go incredibly far in this respect, it is true, but linguistic history shows conclusively that sooner or later the less frequently occurring associations are ironed out at the expense of the more vital ones. In other words, all languages have an inherent tendency to economy of expression. Were this tendency entirely inoperative, there would be no grammar. The fact of grammar, a universal trait of language, is simply a generalized expression of the feeling that analogous concepts and relations are most conveniently symbolized in analogous forms. Were a language ever completely "grammatical," it would be a perfect engine of conceptual expression. Unfortunately, or luckily, no language is tyrannically consistent. All grammars leak.

Up to the present we have been assuming that the material of language reflects merely the world of concepts and, on what I have ventured to call the "prerational" plane, of images, which are the raw material of concepts. We have, in other words, been assuming that language moves entirely in the ideational or cognitive sphere. It is time that we amplified the picture. The volitional aspect of consciousness also is to some extent explicitly provided for in language. Nearly all languages have special means for the expression of commands (in the imperative forms of the verb, for example) and of desires, unattained or unattainable (*Would he might come!* or *Would he were here!*) The emotions, on the whole, seem to be given a less adequate outlet. Emotion, indeed, is proverbially inclined to speechlessness. Most, if not all, the interjections are to be put to the credit of emotional expression, also, it may be, a number of linguistic elements expressing certain modalities, such as dubitative or potential forms, which may be interpreted as reflecting the emotional states of hesitation or doubt—attenuated fear. On the whole, it must be admitted that ideation reigns supreme in language, that volition and emotion come in as distinctly secondary factors. This, after all, s perfectly intelligible. The world of image and concept, the endless and ever-shifting picture of objective reality, is the unavoidable subject-matter of human communication, for it is only, or mainly, in terms of this world that effective action is possible. Desire, purpose, emotion are the personal color of the objective world; they are applied privately by the individual soul and are of relatively little importance to the neighboring one. All this does not mean that volition and emotion are not expressed. They are, strictly speaking, never absent from normal speech, but their expression is not of a truly linguistic nature. The nuances of emphasis, tone, and phrasing, the varying speed and continuity of utterance, the accompanying bodily movements, all these express something of the inner life of impulse and feeling, but as these means of expression are, at last analysis, but modified forms of the instinctive utterance that man shares with the lower animals, they cannot be considered as forming part of the essential cultural conception of language, however much they may be inseparable from its actual life. And this instinctive expression of volition and emotion is, for the most part, sufficient, often more than sufficient, for the purposes of communication.

There are, it is true, certain writers on the psychology of language[9] who deny its prevailing cognitive character but attempt, on the contrary, to demonstrate the origin of most linguistic elements within the domain of feeling. I confess that I am utterly unable to follow them. What there is of truth in their contentions may be summed up, it seems to me, by saying that most words, like practically all elements of consciousness, have an associated feeling-tone, a mild, yet none the less real and at times insidiously powerful, derivative of pleasure or pain. This feeling-tone, however, is not as a rule an inherent value in the word itself; it is rather a sentimental growth on

[9] E.g., the brilliant Dutch writer, Jac van Ginneken.

the word's true body, on its conceptual kernel. No
only may the feeling-tone change from one age to
another (this, of course, is true of the conceptua
content as well), but it varies remarkably from indi
vidual to individual according to the personal associa
tions of each, varies, indeed, from time to time ir
a single individual's consciousness as his experience:
mold him and his moods change. To be sure, there
are socially accepted feeling-tones, or ranges of feeling
tone, for many words over and above the force of in
dividual association, but they are exceedingly variable
and elusive things at best. They rarely have the ri
gidity of the central, primary fact. We all grant, for
instance, that *storm, tempest,* and *hurricane,* quite
aside from their slight differences of actual meaning,
have distinct feeling-tones, tones that are felt by all
sensitive speakers and readers of English in a roughly
equivalent fashion. *Storm,* we feel, is a more general
and a decidedly less "magnificent" word than the other
two; *tempest* is not only associated with the sea but
is likely, in the minds of many, to have obtained
a softened glamour from a specific association with
Shakespeare's great play; *hurricane* has a greater forth-
rightness, a directer ruthlessness than its synonyms.
Yet the individual's feeling-tones for these words are
likely to vary enormously. To some *tempest* and *hurricane* may seem "soft," literary words, the simpler
storm having a fresh, rugged value which the others
do not possess (think of *storm and stress*). If we have
browsed much in our childhood days in books of the
Spanish Main, *hurricane* is likely to have a pleasurably
bracing tone; if we have had the misfortune to be
caught in one, we are not unlikely to feel the word as
cold, cheerless, sinister.

The feeling-tones of words are of no use, strictly
speaking, to science; the philosopher, if he desires to
arrive at truth rather than merely to persuade, finds
them his most insidious enemies. But man is rarely

engaged in pure science, in solid thinking. Generally his mental activities are bathed in a warm current of feeling and he seizes upon the feeling-tones of words as gentle aids to the desired excitation. They are naturally of great value to the literary artist. It is interesting to note, however, that even to the artist they are a danger. A word whose customary feeling-tone is too unquestionably accepted becomes a plushy bit of furniture, a *cliché*. Every now and then the artist has to fight the feeling-tone, to get the word to mean what it nakedly and conceptually should mean, depending for the effect of feeling on the creative power of an individual juxtaposition of concepts or images.

CHAPTER III

The Sounds of Language

We have seen that the mere phonetic framework of speech does not constitute the inner fact of language and that the single sound of articulated speech is not, as such, a linguistic element at all. For all that, speech is so inevitably bound up with sounds and their articulation that we can hardly avoid giving the subject of phonetics some general consideration. Experience has shown that neither the purely formal aspects of a language nor the course of its history can be fully understood without reference to the sounds in which this form and this history are embodied. A detailed survey of phonetics would be both too technical for the general reader and too loosely related to our main theme to warrant the needed space, but we can well afford to consider a few outstanding facts and ideas connected with the sounds of language.

The feeling that the average speaker has of his language is that it is built up, acoustically speaking, of a comparatively small number of distinct sounds, each of which is rather accurately provided for in the current alphabet by one letter or, in a few cases, by two or more alternative letters. As for the languages of foreigners, he generally feels that, aside from a few striking differences that cannot escape even the un

ritical ear, the sounds they use are the same as those
he is familiar with but that there is a mysterious
"accent" to these foreign languages, a certain unana-
yzed phonetic character, apart from the sounds as
uch, that gives them their air of strangeness. This
naïve feeling is largely illusory on both scores. Phonetic analysis convinces one that the number of clearly
distinguishable sounds and nuances of sounds that are
habitually employed by the speakers of a language is
ar greater than they themselves recognize. Probably
not one English speaker out of a hundred has the re-
notest idea that the *t* of a word like *sting* is not at all
the same sound as the *t* of *teem*, the latter *t* having
a fullness of "breath release" that is inhibited in the
former case by the preceding *s;* that the *ea* of *meat* is
of perceptibly shorter duration than the *ea* of *mead;*
or that the final *s* of a word like *heads* is not the full,
buzzing *z* sound of the *s* in such a word as *please*. It is
the frequent failure of foreigners, who have acquired
a practical mastery of English and who have eliminated
all the cruder phonetic shortcomings of their less careful brethren, to observe such minor distinctions that
helps to give their English pronunciation the curiously elusive "accent" that we all vaguely feel. We
do not diagnose the "accent" as the total acoustic
effect produced by a series of slight but specific phonetic errors for the very good reason that we have
never made clear to ourselves our own phonetic stock
in trade. If two languages taken at random, say English and Russian, are compared as to their phonetic
systems, we are more apt than not to find that very
few of the phonetic elements of the one find an exact
analogue in the other. Thus, the *t* of a Russian word
like *tam* "there" is neither the English *t* of *sting* nor
the English *t* of *teem*. It differs from both in its "dental" articulation, in other words, in being produced
by contact of the tip of the tongue with the upper
teeth, not, as in English, by contact of the tongue

back of the tip with the gum ridge above the teeth
moreover, it differs from the *t* of *teem* also in the
absence of a marked "breath release" before the fol
lowing vowel is attached, so that its acoustic effect i
of a more precise, "metallic" nature than in English
Again, the English *l* is unknown in Russian, which
possesses, on the other hand, two distinct *l*-sounds that
the normal English speaker would find it difficul
exactly to reproduce—a "hollow," guttural-like *l* and
a "soft," palatalized *l*-sound that is only very approx
imately rendered, in English terms, as *ly*. Even so
simple and, one would imagine, so invariable a sound
as *m* differs in the two languages. In a Russian word
like *most* "bridge" the *m* is not the same as the *m*
of the English word *most;* the lips are more fully
rounded during its articulation, so that it makes a
heavier, more resonant impression on the ear. The
vowels, needless to say, differ completely in English
and Russian, hardly any two of them being quite the
same.

I have gone into these illustrative details, which
are of little or no specific interest for us, merely in
order to provide something of an experimental basis
to convince ourselves of the tremendous variability of
speech sounds. Yet a complete inventory of the acoustic resources of all the European languages, the languages nearer home, while unexpectedly large, would
still fall far short of conveying a just idea of the true
range of human articulation. In many of the languages of Asia, Africa, and aboriginal America there
are whole classes of sounds that most of us have no
knowledge of. They are not necessarily more difficult
of enunciation than sounds more familiar to our ears;
they merely involve such muscular adjustments of the
organs of speech as we have never habituated ourselves to. It may be safely said that the total number
of possible sounds is greatly in excess of those actually
in use. Indeed, an experienced phonetician should

have no difficulty in inventing sounds that are unknown to objective investigation. One reason why we find it difficult to believe that the range of possible speech sounds is indefinitely large is our habit of conceiving the sound as a simple, unanalyzable impression instead of as the resultant of a number of distinct muscular adjustments that take place simultaneously. A slight change in any one of these adjustments gives us a new sound which is akin to the old one, because of the continuance of the other adjustments, but which is acoustically distinct from it, so sensitive has the human ear become to the nuanced play of the vocal mechanism. Another reason for our lack of phonetic imagination is the fact that, while our ear is delicately responsive to the sounds of speech, the muscles of our speech organs have early in life become exclusively accustomed to the particular adjustments and systems of adjustment that are required to produce the traditional sounds of the language. All or nearly all other adjustments have become permanently inhibited, whether through inexperience or through gradual elimination. Of course the power to produce these inhibited adjustments is not entirely lost, but the extreme difficulty we experience in learning the new sounds of foreign languages is sufficient evidence of the strange rigidity that has set in for most people in the voluntary control of the speech organs. The point may be brought home by contrasting the comparative lack of freedom of voluntary speech movements with the all but perfect freedom of voluntary gesture.[1] Our rigidity in articulation is the price we have had to pay for easy mastery of a highly necessary symbolism. One cannot be both splen-

[1] Observe the "voluntary." When we shout or grunt or otherwise allow our voices to take care of themselves, as we are likely to do when alone in the country on a fine spring day, we are no longer fixing vocal adjustments by voluntary control. Under these circumstances we are almost certain to hit on speech sounds that we could never learn to control in actual speech.

didly free in the random choice of movements and selective with deadly certainty.[2]

There are, then, an indefinitely large number of articulated sounds available for the mechanics of speech; any given language makes use of an explicit, rigidly economical selection of these rich resources; and each of the many possible sounds of speech is conditioned by a number of independent muscular adjustments that work together simultaneously towards its production. A full account of the activity of each of the organs of speech—in so far as its activity has a bearing on language—is impossible here, nor can we concern ourselves in a systematic way with the classification of sounds on the basis of their mechanics.[3] A few bold outlines are all that we can attempt. The organs of speech are the lungs and bronchial tubes; the throat, particularly that part of it which is known as the larynx or, in popular parlance, the "Adam's apple"; the nose; the uvula, which is the soft, pointed, and easily movable organ that depends from the rear of the palate; the palate, which is divided into a pos-

[2] If speech, in its acoustic and articulatory aspect, is indeed a rigid system, how comes it, one may plausibly object, that no two people speak alike? The answer is simple. All that part of speech which falls out of the rigid articulatory framework is not speech in idea, but is merely a superadded, more or less instinctively determined vocal complication inseparable from speech in practice. All the individual color of speech—personal emphasis, speed, personal cadence, personal pitch—is a non-linguistic fact, just as the incidental expression of desire and emotion are, for the most part, alien to linguistic expression. Speech, like all elements of culture, demands conceptual selection, inhibition of the randomness of instinctive behavior. That its "idea" is never realized as such in practice, its carriers being instinctively animated organisms, is of course true of each and every aspect of culture.

[3] Purely acoustic classifications, such as more easily suggest themselves to a first attempt at analysis, are now in less favor among students of phonetics than organic classifications. The latter have the advantage of being more objective. Moreover, the acoustic quality of a sound is dependent on the articulation, even though in linguistic consciousness this quality is the primary, not the secondary, fact.

erior, movable "soft palate" or velum and a "hard
palate"; the tongue; the teeth; and the lips. The
palate, lower palate, tongue, teeth, and lips may be
looked upon as a combined resonance chamber, whose
constantly varying shape, chiefly due to the extreme
mobility of the tongue, is the main factor in giving
the outgoing breath its precise quality[4] of sound.

The lungs and bronchial tubes are organs of speech
only in so far as they supply and conduct the current
of outgoing air without which audible articulation is
impossible. They are not responsible for any specific
sound or acoustic feature of sounds except, possibly,
accent or stress. It may be that differences of stress
are due to slight differences in the contracting force
of the lung muscles, but even this influence of the
lungs is denied by some students, who explain the
fluctuations of stress that do so much to color speech
by reference to the more delicate activity of the glottal
cords. These glottal cords are two small, nearly hori-
zontal, and highly sensitive membranes within the
larynx, which consists, for the most part, of two large
and several smaller cartilages and of a number of
small muscles that control the action of the cords.

The cords, which are attached to the cartilages, are
to the human speech organs what the two vibrating
reeds are to an oboe or the strings to a violin. They
are capable of at least three distinct types of movement, each of which is of the greatest importance for
speech. They may be drawn towards or away from
each other, they may vibrate like reeds or strings, and
they may become lax or tense in the direction of their
length. The last class of these movements allows the
cords to vibrate at different "lengths" or degrees of
tenseness and is responsible for the variations in pitch

---

[4] By "quality" is here meant the inherent nature and resonance of the sound as such. The general "quality" of the individual's voice is another matter altogether. This is chiefly determined by the individual anatomical characteristics of the
larynx and is of no linguistic interest whatever.

which are present not only in song but in the more
elusive modulations of ordinary speech. The two other
types of glottal action determine the nature of the
voice, "voice" being a convenient term for breath as
utilized in speech. If the cords are well apart, allowing
the breath to escape in unmodified form, we have the
condition technically known as "voicelessness." All
sounds produced under these circumstances are "voiceless" sounds. Such are the simple, unmodified breath
as it passes into the mouth, which is, at least approximately, the same as the sound that we write *h,* also
a large number of special articulations in the mouth
chamber, like *p* and *s.* On the other hand, the glottal
cords may be brought tight together, without vibrating. When this happens, the current of breath is
checked for the time being. The slight choke or
"arrested cough" that is thus made audible is not recognized in English as a definite sound but occurs
nevertheless not infrequently.[5] This momentary check,
technically known as a "glottal stop," is an integral
element of speech in many languages, as Danish, Let-
tish, certain Chinese dialects, and nearly all American
Indian languages. Between the two extremes of voicelessness, that of completely open breath and that of
checked breath, lies the position of true voice. In this
position the cords are close together, but not so tightly
as to prevent the air from streaming through; the
cords are set vibrating and a musical tone of varying pitch results. A tone so produced is known as a
"voiced sound." It may have an indefinite number of
qualities according to the precise position of the upper
organs of speech. Our vowels, nasals (such as *m* and
n), and such sounds as *b, z,* and *l* are all voiced sounds.
The most convenient test of a voiced sound is the possibility of pronouncing it on any given pitch, in other

---

[5] As at the end of the snappily pronounced *no!* (sometimes
written *nope!*) or in the over-carefully pronounced *at all,* where
one may hear a slight check between the *t* and the *a.*

words, of singing on it.[6] The voiced sounds are the most clearly audible elements of speech. As such they are the carriers of practically all significant differences in stress, pitch, and syllabification. The voiceless sounds are articulated noises that break up the stream of voice with fleeting moments of silence. Acoustically intermediate between the freely unvoiced and the voiced sounds are a number of other characteristic types of voicing, such as murmuring and whisper.[7] These and still other types of voice are relatively unimportant in English and most other European languages, but there are languages in which they rise to some prominence in the normal flow of speech.

The nose is not an active organ of speech, but it is highly important as a resonance chamber. It may be disconnected from the mouth, which is the other great resonance chamber, by the lifting of the movable part of the soft palate so as to shut off the passage of the breath into the nasal cavity; or, if the soft palate is allowed to hang down freely and unobstructively, so that the breath passes into both the nose and the mouth, these make a combined resonance chamber. Such sounds as *b* and *a* (as in *father*) are voiced "oral" sounds, that is, the voiced breath does not receive a nasal resonance. As soon as the soft palate is lowered, however, and the nose added as a participating resonance chamber, the sounds *b* and *a* take on a peculiar "nasal" quality and become, respectively, *m* and the nasalized vowel written *an* in French (e.g.,

[6] "Singing" is here used in a wide sense. One cannot sing continuously on such a sound as *b* or *d*, but one may easily outline a tune on a series of *b*'s or *d*'s in the manner of the plucked "pizzicato" on stringed instruments. A series of tones executed on continuant consonants, like *m, z,* or *l,* gives the effect of humming, droning, or buzzing. The sound of "humming," indeed, is nothing but a continuous voiced nasal, held on one pitch or varying in pitch, as desired.

[7] The whisper of ordinary speech is a combination of unvoiced sounds and "whispered" sounds, as the term is understood in phonetics.

sang, tant). The only English sounds[8] that normal
receive a nasal resonance are *m, n,* and the *ng* soun
of *sing.* Practically all sounds, however, may be nasa
ized, not only the vowels—nasalized vowels are con
mon in all parts of the world—but such sounds as
or *z.* Voiceless nasals are perfectly possible. The
occur, for instance, in Welsh and in quite a numbe
of American Indian languages.

The organs that make up the oral resonance chan
ber may articulate in two ways. The breath, voiced o
unvoiced, nasalized or unnasalized, may be allowed t
pass through the mouth without being checked or in
peded at any point; or it may be either momentaril
checked or allowed to stream through a greatly na
rowed passage with resulting air friction. There a
also transitions between the two latter types of artic
lation. The unimpeded breath takes on a particula
color or quality in accordance with the varying shap
of the oral resonance chamber. This shape is chiefl
determined by the position of the movable parts—
the tongue and the lips. As the tongue is raised o
lowered, retracted or brought forward, held tense o
lax, and as the lips are pursed ("rounded") in varyin
degree or allowed to keep their position of rest, a larg
number of distinct qualities result. These oral quali
ties are the vowels. In theory their number is infinit
in practice the ear can differentiate only a limited, ye
a surprisingly large, number of resonance position
Vowels, whether nasalized or not, are normally voice
sounds; in not a few languages, however, "voicele
vowels" [9] also occur.

The remaining oral sounds are generally groupe
together as "consonants." In them the stream o
breath is interfered with in some way, so that a lesse

---

[8] Aside from the involuntary nasalizing of all voiced soun
in the speech of those that talk with a "nasal twang."
[9] These may be also defined as free unvoiced breath wit
varying vocalic timbres. In the long Paiute word quoted o
page 30 the first *u* and the final *ü* are pronounced without voic

resonance results, and a sharper, more incisive quality of tone. There are four main types of articulation generally recognized within the consonantal group of sounds. The breath may be completely stopped for a moment at some definite point in the oral cavity. Sounds so produced, like *t* or *d* or *p,* are known as "stops" or "explosives." [10] Or the breath may be continuously obstructed through a narrow passage, not entirely checked. Examples of such "spirants" or "fricatives," as they are called, are *s* and *z* and *y.* The third class of consonants, the "laterals," are semi-stopped. There is a true stoppage at the central point of articulation, but the breath is allowed to escape through the two side passages or through one of them. Our English *d,* for instance, may be readily transformed into *l,* which has the voicing and the position of *d,* merely by depressing the sides of the tongue on either side of the point of contact sufficiently to allow the breath to come through. Laterals are possible in many distinct positions. They may be unvoiced (the Welsh *ll* is an example) as well as voiced. Finally, the stoppage of the breath may be rapidly intermittent; in other words, the active organ of contact—generally the point of the tongue, less often the uvula[11]—may be made to vibrate against or near the point of contact. These sounds are the "trills" or "rolled consonants," of which the normal English *r* is a none too typical example. They are well developed in many languages, however, generally in voiced form, sometimes, as in Welsh and Paiute, in unvoiced form as well.

The oral manner of articulation is naturally not sufficient to define a consonant. The place of articulation must also be considered. Contacts may be formed

[10] Nasalized stops, say *m* or *n,* can naturally not be truly "stopped," as there is no way of checking the stream of breath in the nose by a definite articulation.

[11] The lips also may theoretically so articulate. "Labial trills," however, are certainly rare in natural speech.

at a large number of points, from the root of the tongue to the lips. It is not necessary here to go at length into this somewhat complicated matter. The contact is either between the root of the tongue and the throat,[12] some part of the tongue and a point on the palate (as in *k* or *ch* or *l*), some part of the tongue and the teeth (as in the English *th* of *thick* and *then*), the teeth and one of the lips (practically always the upper teeth and lower lip, as in *f*), or the two lips (as in *p* or English *w*). The tongue articulations are the most complicated of all, as the mobility of the tongue allows various points on its surface, say the tip, to articulate against a number of opposed points of contact. Hence arise many positions of articulation that we are not familiar with, such as the typical "dental" position of Russian or Italian *t* and *d;* or the "cerebral" position of Sanskrit and other languages of India, in which the tip of the tongue articulates against the hard palate. As there is no break at any point between the rims of the teeth back to the uvula nor from the tip of the tongue back to its root, it is evident that all the articulations that involve the tongue form a continuous organic (and acoustic) series. The positions grade into each other, but each language selects a limited number of clearly defined positions as characteristic of its consonantal system, ignoring transitional or extreme positions. Frequently a language allows a certain latitude in the fixing of the required position. This is true, for instance, of the English *k*-sound, which is articulated much further to the front in a word like *kin* than in *cool*. We ignore this difference, psychologically, as a non-essential, mechanical one. Another language might well recognize the difference, or only a slightly greater one, as significant, as paralleling the distinction in position between the *k* of *kin* and the *t* of *tin*.

The organic classification of speech sounds is a

[12] This position, known as "faucal," is not common.

ple matter after what we have learned of their
oduction. Any such sound may be put into its
oper place by the appropriate answer to four main
estions:—What is the position of the glottal cords
ring its articulation? Does the breath pass into the
outh alone or is it also allowed to stream into the
se? Does the breath pass freely through the mouth
· is it impeded at some point and, if so, in what
anner? What are the precise points of articulation
the mouth? [13] This fourfold classification of sounds,
orked out in all its detailed ramifications,[14] is suffi-
ent to account for all, or practically all, the sounds
language.[15]

The phonetic habits of a given language are not ex-
austively defined by stating that it makes use of such
d such particular sounds out of the all but endless
mut that we have briefly surveyed. There remains
e important question of the dynamics of these pho-
etic elements. Two languages may, theoretically, be
uilt up of precisely the same series of consonants and
wels and yet produce utterly different acoustic ef-
cts. One of them may not recognize striking vari-
tions in the lengths or "quantities" of the phonetic
ements, the other may note such variations most
unctiliously (in probably the majority of languages
ng and short vowels are distinguished; in many, as
Italian or Swedish or Ojibwa, long consonants are
cognized as distinct from short ones). Or the one,
y English, may be very sensitive to relative stresses,

[13] "Points of articulation" must be understood to include
ngue and lip positions of the vowels.
[14] Including, under the fourth category, a number of special
esonance adjustments that we have not been able to take up
ecifically.
[15] In so far, it should be added, as these sounds are expiratory,
e., pronounced with the outgoing breath. Certain languages,
ke the South African Hottentot and Bushman, have also a
umber of inspiratory sounds, pronounced by sucking in the
reath at various points of oral contact. These are the so-called
clicks."

while in the other, say French, stress is a very min
consideration. Or, again, the pitch differences whi
are inseparable from the actual practice of langua
may not affect the word as such, but, as in Englis
may be a more or less random or, at best, but a rl
torical phenomenon, while in other languages, as
Swedish, Lithuanian, Chinese, Siamese, and the n
jority of African languages, they may be more fine
graduated and felt as integral characteristics of t
words themselves. Varying methods of syllabifying a
also responsible for noteworthy acoustic difference
Most important of all, perhaps, are the very differe
possibilities of combining the phonetic elements. Ea
language has its peculiarities. The *ts* combination, f
instance, is found in both English and German, b
in English it can only occur at the end of a wo
(as in *hats*), while it occurs freely in German as tl
psychological equivalent of a single sound (as in *Ze.
Katze*). Some languages allow of great heapings
consonants or of vocalic groups (diphthongs), in othe
no two consonants or no two vowels may ever con
together. Frequently a sound occurs only in a speci
position or under special phonetic circumstances. I
English, for instance, the z-sound of *azure* cannot o
cur initially, while the peculiar quality of the *t*
sting is dependent on its being preceded by the
These dynamic factors, in their totality, are as in
portant for the proper understanding of the phonet
genius of a language as the sound system itself, ofte
far more so.

We have already seen, in an incidental way, th
phonetic elements or such dynamic features as qua
tity and stress have varying psychological "values.
The English *ts* of *hats* is merely a *t* followed by
functionally independent *s*, the *ts* of the German wor
Zeit has an integral value equivalent, say, to the *t*
the English word *tide*. Again, the *t* of *time* is indee
noticeably distinct from that of *sting*, but the di

erence, to the consciousness of an English-speaking erson, is quite irrelevant. It has no "value." If we ompare the *t*-sounds of Haida, the Indian language poken in the Queen Charlotte Islands, we find that recisely the same difference of articulation has a real alue. In such a word as *sting* "two," the *t* is pronounced precisely as in English, but in *sta* "from" he *t* is clearly "aspirated," like that of *time*. In other vords, an objective difference that is irrelevant in English is of functional value in Haida; from its own psychological standpoint the *t* of *sting* is as different rom that of *sta* as, from our standpoint, is the *t* of *ime* from the *d* of *divine*. Further investigation vould yield the interesting result that the Haida ear inds the difference between the English *t* of *sting* and he *d* of *divine* as irrelevant as the naïve English ear inds that of the *t*-sounds of *sting* and *time*. The objective comparison of sounds in two or more languages is, then, of no psychological or historical significance unless these sounds are first "weighted," unless their phonetic "values" are determined. These values, in turn, flow from the general behavior and functioning of the sounds in actual speech.

These considerations as to phonetic value lead to an important conception. Back of the purely objective system of sounds that is peculiar to a language and which can be arrived at only by a painstaking phonetic analysis, there is a more restricted "inner" or "ideal" system which, while perhaps equally unconscious as a system to the naïve speaker, can far more readily than the other be brought to his consciousness as a finished pattern, a psychological mechanism. The inner sound-system, overlaid though it may be by the mechanical or the irrelevant, is a real and an immensely important principle in the life of a language. It may persist as a pattern, involving number, relation, and functioning of phonetic elements, long after its phonetic content is changed. Two his-

torically related languages or dialects may not have a
sound in common, but their ideal sound-systems may
be identical patterns. I would not for a moment wish
to imply that this pattern may not change. It may
shrink or expand or change its functional complexion,
but its rate of change is infinitely less rapid than
that of the sounds as such. Every language, then, is
characterized as much by its ideal system of sounds
and by the underlying phonetic pattern (system, one
might term it, of symbolic atoms) as by a definite
grammatical structure. Both the phonetic and conceptual structures show the instinctive feeling of language for form.[16]

[16] The conception of the ideal phonetic system, the phonetic
pattern, of a language is not as well understood by linguistic
students as it should be. In this respect the unschooled recorder
of language, provided he has a good ear and a genuine instinct
for language, is often at a great advantage as compared with the
minute phonetician, who is apt to be swamped by his mass of
observations. I have already employed my experience in teaching Indians to write their own language for its testing value in
another connection. It yields equally valuable evidence here. I
found that it was difficult or impossible to teach an Indian to
make phonetic distinctions that did not correspond to "points
in the pattern of his language," however these differences might
strike our objective ear, but that subtle, barely audible, phonetic
differences, if only they hit the "points in the pattern," were
easily and voluntarily expressed in writing. In watching my
Nootka interpreter write his language, I often had the curious
feeling that he was transcribing an ideal flow of phonetic elements which he heard, inadequately from a purely objective
standpoint, as the intention of the actual rumble of speech.

CHAPTER IV

Form in Language: Grammatical Processes

○

he question of form in language presents itself under
o aspects. We may either consider the formal meth-
ls employed by a language, its "grammatical proc-
ses," or we may ascertain the distribution of concepts
ith reference to formal expression. What are the
rmal patterns of the language? And what types of
ncepts make up the content of these formal pat-
rns? The two points of view are quite distinct. The
nglish word *unthinkingly* is, broadly speaking, for-
ally parallel to the word *reformers,* each being built
on a radical element which may occur as an
dependent verb *(think, form),* this radical element
ing preceded by an element *(un-, re-)* that conveys
definite and fairly concrete significance but that
nnot be used independently, and followed by two
ements *(-ing, -ly; -er, -s)* that limit the applica-
on of the radical concept in a relational sense. This
rmal pattern—$(b) + A + (c) + (d)$[1]—is a character-
tic feature of the language. A countless number of
nctions may be expressed by it; in other words,
l the possible ideas conveyed by such prefixed and
ffixed elements, while tending to fall into minor
oups, do not necessarily form natural, functional sys-
ms. There is no logical reason, for instance, why the

[1] For the symbolism, see Chapter II.

numeral function of -*s* should be formally express
in a manner that is analogous to the expression of t
idea conveyed by -*ly*. It is perfectly conceivable th
in another language the concept of manner (-*ly*) m
be treated according to an entirely different patte
from that of plurality. The former might have to
expressed by an independent word (say, *thus unthir
ing*), the latter by a prefixed element (say, *plura.
reform-er*). There are, of course, an unlimited nu
ber of other possibilities. Even within the confines
English alone the relative independence of form a
function can be made obvious. Thus, the negati
idea conveyed by *un*- can be just as adequately e
pressed by a suffixed element (-*less*) in such a wo
as *thoughtlessly*. Such a twofold formal expressi
of the negative function would be inconceivable
certain languages, say Eskimo, where a suffixed e
ment would alone be possible. Again, the plural n
tion conveyed by the -*s* of *reformers* is just as definite
expressed in the word *geese*, where an utterly distin
method is employed. Furthermore, the principle
vocalic change (*goose*—*geese*) is by no means confin
to the expression of the idea of plurality; it may al
function as an indicator of difference of time (e.
sing—*sang, throw*—*threw*). But the expression in En
lish of past time is not by any means always bou
up with a change of vowel. In the great majority
cases the same idea is expressed by means of a distin
suffix (*die-d, work-ed*). Functionally, *died* and *sang* a
analogous; so are *reformers* and *geese*. Formally, v
must arrange these words quite otherwise. Both *die
and *re-form-er-s* employ the method of suffixing gra
matical elements; both *sang* and *geese* have gramma
ical form by virtue of the fact that their vowels diff
from the vowels of other words with which they a
closely related in form and meaning (*goose; sin
sung*).

² "*Plural*" is here a symbol for any prefix indicating plurali

Every language possesses one or more formal methods for indicating the relation of a secondary concept to the main concept of the radical element. Some of these grammatical processes, like suffixing, are exceedingly wide-spread; others, like vocalic change, are less common but far from rare; still others, like accent and consonantal change, are somewhat exceptional as functional processes. Not all languages are as irregular as English in the assignment of functions to its stock of grammatical processes. As a rule, such basic concepts as those of plurality and time are rendered by means of one or other method alone, but the rule has so many exceptions that we cannot safely lay it down as a principle. Wherever we go we are impressed by the fact that pattern is one thing, the utilization of pattern quite another. A few further examples of the multiple expression of identical functions in other languages than English may help to make still more vivid this idea of the relative independence of form and function.

In Hebrew, as in other Semitic languages, the verbal idea as such is expressed by three, less often by two or four, characteristic consonants. Thus, the group *sh-m-r* expresses the idea of "guarding," the group *g-n-b* that of "stealing," *n-t-n* that of "giving." Naturally these consonantal sequences are merely abstracted from the actual forms. The consonants are held together in different forms by characteristic vowels that vary according to the idea that it is desired to express. Prefixed and suffixed elements are also frequently used. The method of internal vocalic change is exemplified in *shamar* "he has guarded," *shomer* "guarding," *shamur* "being guarded," *shmor* "(to) guard." Analogously, *ganab* "he has stolen," *goneb* "stealing," *ganub* "being stolen," *gnob* "(to) steal." But not all infinitives are formed according to the type of *shmor* and *gnob* or of other types of internal vowel change. Certain verbs suffix a *t*-element for the infinitive, e.g., *ten-eth* "to give," *heyo-th* "to be." Again, the pronominal ideas may be expressed by independent words (e.g., *anoki* "I"), by prefixed elements (e.g., *e-shmor* "I shall guard"), or by suffixed elements (e.g., *shamar-ti* "I have guarded"). In Nass, an Indian language of British Columbia, plurals are formed by four distinct methods. Most nouns (and verbs) are reduplicated in the plural, that is, part of the radical element is repeated, e.g., *gyat* "person," *gyigyat* "people." A second method is the use of certain characteristic prefixes, e.g., *an'on* "hand," *ka-an'on* "hands"; *wai* "one paddles," *lu-wai* "several paddle." Still other plurals are formed by means of internal vowel change, e.g., *gwula* "cloak," *gwila* "cloaks." Finally, a fourth class of plurals is constituted by such nouns as suffix a grammatical element, e.g., *waky* "brother," *wakykw* "brothers."

From such groups of examples as these—and they might be multiplied *ad nauseam*—we cannot but conclude that linguistic form may and should be studied as types of patterning, apart from the associated functions. We are the more justified in this procedure as all languages evince a curious instinct for the development of one or more particular grammatical processes at the expense of others, tending always to lose sight of any explicit functional value that the process may have had in the first instance, delighting, it would seem, in the sheer play of its means of expression. It does not matter that in such a case as the English *goose—geese, foul—defile, sing—sang—sung* we can prove that we are dealing with historically distinct processes, that the vocalic alternation of *sing* and *sang*, for instance, is centuries older as a specific type of grammatical process than the outwardly parallel one of *goose* and *geese*. It remains true that there is (or was) an inherent tendency in English, at the time such forms as *geese* came into being, for the utilization of vocalic change as a significant linguistic method. Fail-

g the precedent set by such already existing types of
ocalic alternation as *sing—sang—sung,* it is highly
oubtful if the detailed conditions that brought about
e evolution of forms like *teeth* and *geese* from *tooth*
d *goose* would have been potent enough to allow
e native linguistic feeling to win through to an
cceptance of these new types of plural formation as
sychologically possible. This feeling for form as such,
eely expanding along predetermined lines and
eatly inhibited in certain directions by the lack of
ontrolling types of patterning, should be more clearly
nderstood than it seems to be. A general survey of
any diverse types of languages is needed to give us
e proper perspective on this point. We saw in the
eceding chapter that every language has an inner
honetic system of definite pattern. We now learn
at it has also a definite feeling for patterning on the
vel of grammatical formation. Both of these sub-
erged and powerfully controlling impulses to defi-
ite form operate as such, regardless of the need for
xpressing particular concepts or of giving consistent
xternal shape to particular groups of concepts. It
oes without saying that these impulses can find real-
ation only in concrete functional expression. We
ust say something to be able to say it in a certain
anner.

Let us now take up a little more systematically,
owever briefly, the various grammatical processes
hat linguistic research has established. They may be
rouped into six main types: word order; composition;
ffixation, including the use of prefixes, suffixes, and
nfixes; internal modification of the radical or grammatical element, whether this affects a vowel or a
onsonant; reduplication; and accentual differences,
whether dynamic (stress) or tonal (pitch). There are
lso special quantitative processes, like vocalic length-
ening or shortening and consonantal doubling, but
hese may be looked upon as particular sub-types

of the process of internal modification. Possibly still
other formal types exist, but they are not likely to
be of importance in a general survey. It is important
to bear in mind that a linguistic phenomenon cannot
be looked upon as illustrating a definite "process"
unless it has an inherent functional value. The con
sonantal change in English, for instance, of *book-*
and *bag-s* (*s* in the former, *z* in the latter) is of no
functional significance. It is a purely external, me
chanical change induced by the presence of a preceding
voiceless consonant, *k*, in the former case, of a voiced
consonant, *g*, in the latter. This mechanical alterna
tion is objectively the same as that between the noun
house and the verb *to house*. In the latter case, how
ever, it has an important grammatical function, that
of transforming a noun into a verb. The two alterna
tions belong, then, to entirely different psychologica
categories. Only the latter is a true illustration of con
sonantal modification as a grammatical process.

The simplest, at least the most economical, method
of conveying some sort of grammatical notion is to
juxtapose two or more words in a definite sequence
without making any attempt by inherent modification
of these words to establish a connection between
them. Let us put down two simple English words a
random, say *sing praise*. This conveys no finished
thought in English, nor does it clearly establish a
relation between the idea of singing and that of prais
ing. Nevertheless, it is psychologically impossible to
hear or see the two words juxtaposed without strain
ing to give them some measure of coherent signifi
cance. The attempt is not likely to yield an entirely
satisfactory result, but what is significant is that as
soon as two or more radical concepts are put before
the human mind in immediate sequence it strives to
bind them together with connecting values of some
sort. In the case of *sing praise* different individuals
are likely to arrive at different provisional results

ne of the latent possibilities of the juxtaposition,
ressed in currently satisfying form, are: *sing praise
him*)*!* or *singing praise, praise expressed in a song
to sing and praise* or *one who sings a song of praise*
mpare such English compounds as *killjoy*, i.e., *one
o kills joy*) or *he sings a song of praise* (*to him*).
e theoretical possibilities in the way of rounding
t these two concepts into a significant group of con-
ts or even into a finished thought are indefinitely
merous. None of them will quite work in English,
t there are numerous languages where one or other
these amplifying processes is habitual. It depends
irely on the genius of the particular language what
ction is inherently involved in a given sequence of
rds.

ome languages, like Latin, express practically all
ations by means of modifications within the body
the word itself. In these, sequence is apt to be a
torical rather than a strictly grammatical princi-
. Whether I say in Latin *hominem femina videt* or
ina hominem videt* or *hominem videt femina* or
et femina hominem makes little or no difference
ond, possibly, a rhetorical or stylistic one. *The
man sees the man* is the identical significance of
h of these sentences. In Chinook, an Indian lan-
ge of the Columbia River, one can be equally free,
the relation between the verb and the two nouns
as inherently fixed as in Latin. The difference be-
en the two languages is that, while Latin allows
nouns to establish their relation to each other and
the verb, Chinook lays the formal burden entirely
the verb, the full content of which is more or less
quately rendered by *she-him-sees*. Eliminate the
tin case suffixes (*-a* and *-em*) and the Chinook pro-
minal prefixes (*she-him-*) and we cannot afford to
so indifferent to our word order. We need to hus-
d our resources. In other words, word order takes
a real functional value. Latin and Chinook are at

one extreme. Such languages as Chinese, Siamese, a
Annamite, in which each and every word, if it is
function properly, falls into its assigned place, are
the other extreme. But the majority of languages f
between these two extremes. In English, for instan
it may make little grammatical difference whethe
say *yesterday the man saw the dog* or *the man s*
the dog yesterday, but it is not a matter of indiff
ence whether I say *yesterday the man saw the dog*
yesterday the dog saw the man or whether I say *he*
here or *is he here?* In the one case, of the latter gro
of examples, the vital distinction of subject and obj
depends entirely on the placing of certain words
the sentence, in the latter a slight difference of
quence makes all the difference between statement a
question. It goes without saying that in these ca
the English principle of word order is as potent
means of expression as is the Latin use of case suffi
or of an interrogative particle. There is here no qu
tion of functional poverty, but of formal economy.

We have already seen something of the process
composition, the uniting into a single word of two
more radical elements. Psychologically this process
closely allied to that of word order in so far as
relation between the elements is implied, not exp
itly stated. It differs from the mere juxtaposition
words in the sentence in that the compounded e
ments are felt as constituting but parts of a sin
word-organism. Such languages as Chinese and E
lish, in which the principle of rigid sequence is w
developed, tend not infrequently also to the devel
ment of compound words. It is but a step from su
a Chinese word sequence as *jin tak* "man virtue," i.
"the virtue of men," to such more conventionaliz
and psychologically unified juxtapositions as *t'ien*
"heaven son," i.e., "emperor," or *shui fu* "water mar
i.e., "water carrier." In the latter case we may as w
frankly write *shui-fu* as a single word, the meaning

e compound as a whole being as divergent from the
ecise etymological values of its component elements
is that of our English word *typewriter* from the
erely combined values of *type* and *writer*. In English
e unity of the word *typewriter* is further safe-
arded by a predominant accent on the first syllable
d by the possibility of adding such a suffixed ele-
ent as the plural -*s* to the whole word. Chinese also
ifies its compounds by means of stress. However,
en, in its ultimate origins the process of composi-
on may go back to typical sequences of words in the
ntence, it is now, for the most part, a specialized
ethod of expressing relations. French has as rigid
word order as English but does not possess anything
e its power of compounding words into more com-
ex units. On the other hand, classical Greek, in spite
its relative freedom in the placing of words, has a
ry considerable bent for the formation of compound
rms.

It is curious to observe how greatly languages differ
their ability to make use of the process of com-
osition. One would have thought on general prin-
oles that so simple a device as gives us our *type-
-iter* and *blackbird* and hosts of other words would
an all but universal grammatical process. Such is
ot the case. There are a great many languages, like
kimo and Nootka and, aside from paltry excep-
ons, the Semitic languages, that cannot compound
dical elements. What is even stranger is the fact that
any of these languages are not in the least averse to
mplex word-formations, but may on the contrary
fect a synthesis that far surpasses the utmost that
reek and Sanskrit are capable of. Such a Nootka
ord, for instance, as "when, as they say, he had been
sent for four days" might be expected to embody
least three radical elements corresponding to the
ncepts of "absent," "four," and "day." As a matter
fact the Nootka word is utterly incapable of com-

position in our sense. It is invariably built up out of
a single radical element and a greater or less number
of suffixed elements, some of which may have as con
crete a significance as the radical element itself. In
the particular case we have cited the radical element
conveys the idea of "four," the notions of "day" and
"absent" being expressed by suffixes that are as in
separable from the radical nucleus of the word as in
an English element like -er from the *sing* or *hunt* or
such words as *singer* and *hunter*. The tendency to
word synthesis is, then, by no means the same thing
as the tendency to compounding radical elements
though the latter is not infrequently a ready means
for the synthetic tendency to work with.

There is a bewildering variety of types of composi
tion. These types vary according to function, the na
ture of the compounded elements, and order. In
great many languages composition is confined to what
we may call the delimiting function, that is, of the
two or more compounded elements one is given
more precisely qualified significance by the other
which contribute nothing to the formal build of the
sentence. In English, for instance, such compounded
elements as *red* in *redcoat* or *over* in *overlook* merely
modify the significance of the dominant *coat* or *look*
without in any way sharing, as such, in the predica
tion that is expressed by the sentence. Some languages
however, such as Iroquois and Nahuatl,[3] employ the
method of composition for much heavier work than
this. In Iroquois, for instance, the composition of
noun, in its radical form, with a following verb is
typical method of expressing case relations, particu
larly of the subject or object. *I-meat-eat*, for instance
is the regular Iroquois method of expressing the sen
tence *I am eating meat*. In other languages similar
forms may express local or instrumental or still other

[3] The language of the Aztecs, still spoken in large parts
Mexico.

relations. Such English forms as *killjoy* and *marplot* also illustrate the compounding of a verb and a noun, but the resulting word has a strictly nominal, not a verbal, function. We cannot say *he marplots*. Some languages allow the composition of all or nearly all types of elements. Paiute, for instance, may compound noun with noun, adjective with noun, verb with noun to make a noun, noun with verb to make a verb, adverb with verb, verb with verb. Yana, an Indian language of California, can freely compound noun with noun and verb with noun, but not verb with verb. On the other hand, Iroquois can compound only noun with verb, never noun and noun as in English or verb and verb as in so many other languages. Finally, each language has its characteristic types of order of composition. In English the qualifying element regularly precedes; in certain other languages it follows. Sometimes both types are used in the same language, as in Yana, where "beef" is "bitter-venison" but "deer-liver" is expressed by "liver-deer." The compounded object of a verb precedes the verbal element in Paiute, Nahuatl, and Iroquois, follows it in Yana, Tsimshian,[4] and the Algonkin languages.

Of all grammatical processes affixing is incomparably the most frequently employed. There are languages, like Chinese and Siamese, that make no grammatical use of elements that do not at the same time possess an independent value as radical elements, but such languages are uncommon. Of the three types of affixing—the use of prefixes, suffixes, and infixes—suffixing is much the commonest. Indeed, it is a fair guess that suffixes do more of the formative work of language than all other methods combined. It is worth noting that there are not a few affixing languages that make absolutely no use of prefixed elements but possess a complex apparatus of suffixes. Such are Turkish,

---

[4] An Indian language of British Columbia closely related to the Nass already cited.

Hottentot, Eskimo, Nootka, and Yana. Some of these, like the three last mentioned, have hundreds of suffixed elements, many of them of a concreteness of significance that would demand expression in the vast majority of languages by means of radical elements. The reverse case, the use of prefixed elements to the complete exclusion of suffixes, is far less common. A good example is Khmer (or Cambodgian), spoken in French Cochin-China, though even here there are obscure traces of old suffixes that have ceased to function as such and are now felt to form part of the radical element.

A considerable majority of known languages are prefixing and suffixing at one and the same time, but the relative importance of the two groups of affixed elements naturally varies enormously. In some languages, such as Latin and Russian, the suffixes alone relate the word to the rest of the sentence, the prefixes being confined to the expression of such ideas as delimit the concrete significance of the radical element without influencing its bearing in the proposition. A Latin form like *remittebantur* "they were being sent back" may serve as an illustration of this type of distribution of elements. The prefixed element *re-* "back" merely qualifies to a certain extent the inherent significance of the radical element *mitt-* "send," while the suffixes *-eba-, -nt-,* and *-ur* convey the less concrete, more strictly formal, notions of time, person, plurality, and passivity.

On the other hand, there are languages, like the Bantu group of Africa or the Athabaskan languages[5] of North America, in which the grammatically significant elements precede, those that follow the radical element forming a relatively dispensable class. The Hupa word *te-s-e-ya-te* "I will go," for example, consists of a radical element *-ya-* "to go," three essential

---

[5] Including such languages as Navaho, Apache, Hupa, Carrier, Chipewyan, Loucheux.

prefixes and a formally subsidiary suffix. The element *e-* indicates that the act takes place here and there in space or continuously over space; practically, it has no clear-cut significance apart from such verb stems as it is customary to connect it with. The second prefixed element, *-s-*, is even less easy to define. All we can say is that it is used in verb forms of "definite" time and that it marks action as in progress rather than as beginning or coming to an end. The third prefix, *-e-*, is a pronominal element, "I," which can be used only in "definite" tenses. It is highly important to understand that the use of *-e-* is conditional on that of *-s-* or of certain alternative prefixes and that *e-* also is in practice linked with *-s-*. The group *te-s-e-ya* is a firmly knit grammatical unit. The suffix *-te,* which indicates the future, is no more necessary to its formal balance than is the prefixed *re-* of the Latin word; it is not an element that is capable of standing alone but its function is materially delimiting rather than strictly formal.[6]

It is not always, however, that we can clearly set off the suffixes of a language as a group against its prefixes. In probably the majority of languages that use both types of affixes each group has both delimiting and formal or relational functions. The most that we can say is that a language tends to express similar functions in either the one or the other manner. If a certain verb expresses a certain tense by suffixing, the probability is strong that it expresses its other tenses in an analogous fashion and that, indeed, all verbs

[6] This may seem surprising to an English reader. We generally think of time as a function that is appropriately expressed in a purely formal manner. This notion is due to the bias that Latin grammar has given us. As a matter of fact the English future *(I shall go)* is not expressed by affixing at all; moreover, it may be expressed by the present, as in *to-morrow I leave this place,* where the temporal function is inherent in the independent adverb. Though in lesser degree, the Hupa *-te* is as irrelevant to the vital word as is *to-morrow* to the grammatical "feel" of *I leave.*

have suffixed tense elements. Similarly, we normally
expect to find the pronominal elements, so far as they
are included in the verb at all, either consistently pre
fixed or suffixed. But these rules are far from absolute
We have already seen that Hebrew prefixes its pro
nominal elements in certain cases, suffixes them in
others. In Chimariko, an Indian language of California, the position of the pronominal affixes depends on
the verb; they are prefixed for certain verbs, suffixed
for others.

It will not be necessary to give many further examples of prefixing and suffixing. One of each category
will suffice to illustrate their formative possibilities.
The idea expressed in English by the sentence *I came
to give it to her* is rendered in Chinook[7] by *i-n-i-a-l-u-
d-am*. This word—and it is a thoroughly unified word
with a clear-cut accent on the first *a*—consists of a
radical element, *-d-* "to give," six functionally distinct,
if phonetically frail, prefixed elements, and a suffix.
Of the prefixes, *i-* indicates recently past time; *n-*, the
pronominal subject "I"; *-i-*, the pronominal object
"it";[8] *-a-*, the second pronominal object "her"; *-l-*, a
prepositional element indicating that the preceding
pronominal prefix is to be understood as an indirect
object (*-her-to-*, i.e., "to her"); and *-u-*, an element that
it is not easy to define satisfactorily but which, on the
whole, indicates movement away from the speaker.
The suffixed *-am* modifies the verbal content in a
local sense; it adds to the notion conveyed by the
radical element that of "arriving" or "going (or coming) for that particular purpose." It is obvious that
in Chinook, as in Hupa, the greater part of the grammatical machinery resides in the prefixes rather than
in the suffixes.

[7] Wishram dialect.
[8] Really "him," but Chinook, like Latin or French, possesses
grammatical gender. An object may be referred to as "he,"
"she," or "it," according to the characteristic form of its noun.

A reverse case, one in which the grammatically significant elements cluster, as in Latin, at the end of the word is yielded by Fox, one of the better known Algonkin languages of the Mississippi Valley. We may take the form *eh-kiwi-n-a-m-oht-ati-wa-ch(i)* "then they together kept (him) in flight from them." The radical element here is *kiwi-*, a verb stem indicating the general notion of "indefinite movement round about, here and there." The prefixed element *eh-* is hardly more than an adverbial particle indicating temporal subordination; it may be conveniently rendered as "then." Of the seven suffixes included in this highly wrought word, *-n-* seems to be merely a phonetic element serving to connect the verb stem with the following *-a-;*[9] *-a-* is a "secondary stem"[10] denoting the idea of "flight, to flee"; *-m-* denotes causality with reference to an animate object;[11] *-o(ht)-* indicates activity done for the subject (the so-called "middle" or "medio-passive" voice of Greek); *-(a)ti-* is a reciprocal element, "one another"; *-wa-ch(i)* is the third person animate plural (*-wa-*, plural; *-chi,* more properly personal) of so-called "conjunctive" forms. The word may be translated more literally (and yet only approximately as to grammatical feeling) as "then they (animate) caused some animate being to wander about in flight from one another of themselves." Eskimo, Nootka, Yana, and other languages have similarly complex arrays of suffixed elements, though the func-

---

[9] This analysis is doubtful. It is likely that *-n-* possesses a function that still remains to be ascertained. The Algonkin languages are unusually complex and present many unsolved problems of detail.

[10] "Secondary stems" are elements which are suffixes from a formal point of view, never appearing without the support of a true radical element, but whose function is as concrete, to all intents and purposes, as that of the radical element itself. Secondary verb stems of this type are characteristic of the Algonkin languages and of Yana.

[11] In the Algonkin languages all persons and things are conceived of as either animate or inanimate, just as in Latin or German they are conceived of as masculine, feminine, or neuter

tions performed by them and their principles of combination differ widely.

We have reserved the very curious type of affixa-
tion known as "infixing" for separate illustration. It
is utterly unknown in English, unless we consider the
-n- of *stand* (contrast *stood*) as an infixed element. The
earlier Indo-European languages, such as Latin, Greek
and Sanskrit, made a fairly considerable use of infixed
nasals to differentiate the present tense of a certain
class of verbs from other forms (contrast Latin *vinc-o*
"I conquer" with *vic-i* "I conquered"; Greek *lamb-
an-o* "I take" with *e-lab-on* "I took"). There are, however, more striking examples of the process, examples
in which it has assumed a more clearly defined function than in these Latin and Greek cases. It is
particularly prevalent in many languages of southeastern Asia and of the Malay archipelago. Good examples from Khmer (Cambodgian) are *tmeu* "one who
walks" and *daneu* "walking" (verbal noun), both derived from *deu* "to walk." Further examples may
be quoted from Bontoc Igorot, a Filipino language.
Thus, an infixed *-in-* conveys the idea of the product
of an accomplished action, e.g., *kayu* "wood," *kinayu*
"gathered wood." Infixes are also freely used in the
Bontoc Igorot verb. Thus, an infixed *-um-* is characteristic of many intransitive verbs with personal pronominal suffixes, e.g., *sad-* "to wait," *sumid-ak* "I
wait"; *kineg* "silent," *kuminek-ak* "I am silent." In
other verbs it indicates futurity, e.g., *tengao-* "to cele-
brate a holiday," *tumengao-ak* "I shall have a holiday." The past tense is frequently indicated by an
infixed *-in-*; if there is already an infixed *-um-*, the two
elements combine to *-in-m-*, e.g., *kinminek-ak* "I am
silent." Obviously the infixing process has in this (and
related) languages the same vitality that is possessed
by the commoner prefixes and suffixes of other languages. The process is also found in a number of
aboriginal American languages. The Yana plural is

sometimes formed by an infixed element, e.g., *k'uruwi* "medicine-men," *k'uwi* "medicine-man"; in Chinook an infixed *-l-* is used in certain verbs to indicate re-peated activity, e.g., *ksik-ludelk* "she keeps looking at him," *iksik-lutk* "she looked at him" (radical element *-tk*). A peculiarly interesting type of infixation is found in the Siouan languages, in which certain verbs insert the pronominal elements into the very body of the radical element, e.g., Sioux *cheti* "to build a fire," *chewati* "I build a fire"; *shuta* "to miss," *shuunta-pi* "we miss."

A subsidiary but by no means unimportant gram-matical process is that of internal vocalic or conso-nantal change. In some languages, as in English (*sing, sang, sung, song; goose, geese*), the former of these has become one of the major methods of indicating fundamental changes of grammatical function. At any rate, the process is alive enough to lead our children into untrodden ways. We all know of the growing youngster who speaks of having *brung* something, on the analogy of such forms as *sung* and *flung*. In He-brew, as we have seen, vocalic change is of even greater significance than in English. What is true of Hebrew is of course true of all other Semitic lan-guages. A few examples of so-called "broken" plurals from Arabic[12] will supplement the Hebrew verb forms that I have given in another connection. The noun *balad* "place" has the plural form *bilad;* [13] *gild* "hide" forms the plural *gulud; ragil* "man," the plural *rigal; shibbak* "window," the plural *shababik*. Very similar phenomena are illustrated by the Hamitic languages of Northern Africa, e.g., Shilh[14] *izbil* "hair," plural *izbel; a-slem* "fish," plural *i-slim-en; sn* "to know," *sen* "to be knowing"; *rmi* "to become tired," *rumni* "to

[12] Egyptian dialect.
[13] There are changes of accent and vocalic quantity in these forms as well, but the requirements of simplicity force us to neglect them.
[14] A Berber language of Morocco.

be tired"; *ttss*[15] "to fall asleep," *ttoss* "to sleep." Strik
ingly similar to English and Greek alternations of
the type *sing—sang* and *leip-o* "I leave," *leloip-a* "I
have left," are such Somali[16] cases as *al* "I am," *il* "I
was"; *i-dah-a* "I say," *i-di* "I said," *deh* "say!"

Vocalic change is of great significance also in a num
ber of American Indian languages. In the Athabaskan
group many verbs change the quality or quantity of
the vowel of the radical element as it changes its
tense or mode. The Navaho verb for "I put (grain)
into a receptacle" is *bi-hi-sh-ja,* in which *-ja* is the
radical element; the past tense, *bi-hi-ja',* has a long
a-vowel, followed by the "glottal stop";[17] the future
is *bi-h-de-sh-ji* with complete change of vowel. In
other types of Navaho verbs the vocalic changes fol
low different lines, e.g., *yah-a-ni-ye* "you carry (a pack)
into (a stable)"; past, *yah-i-ni-yin* (with long *i* in *-yin;*
-n is here used to indicate nasalization); future, *yah-a-
di-yehl* (with long *e*). In another Indian language,
Yokuts,[18] vocalic modifications affect both noun and
verb forms. Thus, *buchong* "son" forms the plural
bochang-i (contrast the objective *buchong-a*); *enash*
"grandfather," the plural *inash-a;* the verb *engtyim* "to
sleep" forms the continuative *ingetym-ad* "to be sleep
ing" and the past *ingetym-ash.*

Consonantal change as a functional process is prob
ably far less common than vocalic modifications, but
it is not exactly rare. There is an interesting group
of cases in English, certain nouns and corresponding
verbs differing solely in that the final consonant is
voiceless or voiced. Examples are *wreath* (with *th* as
in *think*), but *to wreathe* (with *th* as in *then*); *house,*
but *to house* (with *s* pronounced like *z*). That we have
a distinct feeling for the interchange as a means of

[15] Some of the Berber languages allow consonantal combinations that seem unpronounceable to us.
[16] One of the Hamitic languages of eastern Africa.
[17] See page 48.
[18] Spoken in the south-central part of California.

distinguishing the noun from the verb is indicated by the extension of the principle by many Americans to such a noun as *rise* (e.g., *the rise of democracy*)—pronounced like *rice*—in contrast to the verb *to rise* (*s* like *z*).

In the Celtic languages the initial consonants undergo several types of change according to the grammatical relation that subsists between the word itself and the preceding word. Thus, in modern Irish, a word like *bo* "ox" may, under the appropriate circumstances, take the forms *bho* (pronounce *wo*) or *mo* (e.g., *an bo* "the ox," as a subject, but *tir na mo* "land of the oxen," as a possessive plural). In the verb the principle has as one of its most striking consequences the "aspiration" of initial consonants in the past tense. If a verb begins with *t,* say, it changes the *t* to *th* (now pronounced *h*) in forms of the past; if it begins with *g,* the consonant changes, in analogous forms, to *gh* (pronounced like a voiced spirant[19] *g* or like *y,* according to the nature of the following vowel). In modern Irish the principle of consonantal change, which began in the oldest period of the language as a secondary consequence of certain phonetic conditions, has become one of the primary grammatical processes of the language.

Perhaps as remarkable as these Irish phenomena are the consonantal interchanges of Ful, an African language of the Soudan. Here we find that all nouns belonging to the personal class form the plural by changing their initial *g, j, d, b, k, ch,* and *p* to *y* (or *w*), *y, r, w, h, s* and *f* respectively; e.g., *jim-o* "companion," *yim-'be* "companions"; *pio-o* "beater," *fio-'be* "beaters." Curiously enough, nouns that belong to the class of things form their singular and plural in exactly reverse fashion, e.g., *yola-re* "grass-grown place," *jola-je* "grass-grown places"; *fitan-du* "soul," *pital-i* "souls." In Nootka, to refer to but one other language

[19] See page 51.

in which the process is found, the *t* or *tl* [20] of many verbal suffixes becomes *hl* in forms denoting repetition, e.g., *hita-'ato* "to fall out," *hita-'ahl* "to keep falling out"; *mat-achisht-utl* "to fly on to the water," *mat-achisht-ohl* "to keep flying on to the water." Further, the *hl* of certain elements changes to a peculiar *h*-sound in plural forms, e.g., *yak-ohl* "sore-faced," *yak-oh* "sore-faced (people)."

Nothing is more natural than the prevalence of reduplication, in other words, the repetition of all or part of the radical element. The process is generally employed, with self-evident symbolism, to indicate such concepts as distribution, plurality, repetition, customary activity, increase of size, added intensity, continuance. Even in English it is not unknown, though it is not generally accounted one of the typical formative devices of our language. Such words as *goody-goody* and *to pooh-pooh* have become accepted as part of our normal vocabulary, but the method of duplication may on occasion be used more freely than is indicated by such stereotyped examples. Such locutions as *a big big man* or *Let it cool till it's thick thick* are far more common, especially in the speech of women and children, than our linguistic text-books would lead one to suppose. In a class by themselves are the really enormous number of words, many of them sound-imitative or contemptuous in psychological tone, that consist of duplications with either change of the vowel or change of the initial consonant—words of the type *sing-song, riff-raff, wishy-washy, harum-skarum, roly-poly*. Words of this type are all but universal. Such examples as the Russian *Chudo-Yudo* (a dragon), the Chinese *ping-pang* "rattling of rain on the roof," [21] the Tibetan *kyang-kyong* "lazy," and the Manchu *porpon parpan* "blear-eyed" are curiously reminiscent, both in form and in psy-

[20] These orthographies are but makeshifts for simple sounds.
[21] Whence our *ping-pong*.

chology, of words nearer home. But it can hardly be said that the duplicative process is of a distinctively grammatical significance in English. We must turn to other languages for illustration. Such cases as Hottentot *go-go* "to look at carefully" (from *go* "to see"), Somali *fen-fen* "to gnaw at on all sides" (from *fen* "to gnaw at"), Chinook *iwi iwi* "to look about carefully, to examine" (from *iwi* "to appear"), or Tsimshian *am'am* "several (are) good" (from *am* "good") do not depart from the natural and fundamental range of significance of the process. A more abstract function is illustrated in Ewe,[22] in which both infinitives and verbal adjectives are formed from verbs by duplication; e.g., *yi* "to go," *yiyi* "to go, act of going"; *wo* "to do," *wowo*[23] "done"; *mawomawo* "not to do" (with both duplicated verb stem and duplicated negative particle). Causative duplications are characteristic of Hottentot, e.g., *gam-gam*[24] "to cause to tell" (from *gam* "to tell"). Or the process may be used to derive verbs from nouns, as in Hottentot *khoe-khoe* "to talk Hottentot" (from *khoe-b* "man, Hottentot"), or as in Kwakiutl *metmat* "to eat clams" (radical element *met-* "clam").

The most characteristic examples of reduplication are such as repeat only part of the radical element. It would be possible to demonstrate the existence of a vast number of formal types of such partial duplication, according to whether the process makes use of one or more of the radical consonants, preserves or weakens or alters the radical vowel, or affects the beginning, the middle, or the end of the radical element. The functions are even more exuberantly developed than with simple duplication, though the basic notion, at least in origin, is nearly always one

[22] An African language of the Guinea Coast.
[23] In the verbal adjective the tone of the second syllable differs from that of the first.
[24] Initial "click" (see page 53, note 15) omitted.

of repetition or continuance. Examples illustrating this fundamental function can be quoted from all parts of the globe. Initially reduplicating are, for instance, Shilh *ggen* "to be sleeping" (from *gen* "to sleep"); Ful *pepeu-'do* "liar" (i.e., "one who always lies"), plural *fefeu-'be* (from *fewa* "to lie"); Bontoc Igorot *anak* "child," *ananak* "children"; *kamu-ek* "I hasten," *kakamu-ek* "I hasten more"; Tsimshian *gyad* "person," *gyigyad* "people"; Nass *gyibayuk* "to fly," *gyigyibayuk* "one who is flying." Psychologically comparable, but with the reduplication at the end, are Somali *ur* "body," plural *urar;* Hausa *suna* "name," plural *sunana-ki;* Washo[25] *gusu* "buffalo," *gususu* "buffaloes"; Takelma[26] *himi-d-* "to talk to," *himim-d-* "to be accustomed to talk to." Even more commonly than simple duplication, this partial duplication of the radical element has taken on in many languages functions that seem in no way related to the idea of increase. The best known examples are probably the initial reduplication of our older Indo-European languages, which helps to form the perfect tense of many verbs (e.g., Sanskrit *dadarsha* "I have seen," Greek *leloipa* "I have left," Latin *tetigi* "I have touched," Gothic *lelot* "I have let"). In Nootka reduplication of the radical element is often employed in association with certain suffixes; e.g., *hluch-* "woman" forms *hluhluch-'ituhl* "to dream of a woman," *hluhluch-k'ok* "resembling a woman." Psychologically similar to the Greek and Latin examples are many Takelma cases of verbs that exhibit two forms of the stem, one employed in the present or past, the other in the future and in certain modes and verbal derivatives. The former has final reduplication, which is absent in the latter; e.g., *al-yebeb-i'n* "I show (or showed) to him," *al-yeb-in* "I shall show him."

We come now to the subtlest of all grammatical

---

[25] An Indian language of Nevada.
[26] An Indian language of Oregon.

processes, variations in accent, whether of stress or pitch. The chief difficulty in isolating accent as a functional process is that it is so often combined with alternations in vocalic quantity or quality or complicated by the presence of affixed elements that its grammatical value appears as a secondary rather than as a primary feature. In Greek, for instance, it is characteristic of true verbal forms that they throw the accent back as far as the general accentual rules will permit, while nouns may be more freely accented. There is thus a striking accentual difference between a verbal form like *eluthemen* "we were released," accented on the second syllable of the word, and its participial derivative *lutheis* "released," accented on the last. The presence of the characteristic verbal elements *e-* and *-men* in the first case and of the nominal *-s* in the second tends to obscure the inherent value of the accentual alternation. This value comes out very neatly in such English doublets as *to refund* and *a refund*, *to extract* and *an extract*, *to come down* and *a come down*, *to lack luster* and *lack-luster eyes,* in which the difference between the verb and the noun is entirely a matter of changing stress. In the Athabaskan languages there are not infrequently significant alternations of accent, as in Navaho *ta-di-gis* "you wash yourself" (accented on the second syllable), *ta-di-gis* "he washes himself" (accented on the first).[27]

Pitch accent may be as functional as stress and is perhaps more often so. The mere fact, however, that pitch variations are phonetically essential to the language, as in Chinese (e.g., *feng* "wind" with a level tone, *feng* "to serve" with a falling tone) or as in classical Greek (e.g., *lab-on* "having taken" with a simple or high tone on the suffixed participial *-on*, *gunaik-on* "of women" with a compound or falling tone on the case suffix *-on*) does not necessarily constitute a func-

---

[27] It is not unlikely, however, that these Athabaskan alternations are primarily tonal in character.

tional, or perhaps we had better say grammatical, use of pitch. In such cases the pitch is merely inherent in the radical element or affix, as any vowel or consonant might be. It is different with such Chinese alternations as *chung* (level) "middle" and *chung* (falling) "to hit the middle"; *mai* (rising) "to buy" and *mai* (falling) "to sell"; *pei* (falling) "back" and *pei* (level) "to carry on the back." Examples of this type are not exactly common in Chinese and the language cannot be said to possess at present a definite feeling for tonal differences as symbolic of the distinction between noun and verb.

There are languages, however, in which such differences are of the most fundamental grammatical importance. They are particularly common in the Soudan. In Ewe, for instance, there are formed from *subo* "to serve" two reduplicated forms, an infinitive *subosubo* "to serve," with a low tone on the first two syllables and a high one on the last two, and an adjectival *subo-subo* "serving," in which all the syllables have a high tone. Even more striking are cases furnished by Shilluk, one of the languages of the headwaters of the Nile. The plural of the noun often differs in tone from the singular, e.g., *yit* (high) "ear" but *yit* (low) "ears." In the pronoun three forms may be distinguished by tone alone; *e* "he" has a high tone and is subjective, *-e* "him" (e.g., *a chwol-e* "he called him") has a low tone and is objective, *-e* "his" (e.g., *wod-e* "his house") has a middle tone and is possessive. From the verbal element *gwed-* "to write" are formed *gwed-o* "(he) writes" with a low tone, the passive *gwet* "(it was) written" with a falling tone, the imperative *gwet* "write!" with a rising tone, and the verbal noun *gwet* "writing" with a middle tone. In aboriginal America also pitch accent is known to occur as a grammatical process. A good example of such a pitch language is Tlingit, spoken by the Indians of the southern coast of Alaska. In this language many verbs

ary the tone of the radical element according to
ense; *hun* "to sell," *sin* "to hide," *tin* "to see," and
numerous other radical elements, if low-toned, refer
to past time, if high-toned, to the future. Another type
of function is illustrated by the Takelma forms *hel*
"song," with falling pitch, but *hel* "sing!" with a rising inflection; parallel to these forms are *sel* (falling)
"black paint," *sel* (rising) "paint it!" All in all it
is clear that pitch accent, like stress and vocalic or
consonantal modifications, is far less infrequently employed as a grammatical process than our own habits
of speech would prepare us to believe probable.

CHAPTER V

Form in Language:
Grammatical Concepts

○

We have seen that the single word expresses either
a simple concept or a combination of concepts so
interrelated as to form a psychological unity. We
have, furthermore, briefly reviewed from a strictly
formal standpoint the main processes that are used by
all known languages to affect the fundamental con
cepts—those embodied in unanalyzable words or in
the radical elements of words—by the modifying or
formative influence of subsidiary concepts. In this
chapter we shall look a little more closely into the
nature of the world of concepts, in so far as that
world is reflected and systematized in linguistic struc
ture.

Let us begin with a simple sentence that involves
various kinds of concepts—*the farmer kills the duck
ling*. A rough and ready analysis discloses here the
presence of three distinct and fundamental concepts
that are brought into connection with each other in
a number of ways. These three concepts are "farmer"
(the subject of discourse), "kill" (defining the nature
of the activity which the sentence informs us about),
and "duckling" (another subject[1] of discourse that
takes an important though somewhat passive part in
this activity). We can visualize the farmer and the

[1] Not in its technical sense.

duckling and we have also no difficulty in constructing an image of the killing. In other words, the elements *farmer, kill,* and *duckling* define concepts of a concrete order.

But a more careful linguistic analysis soon brings us to see that the two subjects of discourse, however simply we may visualize them, are not expressed quite as directly, as immediately, as we feel them. A "farmer" is in one sense a perfectly unified concept, in another he is "one who farms." The concept conveyed by the radical element (*farm-*) is not one of personality at all but of an industrial activity (*to farm*), itself based on the concept of a particular type of object (*a farm*). Similarly, the concept of *duckling* is at one remove from that which is expressed by the radical element of the word, *duck*. This element, which may occur as an independent word, refers to a whole class of animals, big and little, while *duckling* is limited in its application to the young of that class. The word *farmer* has an "agentive" suffix *-er* that performs the function of indicating the one that carries out a given activity, in this case that of farming. It transforms the verb *to farm* into an agentive noun precisely as it transforms the verbs *to sing, to paint, to teach* into the corresponding agentive nouns *singer, painter, teacher*. The element *-ling* is not so freely used, but its significance is obvious. It adds to the basic concept the notion of smallness (as also in *gosling, fledgeling*) or the somewhat related notion of "contemptible" (as in *weakling, princeling, hireling*). The agentive *-er* and the diminutive *-ling* both convey fairly concrete ideas (roughly those of "doer" and "little"), but the concreteness is not stressed. They do not so much define distinct concepts as mediate between concepts. The *-er* of *farmer* does not quite say "one who (farms)"; it merely indicates that the sort of person we call a "farmer" is closely enough associated with activity on a farm to be conventionally thought of as always so occupied. He may, as a matter of fact, go to town and engage in any pursuit but farming, yet his linguistic label remains "farmer." Language here betrays a certain helplessness or, if one prefers, a stubborn tendency to look away from the immediately suggested function, trusting to the imagination and to usage to fill in the transitions of thought and the details of application that distinguish one concrete concept (*to farm*) from another "derived" one (*farmer*). It would be impossible for any language to express every concrete idea by an independent word or radical element. The concreteness of experience is infinite, the resources of the richest language are strictly limited. It must perforce throw countless concepts under the rubric of certain basic ones, using other concrete or semi-concrete ideas as functional mediators. The ideas expressed by these mediating elements—they may be independent words, affixes, or modifications of the radical element—may be called "derivational" or "qualifying." Some concrete concepts, such as *kill,* are expressed radically; others, such as *farmer* and *duckling,* are expressed derivatively. Corresponding to these two modes of expression we have two types of concepts and of linguistic elements, radical (*farm, kill, duck*) and derivational (*-er, -ling*). When a word (or unified group of words) contains a derivational element (or word) the concrete significance of the radical element (*farm-, duck-*) tends to fade from consciousness and to yield to a new concreteness (*farmer, duckling*) that is synthetic in expression rather than in thought. In our sentence the concepts of *farm* and *duck* are not really involved at all; they are merely latent, for formal reasons, in the linguistic expression.

Returning to this sentence, we feel that the analysis of *farmer* and *duckling* is practically irrelevant to an understanding of its content and entirely irrelevant to a feeling for the structure of the sentence as a

whole. From the standpoint of the sentence the derivational elements *-er* and *-ling* are merely details in
the local economy of two of its terms (*farmer, duckling*) that it accepts as units of expression. This in-
difference of the sentence as such to some part of the
analysis of its words is shown by the fact that if we
substitute such radical words as *man* and *chick* for
farmer and *duckling*, we obtain a new material content, it is true, but not in the least a new structural
mold. We can go further and substitute another activity for that of "killing," say "taking." The new sentence, *the man takes the chick*, is totally different
from the first sentence in what it conveys, not in how
it conveys it. We feel instinctively, without the
slightest attempt at conscious analysis, that the two
sentences fit precisely the same pattern, that they are
really the same fundamental sentence, differing only
in their material trappings. In other words, they express identical relational concepts in an identical
manner. The manner is here threefold—the use of
an inherently relational word (*the*) in analogous positions, the analogous sequence (subject; predicate, con-
sisting of verb and object) of the concrete terms of
the sentence, and the use of the suffixed element *-s*
in the verb.

Change any of these features of the sentence and it
becomes modified, slightly or seriously, in some purely
relational, non-material regard. If *the* is omitted
(*farmer kills duckling, man takes chick*), the sentence
becomes impossible; it falls into no recognized formal
pattern and the two subjects of discourse seem to hang
incompletely in the void. We feel that there is no
relation established between either of them and what
is already in the minds of the speaker and his auditor.
As soon as a *the* is put before the two nouns, we feel
relieved. We know that the farmer and duckling
which the sentence tells us about are the same farmer
and duckling that we had been talking about or hear-

ing about or thinking about some time before. If
meet a man who is not looking at and knows nothin,
about the farmer in question, I am likely to be stare(
at for my pains if I announce to him that "the farme
[what farmer?] kills the duckling [didn't know he ha(
any, whoever he is]." If the fact nevertheless seem
interesting enough to communicate, I should be com
pelled to speak of "*a farmer* up my way" and of "*
duckling* of his." These little words, *the* and *a,* hav
the important function of establishing a definite or a₁
indefinite reference.

If I omit the first *the* and also leave out the suffixe(
-*s,* I obtain an entirely new set of relations. *Farmer
kill the duckling* implies that I am now speaking t(
the farmer, not merely about him; further, that he i
not actually killing the bird, but is being ordered b
me to do so. The subjective relation of the first sen
tence has become a vocative one, one of address, an(
the activity is conceived in terms of command, not o
statement. We conclude, therefore, that if the farme
is to be merely talked about, the little *the* must g(
back into its place and the -*s* must not be removed
The latter element clearly defines, or rather helps t(
define, statement as contrasted with command. I find
moreover, that if I wish to speak of several farmers,
cannot say *the farmers kills the duckling,* but mus
say *the farmers kill the duckling.* Evidently -*s* in
volves the notion of singularity in the subject. If th(
noun is singular, the verb must have a form to corre
spond; if the noun is plural, the verb has another
corresponding form.[2] Comparison with such forms a
I kill and *you kill* shows, moreover, that the -*s* ha
exclusive reference to a person other than the speake
or the one spoken to. We conclude, therefore, that i
connotes a personal relation as well as the notion o
singularity. And comparison with a sentence like *th(*

[2] It is, of course, an "accident" that -*s* denotes plurality in th
noun, singularity in the verb.

farmer killed the duckling indicates that there is implied in this overburdened *-s* a distinct reference to
present time. Statement as such and personal reference
may well be looked upon as inherently relational concepts. Number is evidently felt by those who speak
English as involving a necessary relation, otherwise
there would be no reason to express the concept
twice, in the noun and in the verb. Time also is
clearly felt as a relational concept; if it were not, we
should be allowed to say *the farmer killed-s* to correspond to *the farmer kill-s*. Of the four concepts inextricably interwoven in the *-s* suffix, all are felt as
relational, two necessarily so. The distinction between
a truly relational concept and one that is so felt and
treated, though it need not be in the nature of things,
will receive further attention in a moment.

Finally, I can radically disturb the relational cut of
the sentence by changing the order of its elements.
If the positions of *farmer* and *kills* are interchanged,
the sentence reads *kills the farmer the duckling,* which
is most naturally interpreted as an unusual but not
unintelligible mode of asking the question, *does the
farmer kill the duckling?* In this new sentence the act
is not conceived as necessarily taking place at all. It
may or it may not be happening, the implication being that the speaker wishes to know the truth of the
matter and that the person spoken to is expected to
give him the information. The interrogative sentence
possesses an entirely different "modality" from the
declarative one and implies a markedly different attitude of the speaker towards his companion. An even
more striking change in personal relations is effected
if we interchange *the farmer* and *the duckling. The
duckling kills the farmer* involves precisely the same
subjects of discourse and the same type of activity as
our first sentence, but the rôles of these subjects of
discourse are now reversed. The duckling has turned,
like the proverbial worm, or, to put it in grammat-

ical terminology, what was "subject" is now "object,"
what was object is now subject.

The following tabular statement analyzes the sen
tence from the point of view of the concepts expressed
in it and of the grammatical processes employed for
their expression.

I. CONCRETE CONCEPTS:
    1. First subject of discourse: *farmer*
    2. Second subject of discourse: *duckling*
    3. Activity: *kill*
    —— analyzable into:
  A. RADICAL CONCEPTS:
    1. Verb: (*to*) *farm*
    2. Noun: *duck*
    3. Verb: *kill*
  B. DERIVATIONAL CONCEPTS:
    1. Agentive: expressed by suffix *-er*
    2. Diminutive: expressed by suffix *-ling*
II. RELATIONAL CONCEPTS:
  Reference:
    1. Definiteness of reference to first subject of dis-
       course: expressed by first *the,* which has pre-
       posed position
    2. Definiteness of reference to second subject of
       discourse: expressed by second *the,* which has
       preposed position
  Modality:
    3. Declarative: expressed by sequence of "sub-
       ject" plus verb; and implied by suffixed *-s*
  Personal relations:
    4. Subjectivity of *farmer:* expressed by position
       of *farmer* before kills; and by suffixed *-s*
    5. Objectivity of *duckling:* expressed by position
       of *duckling* after *kills*
  Number:
    6. Singularity of first subject of discourse: ex-
       pressed by lack of plural suffix in *farmer;*
       and by suffix *-s* in following verb
    7. Singularity of second subject of discourse: ex-
       pressed by lack of plural suffix in *duckling*

Time:
   8. Present: expressed by lack of preterit suffix in
       verb; and by suffixed -s

In this short sentence of five words there are expressed, therefore, thirteen distinct concepts, of which three are radical and concrete, two derivational, and eight relational. Perhaps the most striking result of the analysis is a renewed realization of the curious lack of accord in our language between function and form. The method of suffixing is used both for derivational and for relational elements; independent words or radical elements express both concrete ideas (objects, activities, qualities) and relational ideas (articles like *the* and *a;* words defining case relations, like *of, to, for, with, by;* words defining local relations, like *in, on, at*); the same relational concept may be expressed more than once (thus, the singularity of *farmer* is both negatively expressed in the noun and positively in the verb); and one element may convey a group of interwoven concepts rather than one definite concept alone (thus the -s of *kills* embodies no less than four logically independent relations).

Our analysis may seem a bit labored, but only because we are so accustomed to our own well-worn grooves of expression that they have come to be felt as inevitable. Yet destructive analysis of the familiar is the only method of approach to an understanding of fundamentally different modes of expression. When one has learned to feel what is fortuitous or illogical or unbalanced in the structure of his own language, he is already well on the way toward a sympathetic grasp of the expression of the various classes of concepts in alien types of speech. Not everything that is "outlandish" is intrinsically illogical or far-fetched. It is often precisely the familiar that a wider perspective reveals as the curiously exceptional. From a purely logical standpoint it is obvious that there is

no inherent reason why the concepts expressed in ou
sentence should have been singled out, treated, an
grouped as they have been and not otherwise. Th
sentence is the outgrowth of historical and of un
reasoning psychological forces rather than of a logica
synthesis of elements that have been clearly graspe
in their individuality. This is the case, to a greate
or less degree, in all languages, though in the form
of many we find a more coherent, a more consisten
reflection than in our English forms of that uncor
scious analysis into individual concepts which is neve
entirely absent from speech, however it may be con
plicated with or overlaid by the more irrational fa
tors.

A cursory examination of other languages, nea
and far, would soon show that some or all of th
thirteen concepts that our sentence happens to en
body may not only be expressed in different form bu
that they may be differently grouped among then
selves; that some among them may be dispensed witl
and that other concepts, not considered worth ex
pressing in English idiom, may be treated as absolutel
indispensable to the intelligible rendering of th
proposition. First as to a different method of handlin
such concepts as we have found expressed in th
English sentence. If we turn to German, we find tha
in the equivalent sentence (*Der Bauer tötet das En
telein*) the definiteness of reference expressed by th
English *the* is unavoidably coupled with three othe
concepts—number (both *der* and *das* are explicitl
singular), case (*der* is subjective; *das* is subjective o
objective, by elimination therefore objective), an
gender, a new concept of the relational order that i
not in this case explicitly involved in English (*der i
masculine, *das* is neuter). Indeed, the chief burde
of the expression of case, gender, and number is in
the German sentence borne by the particles of re
erence rather than by the words that express th
concrete concepts (*Bauer, Entelein*) to which thes

elational concepts ought logically to attach them-
elves. In the sphere of concrete concepts too it is
vorth noting that the German splits up the idea of
"killing" into the basic concept of "dead" (*tot*) and
he derivational one of "causing to do (or be) so and
o" (by the method of vocalic change, *töt-*); the German *töt-et* (analytically *tot-* + vowel change + *-et*)
"causes to be dead" is, approximately, the formal ap-
:quivalent of our *dead-en-s,* though the idiomatic ap-
)lication of this latter word is different.[3]

Wandering still further afield, we may glance at the
Yana method of expression. Literally translated, the
:quivalent Yana sentence would read something like
'kill-s he farmer[4] he to duck-ling," in which "he" and
'to" are rather awkward English renderings of a gen-
:ral third personal pronoun (*he, she, it,* or *they*) and
an objective particle which indicates that the following noun is connected with the verb otherwise than
as subject. The suffixed element in "kill-s" corresponds
o the English suffix with the important exceptions
:hat it makes no reference to the number of the subject and that the statement is known to be true, that
t is vouched for by the speaker. Number is only
indirectly expressed in the sentence in so far as there
is no specific verb suffix indicating plurality of the
subject nor specific plural elements in the two nouns.
Had the statement been made on another's authority,
a totally different "tense-modal" suffix would have had
to be used. The pronouns of reference ("he") imply
nothing by themselves as to number, gender, or case.
Gender, indeed, is completely absent in Yana as a
relational category.

The Yana sentence has already illustrated the point

---

[3] "To cause to be dead" or "to cause to die" in the sense of
'to kill" is an exceedingly wide-spread usage. It is found, for
instance, also in Nootka and Sioux.

[4] Agriculture was not practised by the Yana. The verbal idea
of "to farm" would probably be expressed in some such synthetic manner as "to dig-earth" or "to grow-cause." These are
suffixed elements corresponding to *-er* and *-ling.*

that certain of our supposedly essential concepts may
be ignored; both the Yana and the German sentence
illustrate the further point that certain concepts may
need expression for which an English-speaking per
son, or rather the English-speaking habit, finds no
need whatever. One could go on and give endless
examples of such deviations from English form, but
we shall have to content ourselves with a few more
indications. In the Chinese sentence "Man kill duck,"
which may be looked upon as the practical equivalent
of "The man kills the duck," there is by no means
present for the Chinese consciousness that childish,
halting, empty feeling which we experience in the
literal English translation. The three concrete con
cepts—two objects and an action—are each directly
expressed by a monosyllabic word which is at the
same time a radical element; the two relational con
cepts—"subject" and "object"—are expressed solely
by the position of the concrete words before and after
the word of action. And that is all. Definiteness or
indefiniteness of reference, number, personality as an
inherent aspect of the verb, tense, not to speak of
gender—all these are given no expression in the
Chinese sentence, which, for all that, is a perfectly
adequate communication—provided, of course, there
is that context, that background of mutual under
standing that is essential to the complete intelligibility
of all speech. Nor does this qualification impair our
argument, for in the English sentence too we leave
unexpressed a large number of ideas which are either
taken for granted or which have been developed or
are about to be developed in the course of the con
versation. Nothing has been said, for example, in the
English, German, Yana, or Chinese sentence as to the
place relations of the farmer, the duck, the speaker,
and the listener. Are the farmer and the duck both
visible or is one or the other invisible from the point
of view of the speaker, and are both placed within

ie horizon of the speaker, the listener, or of some
idefinite point of reference "off yonder"? In other
ords, to paraphrase awkwardly certain latent "de-
ionstrative" ideas, does this farmer (invisible to us
ut standing behind a door not far away from me, you
eing seated yonder well out of reach) kill that duck-
ng (which belongs to you)? or does that farmer (who
ves in your neighborhood and whom we see over
iere) kill that duckling (that belongs to him)? This
ype of demonstrative elaboration is foreign to our
ay of thinking, but it would seem very natural, in-
eed unavoidable, to a Kwakiutl Indian.

What, then, are the absolutely essential concepts
1 speech, the concepts that must be expressed if
inguage is to be a satisfactory means of communica-
on? Clearly we must have, first of all, a large stock
f basic or radical concepts, the concrete wherewithal
f speech. We must have objects, actions, qualities to
ilk about, and these must have their corresponding
ymbols in independent words or in radical elements.
Io proposition, however abstract its intent, is hu-
ianly possible without a tying on at one or more
oints to the concrete world of sense. In every intel-
igible proposition at least two of these radical ideas
iust be expressed, though in exceptional cases one or
ven both may be understood from the context. And,
econdly, such relational concepts must be expressed
s moor the concrete concepts to each other and con-
truct a definite, fundamental form of proposition. In
his fundamental form there must be no doubt as to
he nature of the relations that obtain between the
oncrete concepts. We must know what concrete con-
ept is directly or indirectly related to what other,
nd how. If we wish to talk of a thing and an action,
ve must know if they are coördinately related to each
ither (e.g., "He is fond of *wine and gambling*"); or
f the thing is conceived of as the starting point, the
doer" of the action, or, as it is customary to say, the

"subject" of which the action is predicated; or if, o
the contrary, it is the end point, the "object" of th
action. If I wish to communicate an intelligible ide
about a farmer, a duckling, and the act of killing, i
is not enough to state the linguistic symbols for thes
concrete ideas in any order, higgledy-piggledy, trus
ing that the hearer may construct some kind of
relational pattern out of the general probabilities o
the case. The fundamental syntactic relations mus
be unambiguously expressed. I can afford to be silen
on the subject of time and place and number an
of a host of other possible types of concepts, but
can find no way of dodging the issue as to who i
doing the killing. There is no known language tha
can or does dodge it, any more than it succeeds i
saying something without the use of symbols for th
concrete concepts.

We are thus once more reminded of the distinctio
between essential or unavoidable relational concept
and the dispensable type. The former are universall
expressed, the latter are but sparsely developed i
some languages, elaborated with a bewildering exu
berance in others. But what prevents us from throw
ing in these "dispensable" or "secondary" relationa
concepts with the large, floating group of derivational
qualifying concepts that we have already discussed
Is there, after all is said and done, a fundamental di
ference between a qualifying concept like the nega
tive in *unhealthy* and a relational one like the num
ber concept in *books?* If *unhealthy* may be roughl
paraphrased as *not healthy,* may *not books* be just a
legitimately paraphrased, barring the violence to Eng
lish idiom, as *several book?* There are, indeed, lan
guages in which the plural, if expressed at all, i
conceived of in the same sober, restricted, one migh
almost say casual, spirit in which we feel the negativ
in *unhealthy.* For such languages the number concep
has no syntactic significance whatever, is not essen

ally conceived of as defining a relation, but falls into
the group of derivational or even of basic concepts. In
English, however, as in French, German, Latin, Greek
—indeed in all the languages that we have most famil-
iarity with—the idea of number is not merely appended to a given concept of a thing. It may have
something of this merely qualifying value, but its force
extends far beyond. It infects much else in the sentence, molding other concepts, even such as have no
intelligible relation to number, into forms that are
said to correspond to or "agree with" the basic concept to which it is attached in the first instance. If "a
man falls" but "men fall" in English, it is not because
of any inherent change that has taken place in the
nature of the action or because the idea of plurality
inherent in "men" must, in the very nature of ideas,
relate itself also to the action performed by these men.
What we are doing in these sentences is what most
languages, in greater or less degree and in a hundred
varying ways, are in the habit of doing—throwing a
bold bridge between the two basically distinct types
of concept, the concrete and the abstractly relational,
infecting the latter, as it were, with the color and
crossness of the former. By a certain violence of meta-
phor the material concept is forced to do duty for (or
intertwine itself with) the strictly relational.

The case is even more obvious if we take gender as
our text. In the two English phrases, "The white
woman that comes" and "The white men that come,"
we are not reminded that gender, as well as number,
may be elevated into a secondary relational concept. It
would seem a little far-fetched to make of masculinity
and femininity, crassly material, philosophically accidental concepts that they are, a means of relating
quality and person, person and action, nor would it
easily occur to us, if we had not studied the classics,
that it was anything but absurd to inject into two
such highly attenuated relational concepts as are ex-

pressed by "the" and "that" the combined notions c
number and sex. Yet all this, and more, happens i
Latin. *Illa alba femina quae venit* and *illi albi hom
nes qui veniunt,* conceptually translated, amount t
this: *that*-one-feminine-doer[5] one-feminine-*white*-doe
feminine-doing-one-*woman*   *which*-one-feminine-doe
other[6]-one-now-*come;* and: *that*-several-masculine-doe
several-masculine-*white*-doer   masculine-doing-severa
man *which*-several-masculine-doer other-several-now
come. Each word involves no less than four concept
a radical concept (either properly concrete—*whit
man, woman, come*—or demonstrative—*that, which*
and three relational concepts, selected from the cate
gories of case, number, gender, person, and tense
Logically, only case[7] (the relation of *woman* or *me
to a following verb, of *which* to its antecedent, of *tha
and *white* to *woman* or *men,* and of *which* to *come
imperatively demands expression, and that only i
connection with the concepts directly affected (ther
is, for instance, no need to be informed that the white
ness is a doing or doer's whiteness[8]). The other rela

[5] "Doer," not "done to." This is a necessarily clumsy tag t
represent the "nominative" (subjective) in contrast to the "accu
sative" (objective).

[6] I.e., not you or I.

[7] By "case" is here meant not only the subjective-objective rela
tion but also that of attribution.

[8] Except in so far as Latin uses this method as a rather awk
ward, roundabout method of establishing the attribution of th
color to the particular object or person. In effect one canno
in Latin directly say that a person is white, merely that wha
is white is identical with the person who is, acts, or is acte
upon in such and such a manner. In origin the feel of the Lati
illa alba femina is really "that-one, the-white-one, (namely
the-woman"—three substantive ideas that are related to eac
other by a juxtaposition intended to convey an identity. Englis
and Chinese express the attribution directly by means of orde
In Latin the *illa* and *alba* may occupy almost any position i
the sentence. It is important to observe that the subjective form
of *illa* and *alba* does not truly define a relation of these qualify
ing concepts to *femina.* Such a relation might be formally ex
pressed *via* an attributive case, say the genitive (*woman o
whiteness*). In Tibetan both the methods of order and of tru

8

onal concepts are either merely parasitic (gender throughout; number in the demonstrative, the adjective, the relative, and the verb) or irrelevant to the essential syntactic form of the sentence (number in the noun; person; tense). An intelligent and sensitive Chinaman, accustomed as he is to cut to the very bone of linguistic form, might well say of the Latin sentence, "How pedantically imaginative!" It must be difficult for him, when first confronted by the illogical complexities of our European languages, to feel at home in an attitude that so largely confounds the subject-matter of speech with its formal pattern or, to be more accurate, that turns certain fundamentally concrete concepts to such attenuated relational uses.

I have exaggerated somewhat the concreteness of our subsidiary or rather non-syntactical relational concepts in order that the essential facts might come out in bold relief. It goes without saying that a Frenchman has no clear sex notion in his mind when he speaks of *un arbre* ("a-masculine tree") or of *une pomme* ("a-feminine apple"). Nor have we, despite the grammarians, a very vivid sense of the present as contrasted with all past and all future time when we say *He comes.*[9] This is evident from our use of the present to indicate both future time ("He comes to-morrow") and general activity unspecified as to time ("Whenever he comes, I am glad to see him," where "comes" refers to past occurrences and possible future ones rather than to present activity). In both the French and English instances the primary ideas of sex and time have become diluted by form-analogy and by extensions into the relational sphere, the concepts ostensibly indicated being now so vaguely delimited

case relation may be employed: *woman white* (i.e., "white woman") or *white-of woman* (i.e., "woman of whiteness, woman who is white, white woman").

[9] Aside, naturally, from the life and imminence that may be created for such a sentence by a particular context.

that it is rather the tyranny of usage than the nee
of their concrete expression that sways us in the s
lection of this or that form. If the thinning-out pro
ess continues long enough, we may eventually be le
with a system of forms on our hands from which a
the color of life has vanished and which merely pe
sist by inertia, duplicating each other's secondary, syr
tactic functions with endless prodigality. Hence, i
part, the complex conjugational systems of so man
languages, in which differences of form are attende
by no assignable differences of function. There mus
have been a time, for instance, though it antedate
our earliest documentary evidence, when the type c
tense formation represented by *drove* or *sank* differe
in meaning, in however slightly nuanced a degre
from the type (*killed, worked*) which has now becom
established in English as the prevailing preterit fo
mation, very much as we recognize a valuable distin
tion at present between both these types and the "pe
fect" (*has driven, has killed*) but may have ceased t
do so at some point in the future.[10] Now form live
longer than its own conceptual content. Both ar
ceaselessly changing, but, on the whole, the form tend
to linger on when the spirit has flown or changed it
being. Irrational form, form for form's sake—howeve
we term this tendency to hold on to formal distinc
tions once they have come to be—is as natural to th
life of language as is the retention of modes of con
duct that have long outlived the meaning they onc
had.

There is another powerful tendency which make
for a formal elaboration that does not strictly corre
spond to clear-cut conceptual differences. This is th
tendency to construct schemes of classification int
which all the concepts of language must be fitted

---

[10] This has largely happened in popular French and German
where the difference is stylistic rather than functional. Th
preterits are more literary or formal in tone than the perfects

Once we have made up our minds that all things are either definitely good or bad or definitely black or white, it is difficult to get into the frame of mind that recognizes that any particular thing may be both good and bad (in other words, indifferent) or both black and white (in other words, gray), still more difficult to realize that the good-bad or black-white categories may not apply at all. Language is in many respects as unreasonable and stubborn about its classifications as is such a mind. It must have its perfectly exclusive pigeon-holes and will tolerate no flying vagrants. Any concept that asks for expression must submit to the classificatory rules of the game, just as there are statistical surveys in which even the most convinced atheist must perforce be labeled Catholic, Protestant, or Jew or get no hearing. In English we have made up our minds that all action must be conceived of in reference to three standard times. If, therefore, we desire to state a proposition that is as true to-morrow as it was yesterday, we have to pretend that the present moment may be elongated fore and aft so as to take in all eternity.[11] In French we know once for all that an object is masculine or feminine, whether it be living or not; just as in many American and East Asiatic languages it must be understood to belong to a certain form-category (say, ring-round, ball-round, long and slender, cylindrical, sheet-like, in mass like sugar) before it can be enumerated (e.g., "two ball-class potatoes," "three sheet-class carpets") or even said to "be" or "be handled in a definite way" (thus, in the Athabaskan languages and in Yana, "to carry" or "throw" a pebble is quite another thing than to carry or throw a log, linguistically no less than in terms of muscular experience). Such instances might be multi-

[11] Hence, "the square root of 4 *is* 2," precisely as "my uncle *is* here now." There are many "primitive" languages that are more philosophical and distinguish between a true "present" and a "customary" or "general" tense.

plied at will. It is almost as though at some period in the past the unconscious mind of the race had made a hasty inventory of experience, committed itself to a premature classification that allowed of no revision, and saddled the inheritors of its language with a science that they no longer quite believed in nor had the strength to overthrow. Dogma, rigidly prescribed by tradition, stiffens into formalism. Linguistic categories make up a system of surviving dogma—dogma of the unconscious. They are often but half real as concepts; their life tends ever to languish away into form for form's sake.

There is still a third cause for the rise of this non-significant form, or rather of non-significant differences of form. This is the mechanical operation of phonetic processes, which may bring about formal distinctions that have not and never had a corresponding functional distinction. Much of the irregularity and general formal complexity of our declensional and conjugational systems is due to this process. The plural of *hat* is *hats,* the plural of *self* is *selves.* In the former case we have a true *-s* symbolizing plurality, in the latter a *z*-sound coupled with a change in the radical element of the word of *f* to *v*. Here we have not a falling together of forms that originally stood for fairly distinct concepts—as we saw was presumably the case with such parallel forms as *drove* and *worked* —but a merely mechanical manifolding of the same formal element without a corresponding growth of a new concept. This type of form development, therefore, while of the greatest interest for the general history of language, does not directly concern us now in our effort to understand the nature of grammatical concepts and their tendency to degenerate into purely formal counters.

We may now conveniently revise our first classification of concepts as expressed in language and suggest the following scheme:

14 062.

I. *Basic (Concrete) Concepts* (such as objects, actions, qualities): normally expressed by independent words or radical elements; involve no relation as such[12]

II. *Derivational Concepts* (less concrete, as a rule, than I, more so than III): normally expressed by affixing non-radical elements to radical elements or by inner modification of these; differ from type I in defining ideas that are irrelevant to the proposition as a whole but that give a radical element a particular increment of significance and that are thus inherently related in a specific way to concepts of type I [13]

III. *Concrete Relational Concepts* (still more abstract, yet not entirely devoid of a measure of concreteness): normally expressed by affixing non-radical elements to radical elements, but generally at a greater remove from these than is the case with elements of type II, or by inner modification of radical elements; differ fundamentally from type II in indicating or implying relations that transcend the particular word to which they are immediately attached, thus leading over to

IV. *Pure Relational Concepts* (purely abstract): normally expressed by affixing non-radical elements to radical elements (in which case these concepts are frequently intertwined with those of type III) or by their inner modification, by independent words, or by position; serve to relate the concrete elements of the proposition to each other, thus giving it definite syntactic form.

---

[12] Except, of course, the fundamental selection and contrast necessarily implied in defining one concept as against another. "Man" and "white" possess an inherent relation to "woman" and "black," but it is a relation of conceptual content only and is of no direct interest to grammar.

[13] Thus, the *-er* of *farmer* may be defined as indicating that particular substantive concept (object or thing) that serves as the habitual subject of the particular verb to which it is affixed. This relation of "subject" (*a farmer farms*) is inherent in and specific to the word; it does not exist for the sentence as a whole. In the same way the *-ling* of *duckling* defines a specific relation of attribution that concerns only the radical element, not the sentence.

The nature of these four classes of concepts as regards
their concreteness or their power to express syntactic
relations may be thus symbolized:

$$\left.\begin{array}{l} \textit{Material} \\ \textit{Content} \end{array}\right\} \begin{array}{l} \text{I. Basic Concepts} \\ \text{II. Derivational Concepts} \end{array}$$

$$\textit{Relation} \left\{ \begin{array}{l} \text{III. Concrete Relational Concepts} \\ \text{IV. Pure Relational Concepts} \end{array}\right.$$

These schemes must not be worshipped as fetiches.
In the actual work of analysis difficult problems frequently arise and we may well be in doubt as to how
to group a given set of concepts. This is particularly
apt to be the case in exotic languages, where we may
be quite sure of the analysis of the words in a sentence and yet not succeed in acquiring that inner
"feel" of its structure that enables us to tell infallibly
what is "material content" and what is "relation."
Concepts of class I are essential to all speech, also concepts of class IV. Concepts II and III are both common, but not essential; particularly group III, which
represents, in effect, a psychological and formal con-
fusion of types II and IV or of types I and IV, is an
avoidable class of concepts. Logically there is an im-
passable gulf between I and IV, but the illogical, meta-
phorical genius of speech has wilfully spanned the
gulf and set up a continuous gamut of concepts and
forms that leads imperceptibly from the crudest of
materialities ("house" or "John Smith") to the most
subtle of relations. It is particularly significant that
the unanalyzable independent word belongs in most
cases to either group I or group IV, rather less commonly to II or III. It is possible for a concrete concept, represented by a simple word, to lose its material
significance entirely and pass over directly into the
relational sphere without at the same time losing its
independence as a word. This happens, for instance,
in Chinese and Cambodgian when the verb "give" is
used in an abstract sense as a mere symbol of the "indirect objective" relation (e.g., Cambodgian "We make

story this give all that person who have child," i.e.,
"We have made this story *for* all those that have children").

There are, of course, also not a few instances of transitions between groups I and II and I and III, as well as of the less radical one between II and III. To the first of these transitions belongs that whole class of examples in which the independent word, after passing through the preliminary stage of functioning as the secondary or qualifying element in a compound, ends up by being a derivational affix pure and simple, yet without losing the memory of its former independence. Such an element and concept is the *full* of *teaspoonful*, which hovers psychologically between the status of an independent, radical concept (compare *full*) or of a subsidiary element in a compound (cf. *brim-full*) and that of a simple suffix (cf. *dutiful*) in which the primary concreteness is no longer felt. In general, the more highly synthetic our linguistic type, the more difficult and even arbitrary it becomes to distinguish groups I and II.

Not only is there a gradual loss of the concrete as we pass through from group I to group IV, there is also a constant fading away of the feeling of sensible reality within the main groups of linguistic concepts themselves. In many languages it becomes almost imperative, therefore, to make various sub-classifications, to segregate, for instance, the more concrete from the more abstract concepts of group II. Yet we must always beware of reading into such abstracter groups that purely formal, relational feeling that we can hardly help associating with certain of the abstracter concepts which, with us, fall in group III, unless, indeed, there is clear evidence to warrant such a reading in. An example or two should make clear these all-important distinctions.[14] In Nootka we have an

[14] It is precisely the failure to feel the "value" or "tone," as distinct from the outer significance, of the concept expressed by a given grammatical element that has so often led students to

unusually large number of derivational affixes (expressing concepts of group II). Some of these are quite material in content (e.g., "in the house," "to dream of"), others, like an element denoting plurality and a diminutive affix, are far more abstract in content. The former type are more closely welded with the radical element than the latter, which can only be suffixed to formations that have the value of complete words. If, therefore, I wish to say "the small fires in the house" —and I can do this in one word—I must form the word "fire-in-the-house," to which elements corresponding to "small," our plural, and "the" are appended. The element indicating the definiteness of reference that is implied in our "the" comes at the very end of the word. So far, so good. "Fire-in-the-house-the" is an intelligible correlate of our "the house-fire." [15] But is the Nootka correlate of "the small fires in the house" the true equivalent of an English *"the house-firelets"*? [16] By no means. First of all, the plural element precedes the diminutive in Nootka: "fire-in-the-house-plural-small-the," in other words "the house-fireslet," which at once reveals the important fact that the plural concept is not as abstractly, as relationally, felt as in English. A more adequate rendering would be "the house-fire-several-let," in which, however, "several" is too gross a word, "-let" too choice an element ("small" again is too gross). In truth we cannot carry over into English the inherent feeling of the Nootka word, which seems to hover somewhere between "the house-firelets" and "the

misunderstand the nature of languages profoundly alien to their own. Not everything that calls itself "tense" or "mode" or "number" or "gender" or "person" is genuinely comparable to what we mean by these terms in Latin or French.

[15] Suffixed articles occur also in Danish and Swedish and in numerous other languages. The Nootka element for "in the house" differs from our "house-" in that it is suffixed and cannot occur as an independent word; nor is it related to the Nootka word for "house."

[16] Assuming the existence of a word "firelet."

house-fire-several-small." But what more than anything else cuts off all possibility of comparison between the English -*s* of "house-firelets" and the "-several-small" of the Nootka word is this, that in Nootka neither the plural nor the diminutive affix corresponds or refers to anything else in the sentence. In English "the house-firelets burn" (not "burns"), in Nootka neither verb, nor adjective, nor anything else in the proposition is in the least concerned with the plurality or the diminutiveness of the fire. Hence, while Nootka recognizes a cleavage between concrete and less concrete concepts within group II, the less concrete do not transcend the group and lead us into that abstracter air into which our plural -*s* carries us. But at any rate, the reader may object, it is something that the Nootka plural affix is set apart from the concreter group of affixes; and may not the Nootka diminutive have a slenderer, a more elusive content than our -*let* or -*ling* or the German -*chen* or -*lein*? [17]

Can such a concept as that of plurality ever be classified with the more material concepts of group II? Indeed it can be. In Yana the third person of the verb makes no formal distinction between singular and plural. Nevertheless the plural concept can be, and nearly always is, expressed by the suffixing of an element (-*ba*-) to the radical element of the verb. "It burns in the east" is rendered by the verb *ya-hau-si* "burn-east-s." [18] "They burn in the east" is *ya-ba-hau-si*. Note that the plural affix immediately follows the radical element (*ya*-), disconnecting it from the local element (-*hau*-). It needs no labored argument

[17] The Nootka diminutive is doubtless more of a feeling-element, an element of nuance, than our -*ling*. This is shown by the fact that it may be used with verbs as well as with nouns. In speaking to a child, one is likely to add the diminutive to any word in the sentence, regardless of whether there is an inherent diminutive meaning in the word or not.

[18] -*si* is the third person of the present tense. -*hau*- "east" is an affix, not a compounded radical element.

to prove that the concept of plurality is here hardly less concrete than that of location "in the east," and that the Yana form corresponds in feeling not so much to our "They burn in the east" (*ardunt oriente*) as to a "Burn-several-east-s, it plurally burns in the east," an expression which we cannot adequately assimilate for lack of the necessary form-grooves into which to run it.

But can we go a step farther and dispose of the category of plurality as an utterly material idea, one that would make of "books" a "plural book," in which the "plural," like the "white" of "white book," falls contentedly into group I? Our "many books" and "several books" are obviously not cases in point. Even if we could say "many book" and "several book" (as we can say "many a book" and "each book"), the plural concept would still not emerge as clearly as it should for our argument; "many" and "several" are contaminated by certain notions of quantity or scale that are not essential to the idea of plurality itself. We must turn to central and eastern Asia for the type of expression we are seeking. In Tibetan, for instance, *nga-s mi mthong*[19] "I-by man see, by me a man is seen, I see a man" may just as well be understood to mean "I see men," if there happens to be no reason to emphasize the fact of plurality.[20] If the fact is worth expressing, however, I can say *nga-s mi rnams mthong* "by me man plural see," where *rnams* is the perfect conceptual analogue of *-s* in *books*, divested of all relational strings. *Rnams* follows its noun as would any other attributive word—"man plural" (whether two or a million) like "man white." No need to bother about his plurality any more than about his whiteness unless we insist on the point.

What is true of the idea of plurality is naturally

---

[19] These are classical, not modern colloquial, forms.
[20] Just as in English "He has written books" makes no commitment on the score of quantity ("a few, several, many").

just as true of a great many other concepts. They do not necessarily belong where we who speak English are in the habit of putting them. They may be shifted towards I or towards IV, the two poles of linguistic expression. Nor dare we look down on the Nootka Indian and the Tibetan for their material attitude towards a concept which to us is abstract and relational, lest we invite the reproaches of the Frenchman who feels a subtlety of relation in *femme blanche* and *homme blanc* that he misses in the coarser-grained *white woman* and *white man*. But the Bantu Negro, were he a philosopher, might go further and find it strange that we put in group II a category, the diminutive, which he strongly feels to belong to group III and which he uses, along with a number of other classificatory concepts,[21] to relate his subjects and objects, attributes and predicates, as a Russian or a German handles his genders and, if possible, with an even greater finesse.

It is because our conceptual scheme is a sliding scale rather than a philosophical analysis of experience that we cannot say in advance just where to put a given concept. We must dispense, in other words, with a well-ordered classification of categories. What boots it to put tense and mode here or number there when the next language one handles puts tense a peg "lower down" (towards I), mode and number a peg "higher up" (towards IV)? Nor is there much to be gained in a summary work of this kind from a general inventory of the types of concepts generally found in groups II, III, and IV. There are too many possibilities. It would be interesting to show what are the most typical noun-forming and verb-forming elements of group II; how variously nouns may be classified (by gender; personal and non-personal; animate and inanimate; by form; common and proper); how the concept of

[21] Such as person class, animal class, instrument class, augmentative class.

number is elaborated (singular and plural; singular, dual, and plural; singular, dual, trial, and plural; single, distributive, and collective); what tense distinctions may be made in verb or noun (the "past," for instance, may be an indefinite past, immediate, remote, mythical, completed, prior); how delicately certain languages have developed the idea of "aspect" [22] (momentaneous, durative, continuative, inceptive, cessative, durative-inceptive, iterative, momentaneous-iterative, durative-iterative, resultative, and still others); what modalities may be recognized (indicative, imperative, potential, dubitative, optative, negative, and a host of others[23]); what distinctions of person are possible (is "we," for instance, conceived of as a plurality of "I" or is it as distinct from "I" as either is from "you" or "he"?—both attitudes are illustrated in language; moreover, does "we" include you to whom I speak or not?—"inclusive" and "exclusive" forms); what may be the general scheme of orientation, the so-called demonstrative categories ("this" and "that" in an endless procession of nuances);[24] how frequently the form expresses the source or nature of the speaker's knowledge (known by actual experience,

[22] A term borrowed from Slavic grammar. It indicates the lapse of action, its nature from the standpoint of continuity. Our "cry" is indefinite as to aspect, "be crying" is durative, "cry out" is momentaneous, "burst into tears" is inceptive, "keep crying" is continuative, "start in crying" is durative-inceptive, "cry now and again" is iterative, "cry out every now and then" or "cry in fits and starts" is momentaneous-iterative. "To put on a coat" is momentaneous, "to wear a coat" is resultative. As our examples show, aspect is expressed in English by all kinds of idiomatic turns rather than by a consistently worked out set of grammatical forms. In many languages aspect is of far greater formal significance than tense, with which the naïve student is apt to confuse it.

[23] By "modalities" I do not mean the matter of fact statement, say, of negation or uncertainty as such, rather their implication in terms of form. There are languages, for instance, which have as elaborate an apparatus of negative forms for the verb as Greek has of the optative or wish-modality.

[24] Compare page 93.

by hearsay,[25] by inference); how the syntactic relations may be expressed in the noun (subjective and objective; agentive, instrumental, and person affected;[26] various types of "genitive" and indirect relations) and, correspondingly, in the verb (active and passive; active and static; transitive and intransitive; impersonal, reflexive, reciprocal, indefinite as to object, and many other special limitations on the starting-point and end-point of the flow of activity). These details, important as many of them are to an understanding of the "inner form" of language, yield in general significance to the more radical group-distinctions that we have set up. It is enough for the general reader to feel that language struggles towards two poles of linguistic expression—material content and relation— and that these poles tend to be connected by a long series of transitional concepts.

In dealing with words and their varying forms we have had to anticipate much that concerns the sentence as a whole. Every language has its special method or methods of binding words into a larger unity. The importance of these methods is apt to vary with the complexity of the individual word. The

[25] It is because of this classification of experience that in many languages the verb forms which are proper, say, to a mythical narration differ from those commonly used in daily intercourse. We leave these shades to the context or content ourselves with a more explicit and roundabout mode of expression, e.g., "He is dead, as I happen to know," "They say he is dead," "He must be dead by the looks of things."

[26] We say *"I sleep"* and *"I go,"* as well as *"I kill him,"* but *"he kills me."* Yet *me* of the last example is at least as close psychologically to *I* of "I sleep" as is the latter to *I* of "I kill him." It is only by form that we can classify the "I" notion of "I sleep" as that of an acting subject. Properly speaking, I am handled by forces beyond my control when I sleep just as truly as when some one is killing me. Numerous languages differentiate clearly between active subject and static subject (*I go* and *I kill him* as distinct from *I sleep, I am good, I am killed*) or between transitive subject and intransitive subject (*I kill him* as distinct from *I sleep, I am good, I am killed, I go*). The intransitive or static subjects may or may not be identical with the object of the transitive verb.

more synthetic the language, in other words, the more clearly the status of each word in the sentence is indicated by its own resources, the less need is there for looking beyond the word to the sentence as a whole. The Latin *agit* "(he) acts" needs no outside help to establish its place in a proposition. Whether I say *agit dominus* "the master acts" or *sic femina agit* "thus the woman acts," the net result as to the syntactic feel of the *agit* is practically the same. It can only be a verb, the predicate of a proposition, and it can only be conceived as a statement of activity carried out by a person (or thing) other than you or me. It is not so with such a word as the English *act*. *Act* is a syntactic waif until we have defined its status in a proposition—one thing in "they act abominably," quite another in "that was a kindly act." The Latin sentence speaks with the assurance of its individual members, the English word needs the prompting of its fellows. Roughly speaking, to be sure. And yet to say that a sufficiently elaborate word-structure compensates for external syntactic methods is perilously close to begging the question. The elements of the word are related to each other in a specific way and follow each other in a rigorously determined sequence. This is tantamount to saying that a word which consists of more than a radical element is a crystallization of a sentence or of some portion of a sentence, that a form like *agit* is roughly the psychological [27] equivalent of a form like *age is* "act he." Breaking down, then, the wall that separates word and sentence, we may ask: What, at last analysis, are the fundamental methods of relating word to word and element to element, in short, of passing from the isolated notions symbolized by each word and by each element to the unified proposition that corresponds to a thought?

The answer is simple and is implied in the preceding remarks. The most fundamental and the most

[27] Ultimately, also historical—say, *age to* "act that (one)."

powerful of all relating methods is the method of order. Let us think of some more or less concrete idea, say a color, and set down its symbol—*red;* of another concrete idea, say a person or object, setting down its symbol—*dog;* finally, of a third concrete idea, say an action, setting down its symbol—*run.* It is hardly possible to set down these three symbols—*red dog run* —without relating them in some way, for example *(the) red dog run(s).* I am far from wishing to state that the proposition has always grown up in this analytic manner, merely that the very process of juxtaposing concept to concept, symbol to symbol, forces some kind of relational "feeling," if nothing else, upon us. To certain syntactic adhesions we are very sensitive, for example, to the attributive relation of quality *(red dog)* or the subjective relation *(dog run)* or the objective relation *(kill dog),* to others we are more indifferent, for example, to the attributive relation of circumstance *(to-day red dog run* or *red dog to-day run* or *red dog run to-day,* all of which are equivalent propositions or propositions in embryo). Words and elements, then, once they are listed in a certain order, tend not only to establish some kind of relation among themselves but are attracted to each other in greater or in less degree. It is presumably this very greater or less that ultimately leads to those firmly solidified groups of elements (radical element or elements plus one or more grammatical elements) that we have studied as complex words. They are in all likelihood nothing but sequences that have shrunk together and away from other sequences or isolated elements in the flow of speech. While they are fully alive, in other words, while they are functional at every point, they can keep themselves at a psychological distance from their neighbors. As they gradually lose much of their life, they fall back into the embrace of the sentence as a whole and the sequence of independent words regains the importance it had in part

transferred to the crystallized groups of elements
Speech is thus constantly tightening and loosening
its sequences. In its highly integrated forms (Latin
Eskimo) the "energy" of sequence is largely locked
up in complex word formations, it becomes trans
formed into a kind of potential energy that may not
be released for millennia. In its more analytic forms
(Chinese, English) this energy is mobile, ready to hand
for such service as we demand of it.

There can be little doubt that stress has frequently
played a controlling influence in the formation of
element-groups or complex words out of certain sequences in the sentence. Such an English word as
withstand is merely an old sequence *with stand,* i.e.,
"against[28] stand," in which the unstressed adverb was
permanently drawn to the following verb and lost its
independence as a significant element. In the same
way French futures of the type *irai* "(I) shall go" are
but the resultants of a coalescence of originally independent words: *ir[29] a'i* "to-go I-have," under the influence of a unifying accent. But stress has done more
than articulate or unify sequences that in their own
right imply a syntactic relation. Stress is the most natural means at our disposal to emphasize a linguistic
contrast, to indicate the major element in a sequence.
Hence we need not be surprised to find that accent
too, no less than sequence, may serve as the unaided
symbol of certain relations. Such a contrast as that of
go' between ("one who goes between") and *to go between'* may be of quite secondary origin in English,
but there is every reason to believe that analogous
distinctions have prevailed at all times in linguistic
history. A sequence like *see' man* might imply some
type of relation in which *see* qualifies the following

---

[28] For *with* in the sense of "against," compare German *wider*
"against."
[29] Cf. Latin *ire* "to go"; also our English idiom "I have to go,"
i.e., "must go."

word, hence "a seeing man" or "a seen (or visible) man," or is its predication, hence "the man sees" or "the man is seen," while a sequence like *see man'* might indicate that the accented word in some way limits the application of the first, say as direct object, hence "to see a man" or "(he) sees the man." Such alterations of relation, as symbolized by varying stresses, are important and frequent in a number of languages.[30]

It is somewhat venturesome and yet not an altogether unreasonable speculation that sees in word order and stress the primary methods for the expression of all syntactic relations and looks upon the present relational value of specific words and elements as but a secondary condition due to a transfer of values. Thus, we may surmise that the Latin *-m* of words like *feminam, dominum,* and *civem* did not originally[31] denote that "woman," "master," and "citizen" were objectively related to the verb of the proposition but indicated something far more concrete,[32] that the objective relation was merely implied by the position or accent of the word (radical element) immediately preceding the *-m,* and that gradually, as its more concrete significance faded away, it took over a syntactic function that did not originally belong to it. This sort of evolution by transfer is traceable in many instances. Thus, the *of* in an English phrase like "the law of the land" is now as colorless in content, as purely a relational indicator as the "gentive" suffix *-is* in the Latin *lex urbis* "the law of the city." We know, however, that it was originally an adverb of considerable concreteness of meaning,[33] "away, moving from," and that the syntactic relation was originally expressed by

[30] In Chinese no less than in English.
[31] By "originally" I mean, of course, some time antedating the earliest period of the Indo-European languages that we can get at by comparative evidence.
[32] Perhaps it was a noun-classifying element of some sort.
[33] Compare its close historical parallel *off.*

the case form[34] of the second noun. As the case form lost its vitality, the adverb took over its function. If we are actually justified in assuming that the expression of all syntactic relations is ultimately traceable to these two unavoidable, dynamic features of speech—sequence and stress[35]—an interesting thesis results: —All of the actual content of speech, its clusters of vocalic and consonantal sounds, is in origin limited to the concrete; relations were originally not expressed in outward form but were merely implied and articulated with the help of order and rhythm. In other words, relations were intuitively felt and could only "leak out" with the help of dynamic factors that themselves move on an intuitional plane.

There is a special method for the expression of relations that has been so often evolved in the history of language that we must glance at it for a moment. This is the method of "concord" or of like signaling. It is based on the same principle as the password or label. All persons or objects that answer to the same countersign or that bear the same imprint are thereby stamped as somehow related. It makes little difference, once they are so stamped, where they are to be found or how they behave themselves. They are known to belong together. We are familiar with the principle of concord in Latin and Greek. Many of us have been struck by such relentless rhymes as *vidi illum bonum dominum* "I saw that good master" or *quarum dearum saevarum* "of which stern goddesses." Not that sound-echo, whether in the form of rhyme or of alliteration[36] is necessary to concord, though in its most typical and original forms concord is nearly always accompanied by sound repetition. The essence of the principle is simply this, that words (elements) that

---

[34] "Ablative" at last analysis.
[35] Very likely pitch should be understood along with stress.
[36] As in Bantu or Chinook.

belong together, particularly if they are syntactic equivalents or are related in like fashion to another word or element, are outwardly marked by the same or functionally equivalent affixes. The application of the principle varies considerably according to the genius of the particular language. In Latin and Greek, for instance, there is concord between noun and qualifying word (adjective or demonstrative) as regards gender, number, and case, between verb and subject only as regards number, and no concord between verb and object.

In Chinook there is a more far-reaching concord between noun, whether subject or object, and verb. Every noun is classified according to five categories—masculine, feminine, neuter,[37] dual, and plural. "Woman" is feminine, "sand" is neuter, "table" is masculine. If, therefore, I wish to say "The woman put the sand on the table," I must place in the verb certain class or gender prefixes that accord with corresponding noun prefixes. The sentence reads then, "The (fem.)-woman she (fem.)-it (neut.)-it (masc.)-on-put the (neut.)-sand the (masc.)-table." If "sand" is qualified as "much" and "table" as "large," these new ideas are expressed as abstract nouns, each with its inherent class-prefix ("much" is neuter or feminine, "large" is masculine) and with a possessive prefix referring to the qualified noun. Adjective thus calls to noun, noun to verb. "The woman put much sand on the large table," therefore, takes the form: "The (fem.)-woman she (fem.)-it (neut.)-it (masc.)-on-put the (fem.)-thereof (neut.)-quantity the (neut.)-sand the (masc.)-thereof (masc.)-largeness the (masc.)-table." The classification of "table" as masculine is thus three times insisted on—in the noun, in the adjective, and

---

[37] Perhaps better "general." The Chinook "neuter" may refer to persons as well as things and may also be used as a plural. "Masculine" and "feminine," as in German and French, include a great number of inanimate nouns.

in the verb. In the Bantu languages,[38] the principle of concord works very much as in Chinook. In them also nouns are classified into a number of categories and are brought into relation with adjectives, demonstratives, relative pronouns, and verbs by means of prefixed elements that call off the class and make up a complex system of concordances. In such a sentence as "That fierce lion who came here is dead," the class of "lion," which we may call the animal class, would be referred to by concording prefixes no less than six times,—with the demonstrative ("that"), the qualifying adjective, the noun itself, the relative pronoun, the subjective prefix to the verb of the relative clause, and the subjective prefix to the verb of the main clause ("is dead"). We recognize in this insistence on external clarity of reference the same spirit as moves in the more familiar *illum bonum dominum.*

Psychologically the methods of sequence and accent lie at the opposite pole to that of concord. Where they are all for implication, for subtlety of feeling, concord is impatient of the least ambiguity but must have its well-certificated tags at every turn. Concord tends to dispense with order. In Latin and Chinook the independent words are free in position, less so in Bantu. In both Chinook and Bantu, however, the methods of concord and order are equally important for the differentiation of subject and object, as the classifying verb prefixes refer to subject, object, or indirect object according to the relative position they occupy. These examples again bring home to us the significant fact that at some point or other order asserts itself in every language as the most fundamental of relating principles.

The observant reader has probably been surprised

[38] Spoken in the greater part of the southern half of Africa. Chinook is spoken in a number of dialects in the lower Columbia River valley. It is impressive to observe how the human mind has arrived at the same form of expression in two such historically unconnected regions.

at all this time we have had so little to say of the time-honored "parts of speech." The reason for this not far to seek. Our conventional classification of words into parts of speech is only a vague, wavering approximation to a consistently worked out inventory of experience. We imagine, to begin with, that all "verbs" are inherently concerned with action as such, that a "noun" is the name of some definite object or personality that can be pictured by the mind, that all qualities are necessarily expressed by a definite group of words to which we may appropriately apply the term "adjective." As soon as we test our vocabulary, we discover that the parts of speech are far from corresponding to so simple an analysis of reality. We say "it is red" and define "red" as a quality-word or adjective. We should consider it strange to think of an equivalent of "is red" in which the whole predication (adjective and verb of being) is conceived of as a verb in precisely the same way in which we think of "extends" or "lies" or "sleeps" as a verb. Yet as soon as we give the "durative" notion of being red an inceptive or transitional turn, we can avoid the parallel form "it becomes red, it turns red" and say "it reddens." No one denies that "reddens" is as good a verb as "sleeps" or even "walks." Yet "it is red" is related to "it reddens" very much as is "he stands" to "he stands up" or "he rises." It is merely a matter of English or of general Indo-European idiom that we cannot say "it reds" in the sense of "it is red." There are hundreds of languages that can. Indeed there are many that can express what we should call an adjective only by making a participle out of a verb. "Red" in such languages is merely a derivative "being red," as our "sleeping" or "walking" are derivatives of primary verbs.

Just as we can verbify the idea of a quality in such cases as "reddens," so we can represent a quality or an action to ourselves as a thing. We speak of "the

height of a building" or "the fall of an apple" qui
as though these ideas were parallel to "the roof of
building" or "the skin of an apple," forgetting th:
the nouns (*height, fall*) have not ceased to indicate
quality and an act when we have made them spea
with the accent of mere objects. And just as there a
languages that make verbs of the great mass of adje
tives, so there are others that make nouns of them. I
Chinook, as we have seen, "the big table" is "the-tabl
its-bigness"; in Tibetan the same idea may be e
pressed by "the table of bigness," very much as w
may say "a man of wealth" instead of "a rich man."

But are there not certain ideas that it is impossibl
to render except by way of such and such parts c
speech? What can be done with the "to" of "he cam
to the house"? Well, we can say "he reached th
house" and dodge the preposition altogether, givin
the verb a nuance that absorbs the idea of local rel:
tion carried by the "to." But let us insist on givin
independence to this idea of local relation. Must w
not then hold to the preposition? No, we can mak
a noun of it. We can say something like "he reache
the proximity of the house" or "he reached the house
locality." Instead of saying "he looked into the glass
we may say "he scrutinized the glass-interior." Suc
expressions are stilted in English because they do no
easily fit into our formal grooves, but in languag
after language we find that local relations are ex
pressed in just this way. The local relation is nominal
ized. And so we might go on examining the variou
parts of speech and showing how they not merel
grade into each other but are to an astonishing degre
actually convertible into each other. The upshot o
such an examination would be to feel convinced tha
the "part of speech" reflects not so much our intuitiv
analysis of reality as our ability to compose that real
ity into a variety of formal patterns. A part of speecl
outside of the limitations of syntactic form is but :

vill o' the wisp. For this reason no logical scheme of
he parts of speech—their number, nature, and neces-
ary confines—is of the slightest interest to the linguist. Each language has its own scheme. Everything
depends on the formal demarcations which it recognizes.

Yet we must not be too destructive. It is well to remember that speech consists of a series of propositions.
There must be something to talk about and something
must be said about this subject of discourse once it is
selected. This distinction is of such fundamental importance that the vast majority of languages have
emphasized it by creating some sort of formal barrier
between the two terms of the proposition. The subject
of discourse is a noun. As the most common subject of
discourse is either a person or a thing, the noun clusters about concrete concepts of that order. As the
thing predicated of a subject is generally an activity
in the widest sense of the word, a passage from one
moment of existence to another, the form which has
been set aside for the business of predicating, in other
words, the verb, clusters about concepts of activity. No
language wholly fails to distinguish noun and verb,
though in particular cases the nature of the distinction
may be an elusive one. It is different with the other
parts of speech. Not one of them is imperatively required for the life of language.[39]

[39] In Yana the noun and the verb are well distinct, though
there are certain features that they hold in common which tend
to draw them nearer to each other than we feel to be possible.
But there are, strictly speaking, no other parts of speech. The
adjective is a verb. So are the numeral, the interrogative pronoun (e.g., "to be what?"), and certain "conjunctions" and
adverbs (e.g., "to be and" and "to be not"; one says "and-past-
I go," i.e., "and I went"). Adverbs and prepositions are either
nouns or merely derivative affixes in the verb.

CHAPTER VI

Types of Linguistic Structure

❍

So far, in dealing with linguistic form, we have been concerned only with single words and with the relations of words in sentences. We have not envisaged whole languages as conforming to this or that general type. Incidentally we have observed that one language runs to tight-knit synthesis where another contents itself with a more analytic, piece-meal handling of its elements, or that in one language syntactic relations appear pure which in another are combined with certain other notions that have something concrete about them, however abstract they may be felt to be in practice. In this way we may have obtained some inkling of what is meant when we speak of the general form of a language. For it must be obvious to any one who has thought about the question at all or who has felt something of the spirit of a foreign language that there is such a thing as a basic plan, a certain cut, to each language. This type or plan or structural "genius" of the language is something much more fundamental, much more pervasive, than any single feature of it that we can mention, nor can we gain an adequate idea of its nature by a mere recital of the sundry facts that make up the grammar of the language. When we pass from Latin to Russian, we feel that it is approximately the same horizon that

bounds our view, even though the near, familiar land-
marks have changed. When we come to English, we
seem to notice that the hills have dipped down a little, yet we recognize the general lay of the land. And
when we have arrived at Chinese, it is an utterly different sky that is looking down upon us. We can translate these metaphors and say that all languages differ
from one another but that certain ones differ far more
than others. This is tantamount to saying that it is possible to group them into morphological types.

Strictly speaking, we know in advance that it is
impossible to set up a limited number of types that
would do full justice to the peculiarities of the thousands of languages and dialects spoken on the surface
of the earth. Like all human institutions, speech is
too variable and too elusive to be quite safely ticketed.
Even if we operate with a minutely subdivided scale
of types, we may be quite certain that many of our
languages will need trimming before they fit. To get
them into the scheme at all it will be necessary to
overestimate the significance of this or that feature or
to ignore, for the time being, certain contradictions in
their mechanism. Does the difficulty of classification
prove the uselessness of the task? I do not think so. It
would be too easy to relieve ourselves of the burden
of constructive thinking and to take the standpoint
that each language has its unique history, therefore
its unique structure. Such a standpoint expresses only
a half truth. Just as similar social, economic, and religious institutions have grown up in different parts
of the world from distinct historical antecedents, so
also languages, traveling along different roads, have
tended to converge toward similar forms. Moreover,
the historical study of language has proven to us beyond all doubt that a language changes not only gradually but consistently, that it moves unconsciously
from one type towards another, and that analogous
trends are observable in remote quarters of the globe.

From this it follows that broadly similar morphologies must have been reached by unrelated languages, independently and frequently. In assuming the existence of comparable types, therefore, we are not gainsaying the individuality of all historical processes; we are merely affirming that back of the face of history are powerful drifts that move language, like other social products, to balanced patterns, in other words, to types. As linguists we shall be content to realize that there are these types and that certain processes in the life of language tend to modify them. Why similar types should be formed, just what is the nature of the forces that make them and dissolve them—these questions are more easily asked than answered. Perhaps the psychologists of the future will be able to give us the ultimate reasons for the formation of linguistic types.

When it comes to the actual task of classification, we find that we have no easy road to travel. Various classifications have been suggested, and they all contain elements of value. Yet none proves satisfactory. They do not so much enfold the known languages in their embrace as force them down into narrow, straight-backed seats. The difficulties have been of various kinds. First and foremost, it has been difficult to choose a point of view. On what basis shall we classify? A language shows us so many facets that we may well be puzzled. And is one point of view sufficient? Secondly, it is dangerous to generalize from a small number of selected languages. To take, as the sum total of our material, Latin, Arabic, Turkish, Chinese, and perhaps Eskimo or Sioux as an afterthought, is to court disaster. We have no right to assume that a sprinkling of exotic types will do to supplement the few languages nearer home that we are more immediately interested in. Thirdly, the strong craving for a simple formula[1] has been the undoing of linguists.

[1] If possible, a triune formula.

There is something irresistible about a method of classification that starts with two poles, exemplified, say,
by Chinese and Latin, clusters what it conveniently
can about these poles, and throws everything else into
a "transitional type." Hence has arisen the still popular classification of language into an "isolating"
group, an "agglutinative" group, and an "inflective"
group. Sometimes the languages of the American Indians are made to straggle along as an uncomfortable
"polysynthetic" rear-guard to the agglutinative languages. There is justification for the use of all of these
terms, though not perhaps in quite the spirit in which
they are commonly employed. In any case it is very
difficult to assign all known languages to one or other
of these groups, the more so as they are not mutually
exclusive. A language may be both agglutinative and
inflective, or inflective and polysynthetic, or even polysynthetic and isolating, as we shall see a little later on.

There is a fourth reason why the classification of
languages has generally proved a fruitless undertak-
ing. It is probably the most powerful deterrent of all
to clear thinking. This is the evolutionary prejudice
which instilled itself into the social sciences towards
the middle of the last century and which is only now
beginning to abate its tyrannical hold on our mind.
Intermingled with this scientific prejudice and largely
anticipating it was another, a more human one. The
vast majority of linguistic theorists themselves spoke
languages of a certain type, of which the most fully
developed varieties were the Latin and Greek that
they had learned in their childhood. It was not difficult for them to be persuaded that these familiar languages represented the "highest" development that
speech had yet attained and that all other types were
but steps on the way to this beloved "inflective" type.
Whatever conformed to the pattern of Sanskrit and
Greek and Latin and German was accepted as expres-
sive of the "highest," whatever departed from it was

frowned upon as a shortcoming or was at best an in teresting aberration.[2] Now any classification that starts with preconceived values or that works up to senti mental satisfactions is self-condemned as unscientific. A linguist that insists on talking about the Latin type of morphology as though it were necessarily the high-water mark of linguistic development is like the zoölogist that sees in the organic world a huge con spiracy to evolve the race-horse or the Jersey cow. Lan guage in its fundamental forms is the symbolic expres sion of human intuitions. These may shape themselves in a hundred ways, regardless of the material advance ment or backwardness of the people that handle the forms, of which, it need hardly be said, they are in the main unconscious. If, therefore, we wish to understand language in its true inwardness we must disabuse our minds of preferred "values"[3] and accustom ourselves to look upon English and Hottentot with the same cool, yet interested, detachment.

We come back to our first difficulty. What point of view shall we adopt for our classification? After all

[2] One celebrated American writer on culture and language de livered himself of the dictum that, estimable as the speakers of agglutinative languages might be, it was nevertheless a crime for an inflecting woman to marry an agglutinating man. Tre mendous spiritual values were evidently at stake. Champions of the "inflective" languages are wont to glory in the very irra tionalities of Latin and Greek, except when it suits them to emphasize their profoundly "logical" character. Yet the sober logic of Turkish or Chinese leaves them cold. The glorious irrationalities and formal complexities of many "savage" lan guages they have no stomach for. Sentimentalists are difficult people.

[3] I have in mind valuations of form as such. Whether or not a language has a large and useful vocabulary is another matter. The actual size of a vocabulary at a given time is not a thing of real interest to the linguist, as all languages have the re sources at their disposal for the creation of new words, should need for them arise. Furthermore, we are not in the least con cerned with whether or not a language is of great practical value or is the medium of a great culture. All these considerations, important from other standpoints, have nothing to do with form value.

hat we have said about grammatical form in the pre-
eding chapter, it is clear that we cannot now make
he distinction between form languages and formless
anguages that used to appeal to some of the older
writers. Every language can and must express the fundamental syntactic relations even though there is not
a single affix to be found in its vocabulary. We conclude that every language is a form language. Aside
from the expression of pure relation a language may,
of course, be "formless"—formless, that is, in the mechanical and rather superficial sense that it is not
encumbered by the use of non-radical elements. The
attempt has sometimes been made to formulate a distinction on the basis of "inner form." Chinese, for instance, has no formal elements pure and simple, no
"outer form," but it evidences a keen sense of relations, of the difference between subject and object,
attribute and predicate, and so on. In other words, it
has an "inner form" in the same sense in which Latin
possesses it, though it is outwardly "formless" where
Latin is outwardly "formal." On the other hand, there
are supposed to be languages[4] which have no true
grasp of the fundamental relations but content themselves with the more or less minute expression of material ideas, sometimes with an exuberant display of
"outer form," leaving the pure relations to be merely
inferred from the context. I am strongly inclined to
believe that this supposed "inner formlessness" of certain languages is an illusion. It may well be that in
these languages the relations are not expressed in as
immaterial a way as in Chinese or even as in Latin,[5]
or that the principle of order is subject to greater fluctuations than in Chinese, or that a tendency to complex derivations relieves the language of the necessity
of expressing certain relations as explicitly as a more

---

[4] E.g., Malay, Polynesian.
[5] Where, as we have seen, the syntactic relations are by no
means free from an alloy of the concrete.

analytic language would have them expressed.[6] Al
this does not mean that the languages in question
have not a true feeling for the fundamental relations
We shall therefore not be able to use the notion o
"inner formlessness," except in the greatly modified
sense that syntactic relations may be fused with no
tions of another order. To this criterion of classifica
tion we shall have to return a little later.

More justifiable would be a classification according
to the formal processes[7] most typically developed in
the language. Those languages that always identify the
word with the radical element would be set off as an
"isolating" group against such as either affix modifying elements (affixing languages) or possess the power
to change the significance of the radical elements by
internal changes (reduplication; vocalic and consonantal change; changes in quantity, stress, and pitch). The
latter type might be not inaptly termed "symbolic" languages.[8] The affixing languages would naturally subdivide themselves into such as are prevailingly prefixing,
like Bantu or Tlingit, and such as are mainly or
entirely suffixing, like Eskimo or Algonkin or Latin.
There are two serious difficulties with this fourfold
classification (isolating, prefixing, suffixing, symbolic).
In the first place, most languages fall into more than
one of these groups. The Semitic languages, for instance, are prefixing, suffixing, and symbolic at one and

[6] Very much as an English *cod-liver oil* dodges to some extent
the task of explicitly defining the relations of the three nouns.
Contrast French *huile de foie de morue* "oil of liver of cod."
[7] See Chapter IV.
[8] There is probably a real psychological connection between
symbolism and such significant alternations as *drink, drank,
drunk* or Chinese *mai* (with rising tone) "to buy" and *mai* (with
falling tone) "to sell." The unconscious tendency toward symbolism is justly emphasized by recent psychological literature.
Personally I feel that the passage from *sing* to *sang* has very
much the same feeling as the alternation of symbolic colors—
e.g., green for safe, red for danger. But we probably differ
greatly as to the intensity with which we feel symbolism in
linguistic changes of this type.

the same time. In the second place, the classification in its bare form is superficial. It would throw together languages that differ utterly in spirit merely because of a certain external formal resemblance. There is clearly a world of difference between a prefixing language like Cambodgian, which limits itself, so far as its prefixes (and infixes) are concerned, to the expression of derivational concepts, and the Bantu languages, in which the prefixed elements have a far-reaching significance as symbols of syntactic relations. The classification has much greater value if it is taken to refer to the expression of relational concepts[9] alone. In this modified form we shall return to it as a subsidiary criterion. We shall find that the terms "isolating," "affixing," and "symbolic" have a real value. But instead of distinguishing between prefixing and suffixing languages, we shall find that it is of superior interest to make another distinction, one that is based on the relative firmness with which the affixed elements are united with the core of the word.[10]

There is another very useful set of distinctions that can be made, but these too must not be applied exclu-

---

[9] Pure or "concrete relational." See Chapter V.

[10] In spite of my reluctance to emphasize the difference between a prefixing and a suffixing language, I feel that there is more involved in this difference than linguists have generally recognized. It seems to me that there is a rather important psychological distinction between a language that settles the formal status of a radical element before announcing it—and this, in effect, is what such languages as Tlingit and Chinook and Bantu are in the habit of doing—and one that begins with the concrete nucleus of a word and defines the status of this nucleus by successive limitations, each curtailing in some degree the generality of all that precedes. The spirit of the former method has something diagrammatic or architectural about it, the latter is a method of pruning afterthoughts. In the more highly wrought prefixing languages the word is apt to affect us as a crystallization of floating elements, the words of the typical suffixing languages (Turkish, Eskimo, Nootka) are "determinative" formations, each added element determining the form of the whole anew. It is so difficult in practice to apply these elusive, yet important, distinctions that an elementary study has no recourse but to ignore them.

sively, or our classification will again be superficial. I refer to the notions of "analytic," "synthetic," and "polysynthetic." The terms explain themselves. An analytic language is one that either does not combine concepts into single words at all (Chinese) or does so economically (English, French). In an analytic language the sentence is always of prime importance, the word is of minor interest. In a synthetic language (Latin, Arabic, Finnish) the concepts cluster more thickly, the words are more richly chambered, but there is a tendency, on the whole, to keep the range of concrete significance in the single word down to a moderate compass. A polysynthetic language, as its name implies, is more than ordinarily synthetic. The elaboration of the word is extreme. Concepts which we should never dream of treating in a subordinate fashion are symbolized by derivational affixes or "symbolic" changes in the radical element, while the more abstract notions, including the syntactic relations, may also be conveyed by the word. A polysynthetic language illustrates no principles that are not already exemplified in the more familiar synthetic languages. It is related to them very much as a synthetic language is related to our own analytic English.[11] The three terms are purely quantitative—and relative, that is, a language may be "analytic" from one standpoint, "synthetic" from another. I believe the terms are more useful in defining certain drifts than as absolute counters. It is often illuminating to point out that a language has been becoming more and more analytic in the course of its history or that it shows signs of having crystallized from a simple analytic base into a highly synthetic form.[12]

[11] English, however, is only analytic in tendency. Relatively to French, it is still fairly synthetic, at least in certain aspects.
[12] The former process is demonstrable for English, French, Danish, Tibetan, Chinese, and a host of other languages. The latter tendency may be proven, I believe, for a number of American Indian languages, e.g., Chinook, Navaho. Underneath their present moderately polysynthetic form is discernible an analytic base that in the one case may be roughly described as English-like, in the other, Tibetan-like.

We now come to the difference between an "inflective" and an "agglutinative" language. As I have already remarked, the distinction is a useful, even a
necessary, one, but it has been generally obscured by a
number of irrelevancies and by the unavailing effort
to make the terms cover all languages that are not,
like Chinese, of a definitely isolating cast. The meaning that we had best assign to the term "inflective"
can be gained by considering very briefly what are
some of the basic features of Latin and Greek that
have been looked upon as peculiar to the inflective
languages. First of all, they are synthetic rather than
analytic. This does not help us much. Relatively to
many another language that resembles them in broad
structural respects, Latin and Greek are not notably
synthetic; on the other hand, their modern descendants, Italian and Modern Greek, while far more analytic[13] than they, have not departed so widely in
structural outlines as to warrant their being put in a
distinct major group. An inflective language, we must
insist, may be analytic, synthetic, or polysynthetic.

Latin and Greek are mainly affixing in their method,
with the emphasis heavily on suffixing. The agglutinative languages are just as typically affixing as they,
some among them favoring prefixes, others running
to the use of suffixes. Affixing alone does not define
inflection. Possibly everything depends on just what
kind of affixing we have to deal with. If we compare
our English words *farmer* and *goodness* with such
words as *height* and *depth,* we cannot fail to be struck
by a notable difference in the affixing technique of
the two sets. The *-er* and *-ness* are affixed quite mechanically to radical elements which are at the same
time independent words (*farm, good*). They are in
no sense independently significant elements, but they
convey their meaning (agentive, abstract quality) with

[13] This applies more particularly to the Romance group:
Italian, Spanish, Portuguese, French, Roumanian. Modern Greek
is not so clearly analytic.

unfailing directness. Their use is simple and regular and we should have no difficulty in appending them to any verb or to any adjective, however recent in origin. From a verb *to camouflage* we may form the noun *camouflager* "one who camouflages," from an adjective *jazzy* proceeds with perfect ease the noun *jazziness*. It is different with *height* and *depth*. Functionally they are related to *high* and *deep* precisely as is *goodness* to *good,* but the degree of coalescence between radical element and affix is greater. Radical element and affix, while measurably distinct, cannot be torn apart quite so readily as could the *good* and *-ness* of *goodness*. The *-t* of *height* is not the typical form of the affix (compare *strength, length, filth, breadth, youth*), while *dep-* is not identical with *deep*. We may designate the two types of affixing as "fusing" and "juxtaposing." The juxtaposing technique we may call an "agglutinative" one, if we like.

Is the fusing technique thereby set off as the essence of inflection? I am afraid that we have not yet reached our goal. If our language were crammed full of coalescences of the type of *depth,* but if, on the other hand, it used the plural independently of verb concord (e.g., *the books falls* like *the book falls,* or *the book fall* like *the books fall*), the personal endings independently of tense (e.g., *the book fells* like *the book falls,* or *the book fall* like *the book fell*), and the pronouns independently of case (e.g., *I see he* like *he sees me,* or *him see the man* like *the man sees him*), we should hesitate to describe it as inflective. The mere fact of fusion does not seem to satisfy us as a clear indication of the inflective process. There are, indeed, a large number of languages that fuse radical element and affix in as complete and intricate a fashion as one could hope to find anywhere without thereby giving signs of that particular kind of formalism that marks off such languages as Latin and Greek as inflective.

What is true of fusion is equally true of the "symbolic" processes.[14] There are linguists that speak of alternations like *drink* and *drank* as though they represented the high-water mark of inflection, a kind of spiritualized essence of pure inflective form. In such Greek forms, nevertheless, as *pepomph-a* "I have sent," as contrasted with *pemp-o* "I send," with its trebly symbolic change of the radical element (reduplicating *pe-*, change of *e* to *o*, change of *p* to *ph*), it is rather the peculiar alternation of the first person singular *-a* of the perfect with the *-o* of the present that gives them their inflective cast. Nothing could be more erroneous than to imagine that symbolic changes of the radical element, even for the expression of such abstract concepts as those of number and tense, are always associated with the syntactic peculiarities of an inflective language. If by an "agglutinative" language we mean one that affixes according to the juxtaposing technique, then we can only say that there are hundreds of fusing and symbolic languages—non-agglutinative by definition—that are, for all that, quite alien in spirit to the inflective type of Latin and Greek. We can call such languages inflective, if we like, but we must then be prepared to revise radically our notion of inflective form.

It is necessary to understand that fusion of the radical element and the affix may be taken in a broader psychological sense than I have yet indicated. If every noun plural in English were of the type of *book: books,* if there were not such conflicting patterns as *deer: deer, ox: oxen, goose: geese* to complicate the general form picture of plurality, there is little doubt that the fusion of the elements *book* and *-s* into the unified word *books* would be felt as a little less complete than it actually is. One reasons, or feels, unconsciously about the matter somewhat as follows: —If the form pattern represented by the word *books*

[14] See pages 126, 127.

is identical, as far as use is concerned, with that of the word *oxen,* the pluralizing elements *-s* and *-en* cannot have quite so definite, quite so autonomous, a value as we might at first be inclined to suppose. They are plural elements only in so far as plurality is predicated of certain selected concepts. The words *books* and *oxen* are therefore a little other than mechanical combinations of the symbol of a thing (*book, ox*) and a clear symbol of plurality. There is a slight psychological uncertainty or haze about the juncture in *book-s* and *ox-en.* A little of the force of *-s* and *-en* is anticipated by, or appropriated by, the words *book* and *ox* themselves, just as the conceptual force of *-th* in *dep-th* is appreciably weaker than that of *-ness* in *good-ness* in spite of the functional parallelism between *depth* and *goodness.* Where there is uncertainty about the juncture, where the affixed element cannot rightly claim to possess its full share of significance, the unity of the complete word is more strongly emphasized. The mind must rest on something. If it cannot linger on the constituent elements, it hastens all the more eagerly to the acceptance of the word as a whole. A word like *goodness* illustrates "agglutination," *books* "regular fusion," *depth* "irregular fusion," *geese* "symbolic fusion" or "symbolism." [15]

The psychological distinctness of the affixed elements in an agglutinative term may be even more marked than in the *-ness* of *goodness.* To be strictly accurate, the significance of the *-ness* is not quite as inherently determined, as autonomous, as it might be. It is at the mercy of the preceding radical element to this extent, that it requires to be preceded by a par-

---

[15] The following formulæ may prove useful to those that are mathematically inclined. Agglutination: $c = a + b$; regular fusion: $c = a + (b - x) + x$; irregular fusion: $c = (a - x) + (b - y) + (x + y)$; symbolism: $c = (a - x) + x$. I do not wish to imply that there is any mystic value in the process of fusion. It is quite likely to have developed as a purely mechanical product of phonetic forces that brought about irregularities of various sorts.

ticular type of such element, an adjective. Its own power is thus, in a manner, checked in advance. The fusion here, however, is so vague and elementary, so much a matter of course in the great majority of all cases of affixing, that it is natural to overlook its reality and to emphasize rather the juxtaposing or agglutinative nature of the affixing process. If the *-ness* could be affixed as an abstractive element to each and every type of radical element, if we could say *fightness* ("the act or quality of fighting") or *waterness* ("the quality or state of water") or *awayness* ("the state of being away") as we can say *goodness* ("the state of being good"), we should have moved appreciably nearer the agglutinative pole. A language that runs to synthesis of this loose-jointed sort may be looked upon as an example of the ideal agglutinative type, particularly if the concepts expressed by the agglutinated elements are relational or, at the least, belong to the abstracter class of derivational ideas.

Instructive forms may be cited from Nootka. We shall return to our "fire in the house." [16] The Nootka word *inikw-ihl* "fire in the house" is not as definitely formalized a word as its translation suggests. The radical element *inikw-* "fire" is really as much of a verbal as of a nominal term; it may be rendered now by "fire," now by "burn," according to the syntactic exigencies of the sentence. The derivational element *-ihl* "in the house" does not mitigate this vagueness or generality; *inikw-ihl* is still "fire in the house" or "burn in the house." It may be definitely nominalized or verbalized by the affixing of elements that are exclusively nominal or verbal in force. For example, *inikw-ihl-'i,* with its suffixed article, is a clear-cut nominal form: "the burning in the house, the fire in the house"; *inikw-ihl-ma,* with its indicative suffix, is just as clearly verbal: "it burns in the house." How

[16] See page 104.

weak must be the degree of fusion between "fire in the house" and the nominalizing or verbalizing suffix is apparent from the fact that the formally indifferent *inikwihl* is not an abstraction gained by analysis but a full-fledged word, ready for use in the sentence. The nominalizing *-'i* and the indicative *-ma* are not fused form-affixes, they are simply additions of formal import. But we can continue to hold the verbal or nominal nature of *inikwihl* in abeyance long before we reach the *-'i* or *-ma*. We can pluralize it: *inikw-ihl-'minih;* it is still either "fires in the house" or "burn plurally in the house." We can diminutivize this plural: *inikw-ihl-'minih-'is,* "little fires in the house" or "burn plurally and slightly in the house." What if we add the preterit tense suffix *-it*? Is not *inikw-ihl-'minih-'is-it* necessarily a verb: "several small fires were burning in the house"? It is not. It may still be nominalized; *inikwihl'minih'isit-'i* means "the former small fires in the house, the little fires that were once burning in the house." It is not an unambiguous verb until it is given a form that excludes every other possibility, as in the indicative *inikwihl-minih'isit-a* "several small fires were burning in the house." We recognize at once that the elements *-ihl, -'minih, -'is,* and *-it,* quite aside from the relatively concrete or abstract nature of their content and aside, further, from the degree of their outer (phonetic) cohesion with the elements that precede them, have a psychological independence that our own affixes never have. They are typically agglutinated elements, though they have no greater external independence, are no more capable of living apart from the radical element to which they are suffixed, than the *-ness* and *goodness* or the *-s* of *books*. It does not follow that an agglutinative language may not make use of the principle of fusion, both external and psychological, or even of symbolism to a considerable extent. It is a question of tendency. Is the formative slant clearly towards the agglutinative method? Then the language is "agglutinative." As such, it may be prefixing or suffixing, analytic, synthetic, or polysynthetic.

To return to inflection. An inflective language like Latin or Greek uses the method of fusion, and this fusion has an inner psychological as well as an outer phonetic meaning. But it is not enough that the fusion operate merely in the sphere of derivational concepts (group II),[17] it must involve the syntactic relations, which may either be expressed in unalloyed form (group IV) or, as in Latin and Greek, as "concrete relational concepts" (group III).[18] As far as Latin and Greek are concerned, their inflection consists essentially of the fusing of elements that express logically impure relational concepts with radical elements and with elements expressing derivational concepts. Both fusion as a general method and the expression of relational concepts in the word are necessary to the notion of "inflection."

[17] See Chapter V.
[18] If we deny the application of the term "inflective" to fusing languages that express the syntactic relations in pure form, that is, without the admixture of such concepts as number, gender, and tense, merely because such admixture is familiar to us in Latin and Greek, we make of "inflection" an even more arbitrary concept than it need be. At the same time it is true that the method of fusion itself tends to break down the wall between our conceptual groups II and IV, to create group III. Yet the possibility of such "inflective" languages should not be denied. In modern Tibetan, for instance, in which concepts of group II are but weakly expressed, if at all, and in which the relational concepts (e.g., the genitive, the agentive or instrumental) are expressed without alloy of the material, we get many interesting examples of fusion, even of symbolism. *Mi di,* e.g., "man this, the man" is an absolutive form which may be used as the subject of an intransitive verb. When the verb is transitive (really passive), the (logical) subject has to take the agentive form. *Mi di* then becomes *mi di* "by the man," the vowel of the demonstrative pronoun (or article) being merely lengthened. (There is probably also a change in the tone of the syllable.) This, of course, is of the very essence of inflection. It is an amusing commentary on the insufficiency of our current linguistic classification, which considers "inflective" and "isolating" as worlds asunder, that modern Tibetan may be not inaptly described as an isolating language, aside from such examples of fusion and symbolism as the foregoing.

But to have thus defined inflection is to doubt the value of the term as descriptive of a major class. Why emphasize both a technique and a particular content at one and the same time? Surely we should be clear in our minds as to whether we set more store by one or the other. "Fusional" and "symbolic" contrast with "agglutinative," which is not on a par with "inflective" at all. What are we to do with the fusional and symbolic languages that do not express relational concepts in the word but leave them to the sentence? And are we not to distinguish between agglutinative languages that express these same concepts in the word —in so far inflective-like—and those that do not? We dismissed the scale: analytic, synthetic, polysynthetic, as too merely quantitative for our purpose. Isolating, affixing, symbolic—this also seemed insufficient for the reason that it laid too much stress on technical externals. Isolating, agglutinative, fusional, and symbolic is a preferable scheme, but still skirts the external. We shall do best, it seems to me, to hold to "inflective" as a valuable suggestion for a broader and more consistently developed scheme, as a hint for a classification based on the nature of the concepts expressed by the language. The other two classifications, the first based on degree of synthesis, the second on degree of fusion, may be retained as intercrossing schemes that give us the opportunity to subdivide our main conceptual types.

It is well to recall that all languages must needs express radical concepts (group I) and relational ideas (group IV). Of the two other large groups of concepts —derivational (group II) and mixed relational (group III)—both may be absent, both present, or only one present. This gives us at once a simple, incisive, and absolutely inclusive method of classifying all known languages. They are:

A. Such as express only concepts of groups I and IV; in other words, languages that keep the syntactic relations pure and that do not possess the power to modify the significance of their radical elements by means of affixes or internal changes.[19] We may call these *Pure-relational non-deriving languages* or, more tersely, *Simple Pure-relational languages*. These are the languages that cut most to the bone of linguistic expression.

B. Such as express concepts of groups I, II, and IV; in other words, languages that keep the syntactic relations pure and that also possess the power to modify the significance of their radical elements by means of affixes or internal changes. These are the *Pure-relational deriving languages* or *Complex Pure-relational languages*.

C. Such as express concepts of groups I and III;[20] in other words, languages in which the syntactic relations are expressed in necessary connection with concepts that are not utterly devoid of concrete significance but that do not, apart from such mixture, possess the power to modify the significance of their radical elements by means of affixes or internal changes.[21] These are the *Mixed-relational non-deriv-*

[19] I am eliminating entirely the possibility of compounding two or more radical elements into single words or word-like phrases (see pages 64-67). To expressly consider compounding in the present survey of types would be to complicate our problem unduly. Most languages that possess no derivational affixes of any sort may nevertheless freely compound radical elements (independent words). Such compounds often have a fixity that simulates the unity of single words.

[20] We may assume that in these languages and in those of type D all or most of the relational concepts are expressed in "mixed" form, that such a concept as that of subjectivity, for instance, cannot be expressed without simultaneously involving number or gender or that an active verb form must be possessed of a definite tense. Hence group III will be understood to include, or rather absorb, group IV. Theoretically, of course, certain relational concepts may be expressed pure, others mixed, but in practice it will not be found easy to make the distinction.

[21] The line between types C and D cannot be very sharply drawn. It is a matter largely of degree. A language of markedly mixed-relational type, but of little power of derivation pure and simple, such as Bantu or French, may be conveniently put into type C, even though it is not devoid of a number of derivational affixes. Roughly speaking, languages of type C may be considered as highly analytic ("purified") forms of type D.

ing languages or *Simple Mixed-relational languages*.

D. Such as express concepts of groups I, II, and III; in other words, languages in which the syntactic relations are expressed in mixed form, as in C, and that also possess the power to modify the significance of their radical elements, by means of affixes or internal changes. These are the *Mixed-relational deriving languages* or *Complex Mixed-relational languages*. Here belong the "inflective" languages that we are most familiar with as well as a great many "agglutinative" languages, some "polysynthetic," others merely synthetic.

This conceptual classification of languages, I must repeat, does not attempt to take account of the technical externals of language. It answers, in effect, two fundamental questions concerning the translation of concepts into linguistic symbols. Does the language, in the first place, keep its radical concepts pure or does it build up its concrete ideas by an aggregation of inseparable elements (types A and C *versus* types B and D)? And, in the second place, does it keep the basic relational concepts, such as are absolutely unavoidable in the ordering of a proposition, free of an admixture of the concrete or not (types A and B *versus* types C and D)? The second question, it seems to me, is the more fundamental of the two. We can therefore simplify our classification and present it in the following form:

I. Pure-relational Languages	A.	Simple
	B.	Complex
II. Mixed-relational Languages	C.	Simple
	D.	Complex

The classification is too sweeping and too broad for an easy, descriptive survey of the many varieties of human speech. It needs to be amplified. Each of the types A, B, C, D may be subdivided into an agglutinative, a fusional, and a symbolic sub-type, according to

he prevailing method of modification of the radical
lement. In type A we distinguish in addition an
solating sub-type, characterized by the absence of all
ffixes and modifications of the radical element. In the
solating languages the syntactic relations are ex-
ressed by the position of the words in the sentence.
This is also true of many languages of type B, the
erms "agglutinative," "fusional," and "symbolic"
pplying in their case merely to the treatment of the
derivational, not the relational, concepts. Such lan-
uages could be termed "agglutinative-isolating," "fu-
ional-isolating," and "symbolic-isolating."

This brings up the important general consideration
hat the method of handling one group of concepts
need not in the least be identical with that used for
nother. Compound terms could be used to indicate
his difference, if desired, the first element of the compound referring to the treatment of the concepts of
group II, the second to that of the concepts of groups
II and IV. An "agglutinative" language would normally be taken to mean one that agglutinates all of
ts affixed elements or that does so to a preponderating
extent. In an "agglutinative-fusional" language the
derivational elements are agglutinated, perhaps in the
orm of prefixes, while the relational elements (pure
or mixed) are fused with the radical element, possibly
as another set of prefixes following the first set or in
the form of suffixes or as part prefixes and part suffixes.
By a "fusional-agglutinative" language we would understand one that fuses its derivational elements but
allows a greater independence to those that indicate
relations. All these and similar distinctions are not
merely theoretical possibilities, they can be abun-
dantly illustrated from the descriptive facts of linguistic morphology. Further, should it prove desirable
to insist on the degree of elaboration of the word, the
terms "analytic," "synthetic," and "polysynthetic" can
be added as descriptive terms. It goes without saying

that languages of type A are necessarily analytic and
that languages of type C also are prevailingly analytic
and are not likely to develop beyond the synthetic
stage.

But we must not make too much of terminology.
Much depends on the relative emphasis laid on this
or that feature or point of view. The method of
classifying languages here developed has this great
advantage, that it can be refined or simplified according to the needs of a particular discussion. The degree
of synthesis may be entirely ignored; "fusion" and
"symbolism" may often be combined with advantage
under the head of "fusion"; even the difference between agglutination and fusion may, if desired, be
set aside as either too difficult to draw or as irrelevant
to the issue. Languages, after all, are exceedingly complex historical structures. It is of less importance to
put each language in a neat pigeon-hole than to have
evolved a flexible method which enables us to place
it, from two or three independent standpoints, relatively to another language. All this is not to deny that
certain linguistic types are more stable and frequently
represented than others that are just as possible from
a theoretical standpoint. But we are too ill-informed
as yet of the structural spirit of great numbers of
languages to have the right to frame a classification
that is other than flexible and experimental.

The reader will gain a somewhat livelier idea of
the possibilities of linguistic morphology by glancing
down the subjoined analytical table of selected types.
The columns II, III, IV refer to the groups of concepts so numbered in the preceding chapter. The letters *a, b, c, d* refer respectively to the processes of
isolation (position in the sentence), agglutination,
fusion, and symbolism. Where more than one technique is employed, they are put in the order of their
importance.[22]

---

[22] In defining the type to which a language belongs one must
be careful not to be misled by structural features which are

I need hardly point out that these examples are far from exhausting the possibilities of linguistic structure. Nor that the fact that two languages are similarly classified does not necessarily mean that they present a great similarity on the surface. We are here concerned with the most fundamental and generalized features of the spirit, the technique, and the degree of elaboration of a given language. Nevertheless, in numerous instances we may observe this highly suggestive and remarkable fact, that languages that fall into the same class have a way of paralleling each other in many details or in structural features not envisaged by the scheme of classification. Thus, a most interesting parallel could be drawn on structural lines between Takelma and Greek,[23] languages that are as geographically remote from each other and as unconnected in a historical sense as two languages selected at random can well be. Their similarity goes beyond the generalized facts registered in the table. It would almost seem that linguistic features that are easily thinkable apart from each other, that seem to have no necessary connection in theory, have nevertheless a

mere survivals of an older stage, which have no productive life and do not enter into the unconscious patterning of the language. All languages are littered with such petrified bodies. The English -*ster* of *spinster* and *Webster* is an old agentive suffix, but, as far as the feeling of the present English-speaking generation is concerned, it cannot be said to really exist at all; *spinster* and *Webster* have been completely disconnected from the etymological group of *spin* and of *weave* (*web*). Similarly, there are hosts of related words in Chinese which differ in the initial consonant, the vowel, the tone, or in the presence or absence of a final consonant. Even where the Chinaman feels the etymological relationship, as in certain cases he can hardly help doing, he can assign no particular function to the phonetic variation as such. Hence it forms no live feature of the language-mechanism and must be ignored in defining the general form of the language. The caution is all the more necessary, as it is precisely the foreigner, who approaches a new language with a certain prying inquisitiveness, that is most apt to see life in vestigial features which the native is either completely unaware of or feels merely as dead form.

[23] Not Greek specifically, of course, but as a typical representative of Indo-European.

Fundamental Type	II	III	IV	Technique	Synthesis	Examples
A (Simple Pure-relational)	—	—	a	Isolating	Analytic	Chinese; Annamite
	(d)	—	a, b	Isolating (weakly agglutinative)	Analytic	Ewe (Guinea Coast)
	(b)	—	a, b, c	Agglutinative (mildly agglutinative-fusional)	Analytic	Modern Tibetan
B (Complex Pure-relational)	b, (d)	—	a, (b)	Agglutinative-isolating	Analytic	Polynesian
	c	—	a	Agglutinative-isolating	Polysynthetic	Haida
	b	—	b	Fusional-isolating	Analytic	Cambodgian
	b	—	b	Agglutinative	Synthetic	Turkish
	c, d,	(b)	b	Agglutinative (symbolic tinge)	Polysynthetic	Yana (N. California)
	(b)	—	a, b	Fusional-agglutinative (symbolic tinge)	Synthetic (mildly)	Classical Tibetan
	b	—	c	Agglutinative-fusional	Synthetic (mildly polysynthetic)	Sioux
	c	—	c	Fusional	Synthetic	Salinan (S. W. California)
	d, c	(d)	d, c, a	Symbolic	Analytic	Shilluk (Upper Nile)

NOTE.—Parentheses indicate a weak development of the process in question.

Fundamental Type	II	III	IV	Technique	Synthesis	Examples
C (Simple Mixed-relational)	(b)	b	—	Agglutinative	Synthetic	Bantu
	(c)	c, (d)	a	Fusional	Analytic (mildly synthetic)	French*
D (Complex Mixed-relational)	b, c, d	b	b	Agglutinative (symbolic tinge)	Polysynthetic	Nootka (Vancouver Island)†
	c, (d)	b	—	Fusional-agglutinative	Polysynthetic (mildly)	Chinook (lower Columbia R.)
	c, (d)	c, (d), (b)	—	Fusional	Polysynthetic	Algonkin
	c	c, d	a	Fusional	Analytic	English
	c, d	c, d	—	Fusional (symbolic tinge)	Synthetic	Latin, Greek, Sanskrit
	c, b, d	c, d	(a)	Fusional (strongly symbolic)	Synthetic	Takelma (S. W. Oregon)
	d, c	c, d	(a)	Symbolic-fusional	Synthetic	Semitic (Arabic, Hebrew)

* Might nearly as well have come under D.
† Very nearly complex pure-relational.

tendency to cluster or to follow together in the wake of some deep, controlling impulse to form that dominates their drift. If, therefore, we can only be sure of the intuitive similarity of two given languages, of their possession of the same submerged form-feeling, we need not be too much surprised to find that they seek and avoid certain linguistic developments in common. We are at present very far from able to define just what these fundamental form intuitions are. We can only feel them rather vaguely at best and must content ourselves for the most part with noting their symptoms. These symptoms are being garnered in our descriptive and historical grammars of diverse languages. Some day, it may be, we shall be able to read from them the great underlying ground-plans.

Such a purely technical classification of languages as the current one into "isolating," "agglutinative," and "inflective" (read "fusional") cannot claim to have great value as an entering wedge into the discovery of the intuitional forms of language. I do not know whether the suggested classification into four conceptual groups is likely to drive deeper or not. My own feeling is that it does, but classifications, neat constructions of the speculative mind, are slippery things. They have to be tested at every possible opportunity before they have the right to cry for acceptance. Meanwhile we may take some encouragement from the application of a rather curious, yet simple, historical test. Languages are in constant process of change, but it is only reasonable to suppose that they tend to preserve longest what is most fundamental in their structure. Now if we take great groups of genetically related languages,[24] we find that as we pass from one to another or trace the course of their development we frequently encounter a gradual change of morphological type. This is not surprising, for there is no reason

[24] Such, in other words, as can be shown by documentary or comparative evidence to have been derived from a common source. See Chapter VII.

why a language should remain permanently true to
its original form. It is interesting, however, to note
that of the three intercrossing classifications represented in our table (conceptual type, technique, and
degree of synthesis), it is the degree of synthesis that
seems to change most readily, that the technique is
modifiable but far less readily so, and that the conceptual type tends to persist the longest of all.

The illustrative material gathered in the table is
far too scanty to serve as a real basis of proof, but it
is highly suggestive as far as it goes. The only changes
of conceptual type within groups of related languages
that are to be gleaned from the table are of B to A
(Shilluk as contrasted with Ewe;[25] Classical Tibetan
as contrasted with Modern Tibetan and Chinese) and
of D to C (French as contrasted with Latin[26]). But
types A:B and C:D are respectively related to each
other as a simple and a complex form of a still more
fundamental type (pure-relational, mixed-relational).
Of a passage from a pure-relational to a mixed-relational type or *vice versa* I can give no convincing
examples.

The table shows clearly enough how little relative
permanence there is in the technical features of language. That highly synthetic languages (Latin; Sanskrit) have frequently broken down into analytic forms
(French; Bengali) or that agglutinative languages
(Finnish) have in many instances gradually taken on
"inflective" features are well-known facts, but the
natural inference does not seem to have been often
drawn that possibly the contrast between synthetic

[25] These are far-eastern and far-western representatives of the
"Soudan" group recently proposed by D. Westermann. The
genetic relationship between Ewe and Shilluk is exceedingly
remote at best.
[26] This case is doubtful at that. I have put French in C rather
than in D with considerable misgivings. Everything depends on
how one evaluates elements like *-al* in *national*, *-té* in *bonté*, or
re- in *retourner*. They are common enough, but are they as
alive, as little petrified or bookish, as our English *-ness* and *-ful*
and *un-?*

and analytic or agglutinative and "inflective" (fu
sional) is not so fundamental after all. Turning to th
Indo-Chinese languages, we find that Chinese is a
near to being a perfectly isolating language as an
example we are likely to find, while Classical Tibeta
has not only fusional but strong symbolic feature
(e.g., *g-tong-ba* "to give," past *b-tang*, future *g-tang*
imperative *thong*); but both are pure-relational lan
guages. Ewe is either isolating or only barely aggluti
native, while Shilluk, though soberly analytic, is on
of the most definitely symbolic languages I know
both of these Soudanese languages are pure-relational
The relationship between Polynesian and Cambod
gian is remote, though practically certain; while th
latter has more markedly fusional features than th
former,[27] both conform to the complex pure-relationa
type. Yana and Salinan are superficially very dissimila
languages. Yana is highly polysynthetic and quit
typically agglutinative, Salinan is no more syntheti
than and as irregularly and compactly fusional ("in
flective") as Latin; both are pure-relational. Chinook
and Takelma, remotely related languages of Oregon,
have diverged very far from each other, not only as
regards technique and synthesis in general but in
almost all the details of their structure; both are com
plex mixed-relational languages, though in very differ
ent ways. Facts such as these seem to lend color to the
suspicion that in the contrast of pure-relational and
mixed-relational (or concrete-relational) we are con
fronted by something deeper, more far-reaching, than
the contrast of isolating, agglutinative, and fusional.[28]

[27] In spite of its more isolating cast.
[28] In a book of this sort it is naturally impossible to give an
adequate idea of linguistic structure in its varying forms. Only
a few schematic indications are possible. A separate volume
would be needed to breathe life into the scheme. Such a volume
would point out the salient structural characteristics of a num
ber of languages, so selected as to give the reader an insight
into the formal economy of strikingly divergent types.

CHAPTER VII

Language as a Historical Product:
Drift

❍

Everyone knows that language is variable. Two individuals of the same generation and locality, speaking precisely the same dialect and moving in the same social circles, are never absolutely at one in their speech habits. A minute investigation of the speech of each individual would reveal countless differences of detail—in choice of words, in sentence structure, in the relative frequency with which particular forms or combinations of words are used, in the pronunciation of particular vowels and consonants and of combinations of vowels and consonants, in all those features, such as speed, stress, and tone, that give life to spoken language. In a sense they speak slightly divergent dialects of the same language rather than identically the same language.

There is an important difference, however, between individual and dialectic variations. If we take two closely related dialects, say English as spoken by the "middle classes" of London and English as spoken by the average New Yorker, we observe that, however much the individual speakers in each city differ from each other, the body of Londoners forms a compact, relatively unified group in contrast to the body of New Yorkers. The individual variations are swamped in or absorbed by certain major agreements—say of

pronunciation and vocabulary—which stand out ver
strongly when the language of the group as a whol
is contrasted with that of the other group. This mean
that there is something like an ideal linguistic entit
dominating the speech habits of the members of each
group, that the sense of almost unlimited freedon
which each individual feels in the use of his language
is held in leash by a tacitly directing norm. One in
dividual plays on the norm in a way peculiar to him
self, the next individual is nearer the dead average in
that particular respect in which the first speaker mos
characteristically departs from it but in turn diverge
from the average in a way peculiar to himself, and so
on. What keeps the individual's variations from ris
ing to dialectic importance is not merely the fact that
they are in any event of small moment—there are
well-marked dialectic variations that are of no greater
magnitude than individual variations within a dialec
—it is chiefly that they are silently "corrected" or
canceled by the consensus of usage. If all the speakers
of a given dialect were arranged in order in accord
ance with the degree of their conformity to average
usage, there is little doubt that they would constitute
a very finely intergrading series clustered about a well
defined center or norm. The differences between any
two neighboring speakers of the series[1] would be
negligible for any but the most microscopic linguistic
research. The differences between the outermost mem
bers of the series are sure to be considerable, in all
likelihood considerable enough to measure up to a
true dialectic variation. What prevents us from saying
that these untypical individuals speak distinct dialects
is that their peculiarities, as a unified whole, are not
referable to another norm than the norm of their own
series.

---

[1] In so far as they do not fall out of the normal speech group
by reason of a marked speech defect or because they are iso
lated foreigners that have acquired the language late in life

If the speech of any member of the series could ctually be made to fit into another dialect series,[2] we hould have no true barriers between dialects (and anguages) at all. We should merely have a continu-•us series of individual variations extending over the vhole range of a historically unified linguistic area, nd the cutting up of this large area (in some cases mbracing parts of several continents) into distinct lialects and languages would be an essentially arbi-rary proceeding with no warrant save that of practical onvenience. But such a conception of the nature of lialectic variation does not correspond to the facts as ve know them. Isolated individuals may be found who peak a compromise between two dialects of a lan-ruage, and if their number and importance increases hey may even end by creating a new dialectic norm of their own, a dialect in which the extreme peculiari-:ies of the parent dialects are ironed out. In course of :ime the compromise dialect may absorb the parents, hough more frequently these will tend to linger in-lefinitely as marginal forms of the enlarged dialect area. But such phenomena—and they are common :nough in the history of language—are evidently quite .econdary. They are closely linked with such social developments as the rise of nationality, the formation of literatures that aim to have more than a local ap-peal, the movement of rural populations into the cities, and all those other tendencies that break up the intense localism that unsophisticated man has always found natural.

The explanation of primary dialectic differences is still to seek. It is evidently not enough to say that if a dialect or language is spoken in two distinct lo-calities or by two distinct social strata it naturally

---

[2] Observe that we are speaking of an individual's speech as a whole. It is not a question of isolating some particular pecu-liarity of pronunciation or usage and noting its resemblance to or identity with a feature in another dialect.

takes on distinctive forms, which in time come to be divergent enough to deserve the name of dialects. This is certainly true as far as it goes. Dialects do belong, in the first instance, to very definitely circumscribed social groups, homogeneous enough to secure the common feeling and purpose needed to create a norm. But the embarrassing question immediately arises: If all the individual variations within a dialect are being constantly leveled out to the dialectic norm, if there is no appreciable tendency for the individual's peculiarities to initiate a dialectic schism, why should we have dialectic variations at all? Ought not the norm, wherever and whenever threatened, automatically to reassert itself? Ought not the individual variations of each locality, even in the absence of intercourse between them, to cancel out to the same accepted speech average?

If individual variations "on a flat" were the only kind of variability in language, I believe we should be at a loss to explain why and how dialects arise, why it is that a linguistic prototype gradually breaks up into a number of mutually unintelligible languages. But language is not merely something that is spread out in space, as it were—a series of reflections in individual minds of one and the same timeless picture. Language moves down time in a current of its own making. It has a drift. If there were no breaking up of a language into dialects, if each language continued as a firm, self-contained unity, it would still be constantly moving away from any assignable norm, developing new features unceasingly and gradually transforming itself into a language so different from its starting point as to be in effect a new language. Now dialects arise not because of the mere fact of individual variation but because two or more groups of individuals have become sufficiently disconnected to drift apart, or independently, instead of together. So long as they keep strictly together, no amount of individual variation would lead to the formation of dialects. In practice, of course, no language can be spread over a vast territory or even over a considerable area without showing dialectic variations, for it is impossible to keep a large population from segregating itself into local groups, the language of each of which tends to drift independently. Under cultural conditions such as apparently prevail to-day, conditions that fight localism at every turn, the tendency to dialectic cleavage is being constantly counteracted and in part "corrected" by the uniformizing factors already referred to. Yet even in so young a country as America the dialectic differences are not inconsiderable.

Under primitive conditions the political groups are small, the tendency to localism exceedingly strong. It is natural, therefore, that the languages of primitive folk or of non-urban populations in general are differentiated into a great number of dialects. There are parts of the globe where almost every village has its own dialect. The life of the geographically limited community is narrow and intense; its speech is correspondingly peculiar to itself. It is exceedingly doubtful if a language will ever be spoken over a wide area without multiplying itself dialectically. No sooner are the old dialects ironed out by compromises or ousted by the spread and influence of the one dialect which is culturally predominant when a new crop of dialects arises to undo the leveling work of the past. This is precisely what happened in Greece, for instance. In classical antiquity there were spoken a large number of local dialects, several of which are represented in the literature. As the cultural supremacy of Athens grew, its dialect, the Attic, spread at the expense of the rest, until, in the so-called Hellenistic period following the Macedonian conquest, the Attic dialect, in the vulgarized form known as the "Koine," became the standard speech of all Greece. But this linguistic uniformity[3] did not long continue. During the two millennia that separate the Greek of to-day from its classical prototype the Koine gradually split up into a number of dialects. Now Greece is as richly diversified in speech as in the time of Homer, though the present local dialects, aside from those of Attic itself, are not the lineal descendants of the old dialect of pre-Alexandrian days.[4] The experience of Greece is not exceptional. Old dialects are being continually wiped out only to make room for new ones. Language can change at so many points of phonetics, morphology, and vocabulary that it is not surprising that once the linguistic community is broken it should slip off in different directions. It would be too much to expect a locally diversified language to develop along strictly parallel lines. If once the speech of a locality has begun to drift on its own account, it is practically certain to move further and further away from its linguistic fellows. Failing the retarding effect of dialectic interinfluences, which I have already touched upon, a group of dialects is bound to diverge on the whole, each from all of the others.

In course of time each dialect itself splits up into subdialects, which gradually take on the dignity of dialects proper while the primary dialects develop into mutually unintelligible languages. And so the budding process continues, until the divergences become so great that none but a linguistic student, armed with his documentary evidence and with his comparative or reconstructive method, would infer that the languages in question were genealogically related, represented independent lines of development, in

[3] It is doubtful if we have the right to speak of linguistic uniformity even during the predominance of the Koine. It is hardly conceivable that when the various groups of non-Attic Greeks took on the Koine they did not at once tinge it with dialectic peculiarities induced by their previous speech habits.
[4] The Zaconic dialect of Lacedaemon is the sole exception. It is not derived from the Koine, but stems directly from the Doric dialect of Sparta.

other words, from a remote and common starting point. Yet it is as certain as any historical fact can be that languages so little resembling each other as Modern Irish, English, Italian, Greek, Russian, Armenian, Persian, and Bengali are but end-points in the present of drifts that converge to a meeting-point in the dim past. There is naturally no reason to believe that this earliest "Indo-European" (or "Aryan") prototype which we can in part reconstruct, in part but dimly guess at, is itself other than a single "dialect" of a group that has either become largely extinct or is now further represented by languages too divergent for us, with our limited means, to recognize as clear kin.[5]

All languages that are known to be genetically related, i.e., to be divergent forms of a single prototype, may be considered as constituting a "linguistic stock." There is nothing final about a linguistic stock. When we set it up, we merely say, in effect, that thus far we can go and no farther. At any point in the progress of our researches an unexpected ray of light may reveal the "stock" as but a "dialect" of a larger group. The terms dialect, language, branch, stock—it goes without saying—are purely relative terms. They are convertible as our perspective widens or contracts.[6] It would be vain to speculate as to whether or not we shall ever be able to demonstrate that all languages stem from a common source. Of late years linguists have been able to make larger historical syntheses than were at one time deemed feasible, just as students of culture have been able to show historical connections between culture areas or institutions that were at one time believed to be totally isolated from each other. The human world is contracting not only

[5] Though indications are not lacking of what these remoter kin of the Indo-European languages may be. This is disputed ground, however, and hardly fit subject for a purely general study of speech.

[6] "Dialect" in contrast to an accepted literary norm is a use of the term that we are not considering.

prospectively but to the backward-probing eye of cul-
ture-history. Nevertheless we are as yet far from able
to reduce the riot of spoken languages to a small
number of "stocks." We must still operate with a
quite considerable number of these stocks. Some of
them, like Indo-European or Indo-Chinese, are spoken
over tremendous reaches; others, like Basque,[7]
have a curiously restricted range and are in all likelihood
but dwindling remnants of groups that were at one
time more widely distributed. As for the single or
multiple origin of speech, it is likely enough that
language as a human institution (or, if one prefers,
as a human "faculty") developed but once in the history of the race, that all the complex history of language is a unique cultural event. Such a theory con-
structed "on general principles" is of no real interest,
however, to linguistic science. What lies beyond the
demonstrable must be left to the philosopher or the
romancer.

We must return to the conception of "drift" in language. If the historical changes that take place in a
language, if the vast accumulation of minute modifications which in time results in the complete remodel-
ing of the language, are not in essence identical with
the individual variations that we note on every hand
about us, if these variations are born only to die
without a trace, while the equally minute, or even
minuter, changes that make up the drift are forever
imprinted on the history of the language, are we not
imputing to this history a certain mystical quality?
Are we not giving language a power to change of its
own accord over and above the involuntary tendency
of individuals to vary the norm? And if this drift of
language is not merely the familiar set of individual
variations seen in vertical perspective, that is historically, instead of horizontally, that is in daily experience, what is it? Language exists only in so far as it

[7] Spoken in France and Spain in the region of the Pyrenees.

is actually used—spoken and heard, written and read. What significant changes take place in it must exist, to begin with, as individual variations. This is perfectly true, and yet it by no means follows that the general drift of language can be understood [8] from an exhaustive descriptive study of these variations alone. They themselves are random phenomena,[9] like the waves of the sea, moving backward and forward in purposeless flux. The linguistic drift has direction. In other words, only those individual variations embody it or carry it which move in a certain direction, just as only certain wave movements in the bay outline the tide. The drift of a language is constituted by the unconscious selection on the part of its speakers of those individual variations that are cumulative in some special direction. This direction may be inferred, in the main, from the past history of the language. In the long run any new feature of the drift becomes part and parcel of the common, accepted speech, but for a long time it may exist as a mere tendency in the speech of a few, perhaps of a despised few. As we look about us and observe current usage, it is not likely to occur to us that our language has a "slope," that the changes of the next few centuries are in a sense prefigured in certain obscure tendencies of the present and that these changes, when consummated, will be seen to be but continuations of changes that have been already effected. We feel rather that our language is practically a fixed system and that what slight changes are destined to take place in it are as likely to move in one direction as another. The feeling is fallacious. Our very uncertainty as to the impending details of change makes the eventual consistency of their direction all the more impressive.

[8] Or rather apprehended, for we do not, in sober fact, entirely understand it as yet.
[9] Not ultimately random, of course, only relatively so.

Sometimes we can feel where the drift is taking us even while we struggle against it. Probably the majority of those who read these words feel that it is quite "incorrect" to say "Who did you see?" We readers of many books are still very careful to say "Whom did you see?" but we feel a little uncomfortable (uncomfortably proud, it may be) in the process. We are likely to avoid the locution altogether and to say "Who was it you saw?" conserving literary tradition (the "whom") with the dignity of silence.[10] The folk makes no apology. "Whom did you see?" might do for an epitaph, but "Who did you see?" is the natural form for an eager inquiry. It is of course the uncontrolled speech of the folk to which we must look for advance information as to the general linguistic movement. It is safe to prophesy that within a couple of hundred years from to-day not even the most learned jurist will be saying "Whom did you see?" By that time the "whom" will be as delightfully archaic as the Elizabethan "his" for "its." [11] No logical or historical argument will avail to save this hapless "whom." The demonstration "I:me = he:him = who: whom" will be convincing in theory and will go unheeded in practice.

Even now we may go so far as to say that the majority of us are secretly wishing they could say "Who did you see?" It would be a weight off their unconscious minds if some divine authority, overruling the

[10] In relative clauses too we tend to avoid the objective form of "who." Instead of "The man whom I saw" we are likely to say "The man that I saw" or "The man I saw."

[11] "Its" was at one time as impertinent a departure as the "who" of "Who did you see?" It forced itself into English because the old cleavage between masculine, feminine, and neuter was being slowly and powerfully supplemented by a new one between thing-class and animate-class. The latter classification proved too vital to allow usage to couple males and things ("his") as against females ("her"). The form "its" had to be created on the analogy of words like "man's," to satisfy the growing form feeling. The drift was strong enough to sanction a grammatical blunder.

lifted finger of the pedagogue, gave them *carte blanche*. But we cannot too frankly anticipate the drift and maintain caste. We must affect ignorance of whither we are going and rest content with our mental conflict—uncomfortable conscious acceptance of the "whom," unconscious desire for the "who."[12] Meanwhile we indulge our sneaking desire for the forbidden locution by the use of the "who" in certain twilight cases in which we can cover up our fault by a bit of unconscious special pleading. Imagine that some one drops the remark when you are not listening attentively, "John Smith is coming to-night." You have not caught the name and ask, not "Whom did you say?" but "Who did you say?" There is likely to be a little hesitation in the choice of the form, but the precedent of usages like "Whom did you see?" will probably not seem quite strong enough to induce a "Whom did you say?" Not quite relevant enough, the grammarian may remark, for a sentence like "Who did you say?" is not strictly analogous to "Whom did you see?" or "Whom did you mean?" It is rather an abbreviated form of some such sentence as "Who, did you say, is coming to-night?" This is the special pleading that I have referred to, and it has a certain logic on its side. Yet the case is more hollow than the grammarian thinks it to be, for in reply to such a query as "You're a good hand at bridge, John, aren't you?" John, a little taken aback, might mutter "Did you say me?" hardly "Did you say I?" Yet the logic for the latter ("Did you say I was a good hand at bridge?") is evident. The real point is that there is not enough vitality in the "whom" to carry it over

[12] Psychoanalysts will recognize the mechanism. The mechanisms of "repression of impulse" and of its symptomatic symbolization can be illustrated in the most unexpected corners of individual and group psychology. A more general psychology than Freud's will eventually prove them to be as applicable to the groping for abstract form, the logical or esthetic ordering of experience, as to the life of the fundamental instincts.

such little difficulties as a "me" can compass without a thought. The proportion "I : me = he : him = who : whom" is logically and historically sound, but psychologically shaky. "Whom did you see?" is correct, but there is something false about its correctness.

It is worth looking into the reason for our curious reluctance to use locutions involving the word "whom," particularly in its interrogative sense. The only distinctively objective forms which we still possess in English are *me, him, her* (a little blurred because of its identity with the possessive *her*), *us, them,* and *whom*. In all other cases the objective has come to be identical with the subjective—that is, in outer form, for we are not now taking account of position in the sentence. We observe immediately in looking through the list of objective forms that *whom* is psychologically isolated. *Me, him, her, us,* and *them* form a solid, well-integrated group of objective personal pronouns parallel to the subjective series *I, he, she, we, they*. The forms *who* and *whom* are technically "pronouns" but they are not felt to be in the same box as the personal pronouns. *Whom* has clearly a weak position, an exposed flank, for words of a feather tend to flock together, and if one strays behind, it is likely to incur danger of life. Now the other interrogative and relative pronouns (*which, what, that*), with which *whom* should properly flock, do not distinguish the subjective and objective forms. It is psychologically unsound to draw the line of form cleavage between *whom* and the personal pronouns on the one side, the remaining interrogative and relative pronouns on the other. The form groups should be symmetrically related to, if not identical with, the function groups. Had *which, what,* and *that* objective forms parallel to *whom*, the position of this last would be more secure. As it is, there is something unesthetic about the word. It suggests a form pattern which is not filled out by its fellows. The only way to remedy the irregularity of form distribution is to abandon the *whom* altogether, for we have lost the power to create new objective forms and cannot re-model our *which-what-that* group so as to make it parallel with the smaller group *who-whom*. Once this is done, *who* joins its flock and our unconscious desire for form symmetry is satisfied. We do not secretly chafe at "Whom did you see?" without reason.[13]

But the drift away from *whom* has still other deter-minants. The words *who* and *whom* in their interroga-tive sense are psychologically related not merely to the pronouns *which* and *what,* but to a group of inter-rogative adverbs—*where, when, how*—all of which are invariable and generally emphatic. I believe it is safe to infer that there is a rather strong feeling in English that the interrogative pronoun or adverb, typically an emphatic element in the sentence, should be invari-able. The inflective *-m* of *whom* is felt as a drag upon the rhetorical effectiveness of the word. It needs to be eliminated if the interrogative pronoun is to re-ceive all its latent power. There is still a third, and a very powerful, reason for the avoidance of *whom.* The contrast between the subjective and objective series of personal pronouns (*I, he, she, we, they: me, him, her, us, them*) is in English associated with a difference of position. We say *I see the man* but *the man sees me; he told him,* never *him he told* or *him told he.* Such usages as the last two are distinctly poetic and archaic; they are opposed to the present drift of the language. Even in the interrogative one does not say *Him did you see?* It is only in sentences of the type *Whom did you see?* than an inflected ob-jective before the verb is now used at all. On the

[13] Note that it is different with *whose.* This has not the support of analogous possessive forms in its own functional group, but the analogical power of the great body of possessives of nouns (*man's, boy's*) as well as of certain personal pronouns (*his, its;* as predicated possessive also *hers, yours, theirs*) is suffi-cient to give it vitality.

other hand, the order in *Whom did you see?* is imperative because of its interrogative form; the interrogative pronoun or adverb normally comes first in the sentence (*What are you doing? When did he go? Where are you from?*). In the "whom" of *Whom did you see?* there is concealed, therefore, a conflict between the order proper to a sentence containing an inflected objective and the order natural to a sentence with an interrogative pronoun or adverb. The solution *Did you see whom?* or *You saw whom?* [14] is too contrary to the idiomatic drift of our language to receive acceptance. The more radical solution *Who did you see?* is the one the language is gradually making for.

These three conflicts—on the score of form grouping, of rhetorical emphasis, and of order—are supplemented by a fourth difficulty. The emphatic *whom*, with its heavy build (half-long vowel followed by labial consonant), should contrast with a lightly tripping syllable immediately following. In *whom did*, however, we have an involuntary retardation that makes the locution sound "clumsy." This clumsiness is a phonetic verdict, quite apart from the dissatisfaction due to the grammatical factors which we have analyzed. The same prosodic objection does not apply to such parallel locutions as *what did* and *when did*. The vowels of *what* and *when* are shorter and their final consonants melt easily into the following *d*, which is pronounced in the same tongue position as *t* and *n*. Our instinct for appropriate rhythms makes it as difficult for us to feel content with *whom did* as for a poet to use words like *dreamed* and *hummed* in a rapid line. Neither common feeling nor the poet's choice need be at all conscious. It may be that not all

---

[14] Aside from certain idiomatic usages, as when *You saw whom?* is equivalent to *You saw so and so and that so and so is who?* In such sentences *whom* is pronounced high and lingeringly to emphasize the fact that the person just referred to by the listener is not known or recognized.

are equally sensitive to the rhythmic flow of speech, but it is probable that rhythm is an unconscious linguistic determinant even with those who set little store by its artisic use. In any event the poet's rhythms can only be a more sensitive and stylized application of rhythmic tendencies that are characteristic of the daily speech of his people.

We have discovered no less than four factors which enter into our subtle disinclination to say "Whom did you see?" The uneducated folk that says "Who did you see?" with no twinge of conscience has a more acute flair for the genuine drift of the language than its students. Naturally the four restraining factors do not operate independently. Their separate energies, if we may make bold to use a mechanical concept, are "canalized" into a single force. This force or minute embodiment of the general drift of the language is psychologically registered as a slight hesitation in using the word *whom*. The hesitation is likely to be quite unconscious, though it may be readily acknowledged when attention is called to it. The analysis is certain to be unconscious, or rather unknown, to the normal speaker.[15] How, then, can we be certain in such an analysis as we have undertaken that all of the assigned determinants are really operative and not merely some one of them? Certainly they are not equally powerful in all cases. Their values are variable, rising and falling according to the individual and the locution.[16] But that they really exist, each in its own right, may sometimes be tested

[15] Students of language cannot be entirely normal in their attitude towards their own speech. Perhaps it would be better to say "naïve" than "normal."

[16] It is probably this *variability of value* in the significant compounds of a general linguistic drift that is responsible for the rise of dialectic variations. Each dialect continues the general drift of the common parent, but has not been able to hold fast to constant values for each component of the drift. Deviations as to the drift itself, at first slight, later cumulative, are therefore unavoidable.

by the method of elimination. If one or other of the factors is missing and we observe a slight diminution in the corresponding psychological reaction ("hesitation" in our case), we may conclude that the factor is in other uses genuinely positive. The second of our four factors applies only to the interrogative use of *whom,* the fourth factor applies with more force to the interrogative than to the relative. We can therefore understand why a sentence like *Is he the man whom you referred to?* though not as idiomatic as *Is he the man (that) you referred to?* (remember that it sins against counts one and three), is still not as difficult to reconcile with our innate feeling for English expression as *Whom did you see?* If we eliminate the fourth factor from the interrogative usage,[17] say in *Whom are you looking at?* where the vowel following *whom* relieves this word of its phonetic weight, we can observe, if I am not mistaken, a lesser reluctance to use the *whom. Who are you looking at?* might even sound slightly offensive to ears that welcome *Who did you see?*

We may set up a scale of "hesitation values" somewhat after this fashion:

Value 1: factors 1, 3. "The man whom I referred to."
Value 2: factors 1, 3, 4. "The man whom they referred to."
Value 3: factors 1, 2, 3. "Whom are you looking at?"
Value 4: factors 1, 2, 3, 4. "Whom did you see?"

We may venture to surmise that while *whom* will ultimately disappear from English speech, locutions of the type *Whom did you see?* will be obsolete when phrases like *The man whom I referred to* are still in lingering use. It is impossible to be certain, however, for we can never tell if we have isolated all the determinants of a drift. In our particular case we have

---

[17] Most sentences beginning with interrogative *whom* are likely to be followed by *did* or *does, do*. Yet not all.

ignored what may well prove to be a controlling factor in the history of *who* and *whom* in the relative sense. This is the unconscious desire to leave these words to their interrogative function and to concentrate on *that* or mere word order as expressions of the relative (e.g., *The man that I referred to* or *The man I referred to*). This drift, which does not directly concern the use of *whom* as such (merely of *whom* as a form of *who*), may have made the relative *who* obsolete before the other factors affecting relative *whom* have run their course. A consideration like this is instructive because it indicates that knowledge of the general drift of a language is insufficient to enable us to see clearly what the drift is heading for. We need to know something of the relative potencies and speeds of the components of the drift.

It is hardly necessary to say that the particular drifts involved in the use of *whom* are of interest to us not for their own sake but as symptoms of larger tendencies at work in the language. At least three drifts of major importance are discernible. Each of these has operated for centuries, each is at work in other parts of our linguistic mechanism, each is almost certain to continue for centuries, possibly millennia. The first is the familiar tendency to level the distinction between the subjective and the objective, itself but a late chapter in the steady reduction of the old Indo-European system of syntactic cases. This system, which is at present best preserved in Lithuanian,[18] was already considerably reduced in the old Germanic language of which English, Dutch, German, Danish, and Swedish are modern dialectic forms. The seven Indo-European cases (nominative, genitive, dative, accusative, ablative, locative, instrumental) had been already

[18] Better, indeed, than in our oldest Latin and Greek records. The old Indo-Iranian languages alone (Sanskrit, Avestan) show an equally or more archaic status of the Indo-European parent tongue as regards case forms.

reduced to four (nominative, genitive, dative, accusative). We know this from a careful comparison of and reconstruction based on the oldest Germanic dialects of which we still have records (Gothic, Old Icelandic, Old High German, Anglo-Saxon). In the group of West Germanic dialects, for the study of which Old High German, Anglo-Saxon, Old Frisian, and Old Saxon are our oldest and most valuable sources, we still have these four cases, but the phonetic form of the case syllables is already greatly reduced and in certain paradigms particular cases have coalesced. The case system is practically intact but it is evidently moving towards further disintegration. Within the Anglo-Saxon and early Middle English period there took place further changes in the same direction. The phonetic form of the case syllables became still further reduced and the distinction between the accusative and the dative finally disappeared. The new "objective" is really an amalgam of old accusative and dative forms; thus *him,* the old dative (we still say *I give him the book,* not "abbreviated" from *I give to him;* compare Gothic *imma,* Modern German *ihm*), took over the functions of the old accusative (Anglo-Saxon *hine;* compare Gothic *ina,* Modern German *ihn*) and dative. The distinction between the nominative and accusative was nibbled away by phonetic processes and morphological levelings until only certain pronouns retained distinctive subjective and objective forms.

In later medieval and in modern times there have been comparatively few apparent changes in our case system apart from the gradual replacement of *thou—thee* (singular) and subjective *ye*—objective *you* (plural) by a single undifferentiated form *you.* All the while, however, the case system, such as it is (subjective-objective, really absolute, and possessive in nouns; subjective, objective, and possessive in certain pronouns) has been steadily weakening in psychological respects. At present it is more seriously under-

mined than most of us realize. The possessive has
little vitality except in the pronoun and in animate
nouns. Theoretically we can still say *the moon's
phases* or *a newspaper's vogue;* practically we limit
ourselves pretty much to analytic locutions like *the
phases of the moon* and *the vogue of a newspaper.*
The drift is clearly toward the limitation of possessive
forms to animate nouns. All the possessive pronominal
forms except *its* and, in part, *their* and *theirs,* are also
animate. It is significant that *theirs* is hardly ever used
in reference to inanimate nouns, that there is some
reluctance to so use *their,* and that *its* also is beginning
to give way to *of it. The appearance of it* or *the looks
of it* is more in the current of the language than *its
appearance.* It is curiously significant that *its young*
(referring to an animal's cubs) is idiomatically preferable to *the young of it.* The form is only ostensibly
neuter, in feeling it is animate; psychologically it
belongs with *his children,* not with *the pieces of it.*
Can it be that so common a word as *its* is actually
beginning to be difficult? Is it too doomed to disappear? It would be rash to say that it shows signs of
approaching obsolescence, but that it is steadily weakening is fairly clear.[19] In any event, it is not too much
to say that there is a strong drift towards the restric-
tion of the inflected possessive forms to animate nouns
and pronouns.

How is it with the alternation of subjective and
objective in the pronoun? Granted that *whom* is a
weak sister, that the two cases have been leveled in
you (in *it, that,* and *what* they were never distinct, so
far as we can tell [20]), and that *her* as an objective is a
trifle weak because of its formal identity with the

[19] Should *its* eventually drop out, it will have had a curious
history. It will have played the rôle of a stop-gap between *his*
in its non-personal use (see footnote 11, page 156) and the later
analytic *of it.*
[20] Except in so far as *that* has absorbed other functions than
such as originally belonged to it. It was only a nominative-
accusative neuter to begin with.

possessive *her,* is there any reason to doubt the vitality of such alternations as *I see the man* and *the man sees me?* Surely the distinction between subjective *I* and objective *me,* between subjective *he* and objective *him,* and correspondingly for other personal pronouns, belongs to the very core of the language. We can throw *whom* to the dogs, somehow make shift to do without an *its,* but to level *I* and *me* to a single case—would that not be to un-English our language beyond recognition? There is no drift toward such horrors as *Me see him* or *I see he.* True, the phonetic disparity between *I* and *me, he* and *him, we* and *us,* has been too great for any serious possibility of form leveling. It does not follow that the case distinction as such is still vital. One of the most insidious peculiarities of a linguistic drift is that where it cannot destroy what lies in its way it renders it innocuous by washing the old significance out of it. It turns its very enemies to its own uses. This brings us to the second of the major drifts, the tendency to fixed position in the sentence, determined by the syntactic relation of the word.

We need not go into the history of this all-important drift. It is enough to know that as the inflected forms of English became scantier, as the syntactic relations were more and more inadequately expressed by the forms of the words themselves, position in the sentence gradually took over functions originally foreign to it. *The man* in *the man sees the dog* is subjective; in *the dog sees the man,* objective. Strictly parallel to these sentences are *he sees the dog* and *the dog sees him.* Are the subjective value of *he* and the objective value of *him* entirely, or even mainly, dependent on the difference of form? I doubt it. We could hold to such a view if it were possible to say *the dog sees he* or *him sees the dog.* It was once possible to say such things, but we have lost the power. In other words, at least part of the case feeling in *he* and *him* is to be credited to their position before or after the verb. May it not be, then, that *he* and *him, we* and *us,* are not so much subjective and objective forms as pre-verbal and post-verbal [21] forms, very much as *my* and *mine* are now pre-nominal and post-nominal forms of the possessive (*my father* but *father mine; it is my book* but *the book is mine*)? That this interpretation corresponds to the actual drift of the English language is again indicated by the language of the folk. The folk says *it is me,* not *it is I,* which is "correct" but just as falsely so as the *whom did you see?* that we have analyzed. *I'm the one, it's me; we're the ones, it's us that will win out*—such are the live parallelisms in English to-day. There is little doubt that *it is I* will one day be as impossible in English as *c'est je,* for *c'est moi,* is now in French.

How differently our *I : me* feels than in Chaucer's day is shown by the Chaucerian *it am I.* Here the distinctively subjective aspect of the *I* was enough to influence the form of the preceding verb in spite of the introductory *it;* Chaucer's locution clearly felt more like a Latin *sum ego* than a modern *it is I* or colloquial *it is me.* We have a curious bit of further evidence to prove that the English personal pronouns have lost some share of their original syntactic force. Were *he* and *she* subjective forms pure and simple, were they not striving, so to speak, to become caseless absolutes, like *man* or any other noun, we should not have been able to coin such compounds as *he-goat* and *she-goat,* words that are psychologically analogous to *bull-moose* and *mother-bear.* Again, in inquiring about a new-born baby, we ask *Is it a he or a she?* quite as though *he* and *she* were the equiv-

---

[21] Aside from the interrogative: *am I? is he?* Emphasis counts for something. There is a strong tendency for the old "objective" forms to bear a stronger stress than the "subjective" forms. This is why the stress in locutions like *He didn't go, did he?* and *isn't he?* is thrown back on the verb; it is not a matter of logical emphasis.

alents of *male* and *female* or *boy* and *girl*. All in all, we may conclude that our English case system is weaker than it looks and that, in one way or another, it is destined to get itself reduced to an absolutive (caseless) form for all nouns and pronouns but those that are animate. Animate nouns and pronouns are sure to have distinctive possessive forms for an indefinitely long period.

Meanwhile observe that the old alignment of case forms is being invaded by two new categories—a positional category (pre-verbal, post-verbal) and a classificatory category (animate, inanimate). The facts that in the possessive animate nouns and pronouns are destined to be more and more sharply distinguished from inanimate nouns and pronouns (*the man's,* but *of the house; his,* but *of it*) and that, on the whole, it is only animate pronouns that distinguish pre-verbal and post-verbal forms[22] are of the greatest theoretical interest. They show that, however the language strive for a more and more analytic form, it is by no means manifesting a drift toward the expression of "pure" relational concepts in the Indo-Chinese manner.[23] The insistence on the concreteness of the relational concepts is clearly stronger than the destructive power of the most sweeping and persistent drifts that we know of in the history and prehistory of our language.

The drift toward the abolition of most case distinctions and the correlative drift toward position as an all-important grammatical method are accompanied, in a sense dominated, by the last of the three major drifts that I have referred to. This is the drift toward the invariable word. In analyzing the "whom" sentence I pointed out that the rhetorical emphasis natural to an interrogative pronoun lost something by

---

[22] *They: them* as an inanimate group may be looked upon as a kind of borrowing from the animate, to which, in feeling, it more properly belongs.

[23] See page 146.

its form variability (*who, whose, whom*). This striving for a simple, unnuanced correspondence between idea and word, as invariable as may be, is very strong in English. It accounts for a number of tendencies which at first sight seem unconnected. Certain well-established forms, like the present third person singular *-s* of *works* or the plural *-s* of *books,* have resisted the drift to invariable words, possibly because they symbolize certain stronger form cravings that we do not yet fully understand. It is interesting to note that derivations that get away sufficiently from the concrete notion of the radical word to exist as independent conceptual centers are not affected by this elusive drift. As soon as the derivation runs danger of being felt as a mere nuancing of, a finicky play on, the primary concept, it tends to be absorbed by the radical word, to disappear as such. English words crave spaces between them, they do not like to huddle in clusters of slightly divergent centers of meaning, each edging a little away from the rest. *Goodness,* a noun of quality, almost a noun of relation, that takes its cue from the concrete idea of "good" without necessarily predicating that quality (e.g., *I do not think much of his goodness*) is sufficiently spaced from *good* itself not to need fear absorption. Similarly, *unable* can hold its own against *able* because it destroys the latter's sphere of influence; *unable* is psychologically as distinct from *able* as is *blundering* or *stupid.* It is different with adverbs in *-ly.* These lean too heavily on their adjectives to have the kind of vitality that English demands of its words. *Do it quickly!* drags psychologically. The nuance expressed by *quickly* is too close to that of *quick,* their circles of concreteness are too nearly the same, for the two words to feel comfortable together. The adverbs in *-ly* are likely to go to the wall in the not too distant future for this very reason and in face of their obvious usefulness. Another instance of the sacrifice of highly useful forms to this impatience of nuancing is the group *whence, whither, hence, hither, thence, thither*. They could not persist in live usage because they impinged too solidly upon the circles of meaning represented by the words *where, here* and *there*. In saying *whither* we feel too keenly that we repeat all of *where*. That we add to *where* an important nuance of direction irritates rather than satisfies. We prefer to merge the static and the directive (*Where do you live?* like *Where are you going?*) or, if need be, to overdo a little the concept of direction (*Where are you running to?*).

Now it is highly symptomatic of the nature of the drift away from word clusters that we do not object to nuances as such, we object to having the nuances formally earmarked for us. As a matter of fact our vocabulary is rich in near-synonyms and in groups of words that are psychologically near relatives, but these near-synonyms and these groups do not hang together by reason of etymology. We are satisfied with *believe* and *credible* just because they keep aloof from each other. *Good* and *well* go better together than *quick* and *quickly*. The English vocabulary is a rich medley because each English word wants its own castle. Has English long been peculiarly receptive to foreign words because it craves the staking out of as many word areas as possible, or, conversely, has the mechanical imposition of a flood of French and Latin loan-words, unrooted in our earlier tradition, so dulled our feeling for the possibilities of our native resources that we are allowing these to shrink by default? I suspect that both propositions are true. Each feeds on the other. I do not think it likely, however, that the borrowings in English have been as mechanical and external a process as they are generally represented to have been. There was something about the English drift as early as the period following the Norman Conquest that welcomed the new words. They were a compensation for something that was weakening within.

CHAPTER VIII

Language as a Historical Product:
Phonetic Law

⊙

have preferred to take up in some detail the analysis
f our hesitation in using a locution like "Whom did
ou see?" and to point to some of the English drifts,
articular and general, that are implied by this hesi-
ation than to discuss linguistic change in the abstract.
What is true of the particular idiom that we started
with is true of everything else in language. Nothing
 perfectly static. Every word, every grammatical ele-
nent, every locution, every sound and accent is a
owly changing configuration, molded by the invisible
nd impersonal drift that is the life of language. The
vidence is overwhelming that this drift has a certain
onsistent direction. Its speed varies enormously ac-
ording to circumstances that it is not always easy to
efine. We have already seen that Lithuanian is to-day
earer its Indo-European prototype than was the hypo-
hetical Germanic mother-tongue five hundred or a
housand years before Christ. German has moved more
lowly than English; in some respects it stands roughly
nidway between English and Anglo-Saxon, in others
t has of course diverged from the Anglo-Saxon line.
When I pointed out in the preceding chapter that dia-
ects formed because a language broken up into local
egments could not move along the same drift in all
f these segments, I meant of course that it could not

move along identically the same drift. The gener
drift of a language has its depths. At the surface tl
current is relatively fast. In certain features dialec
drift apart rapidly. By that very fact these features b
tray themselves as less fundamental to the genius
the language than the more slowly modifiable featur
in which the dialects keep together long after th
have grown to be mutually alien forms of speech. B
this is not all. The momentum of the more fundame
tal, the pre-dialectic, drift is often such that languag
long disconnected will pass through the same or stri
ingly similar phases. In many such cases it is perfect
clear that there could have been no dialectic inte
influencing.

These parallelisms in drift may operate in the ph
netic as well as in the morphological sphere, or the
may affect both at the same time. Here is an interes
ing example. The English type of plural represente
by *foot: feet, mouse: mice* is strictly parallel to th
German *Fuss: Füsse, Maus: Mäuse.* One would be i
clined to surmise that these dialectic forms go back t
old Germanic or West-Germanic alternations of th
same type. But the documentary evidence shows cor
clusively that there could have been no plurals of th
type in primitive Germanic. There is no trace of suc
vocalic mutation ("umlaut") in Gothic, our most a
chaic Germanic language. More significant still is th
fact that it does not appear in our oldest Old Hig
German texts and begins to develop only at the ver
end of the Old High German period (circa 1000 A.D.
In the Middle High German period the mutation wa
carried through in all dialects. The typical Old Hig
German forms are singular *fuoss,* plural *fuossi;* [1] singu
lar *mus,* plural *musi.* The corresponding Middle Hig

[1] I have changed the Old and Middle High German orthog
raphy slightly in order to bring it into accord with moder
usage. These purely orthographical changes are immaterial. Th
u of *mus* is a long vowel, very nearly like the *oo* of Englis
moose.

rman forms are *fuoss, füesse; mus, müse.* Modern
rman *Fuss: Füsse, Maus: Mäuse* are the regular
velopments of these medieval forms. Turning to
iglo-Saxon, we find that our modern English forms
rrespond to *fot, fet; mus, mys.*[2] These forms are al-
ady in use in the earliest English monuments that
possess, dating from the eighth century, and thus
itedate the Middle High German forms by three
indred years or more. In other words, on this par-
:ular point it took German at least three hundred
ars to catch up with a phonetic-morphological drift[3]
at had long been under way in English. The mere
ct that the affected vowels of related words (Old
igh German *uo,* Anglo-Saxon *o*) are not always the
me shows that the affection took place at different
riods in German and English.[4] There was evidently
me general tendency or group of tendencies at work
early Germanic, long before English and German
id developed as such, that eventually drove both of
ese dialects along closely parallel paths.

How did such strikingly individual alternations as
t: fet, fuoss: füesse* develop? We have now reached
hat is probably the most central problem in linguis-
: history, gradual phonetic change. "Phonetic laws"
ake up a large and fundamental share of the subject-
atter of linguistics. Their influence reaches far be-

---

[2] The vowels of these four words are long; *o* as in *rode, e* like
of *fade, u* like *oo* of *brood, y* like German *ü.*
[3] Or rather stage in a drift.
[4] Anglo-Saxon *fet* is "unrounded" from an older *föt,* which is
ionetically related to *fot* precisely as is *mys* (i.e., *müs*) to *mus.*
iddle High German *üe* (Modern German *ü*) did not develop
om an "umlauted" prototype of Old High German *uo* and
iglo-Saxon *o,* but was based directly on the dialectic *uo.* The
iaffected prototype was long *o.* Had this been affected in the
rliest Germanic or West-Germanic period, we should have had
pre-German alternation *fot: föti;* this older *ö* could not well
ive resulted in *üe.* Fortunately we do not need inferential evince in this case, yet inferential comparative methods, if han-
ed with care, may be exceedingly useful. They are indeed
dispensable to the historian of language.

yond the proper sphere of phonetics and invades tha
of morphology, as we shall see. A drift that begins a
a slight phonetic readjustment or unsettlement may i
the course of millennia bring about the most profoun
structural changes. The mere fact, for instance, tha
there is a growing tendency to throw the stress aut
matically on the first syllable of a word may eventu
ally change the fundamental type of the language, r
ducing its final syllables to zero and driving it to th
use of more and more analytical or symbolic[5] method
The English phonetic laws involved in the rise of th
words *foot, feet, mouse* and *mice* from their earl
West-Germanic prototypes *fot, foti, mus, musi* [6] may b
briefly summarized as follows:

1. In *foti* "feet" the long *o* was colored by the fo
lowing *i* to long *ö*, that is, *o* kept its lip-rounded qua
ity and its middle height of tongue position but ar
ticipated the front tongue position of the *i*; *ö* is th
resulting compromise. This assimilatory change wa
regular, i.e., every accented long *o* followed by an
in the following syllable automatically developed t
long *ö*; hence *tothi* "teeth" became *töthi*, *fodian* "t
feed" became *födian*. At first there is no doubt the a
ternation between *o* and *ö* was not felt as intrinsicall
significant. It could only have been an unconsciou
mechanical adjustment such as may be observed in th
speech of many to-day who modify the "oo" sound c
words like *you* and *few* in the direction of German
without, however, actually departing far enough fror
the "oo" vowel to prevent their acceptance of *wh*
and *you* as satisfactory rhyming words. Later on th
quality of the *ö* vowel must have departed widel
enough from that of *o* to enable *ö* to rise in consciou
ness[7] as a neatly distinct vowel. As soon as this haj

[5] See page 126.
[6] Primitive Germanic *fot(s)*, *fotiz*, *mus, musiz*; Indo-Europea
pods, podes, *mus, muses*. The vowels of the first syllables are a
long.
[7] Or in that unconscious sound patterning which is ever o
the point of becoming conscious. See page 55.

ened, the expression of plurality in *föti, töthi,* and
nalogous words became symbolic and fusional, not
merely fusional.

2. In *musi* "mice" the long *u* was colored by the
following *i* to long *ü*. This change also was regular;
usi "lice" became *lüsi, kui* "cows" became *küi* (later
implified to *kü;* still preserved as *ki-* in *kine*), *fulian*
to make foul" became *fülian* (still preserved as *-file*
in *defile*). The psychology of this phonetic law is en-
irely analogous to that of 1.

3. The old drift toward reducing final syllables, a
hythmic consequence of the strong Germanic stress
on the first syllable, now manifested itself. The final
i, originally an important functional element, had
ong lost a great share of its value, transferred as that
was to the symbolic vowel change (*o : ö*). It had little
power of resistance, therefore, to the drift. It became
dulled to a colorless *-e; föti* became *föte.*

4. The weak *-e* finally disappeared. Probably the
orms *föte* and *föt* long coexisted as prosodic variants
according to the rhythmic requirements of the sentence, very much as *Füsse* and *Füss'* now coexist in
German.

5. The *ö* of *föt* became "unrounded" to long *e* (our
present *a* of *fade*). The alternation of *fot: foti,* transi-
tionally *fot: föti, föte, föt,* now appears as *fot: fet.*
Analogously, *töth* appears as *teth, födian* as *fedian,*
later *fedan.* The new long *e*-vowel "fell together" with
the older *e*-vowel already existent (e.g., *her* "here,"
he "he"). Henceforward the two are merged and their
later history is in common. Thus our present *he* has
the same vowel as *feet, teeth,* and *feed.* In other words,
the old sound pattern *o, e,* after an interim of *o, ö, e,*
reappeared as *o, e,* except that now the *e* had greater
"weight" than before.

6. *Fot: fet, mus: müs* (written *mys*) are the typical
forms of Anglo-Saxon literature. At the very end of
the Anglo-Saxon period, say about 1050 to 1100 A.D.,
the *ü,* whether long or short, became unrounded to *i.*

Mys was then pronounced *mis* with long *i* (rhymin
with present *niece*). The change is analogous to 5, bu
takes place several centuries later.

7. In Chaucer's day (circa 1350-1400 A.D.) the form
were still *fot: fet* (written *foot, feet*) and *mus: m
(written very variably, but *mous, myse* are typical
About 1500 all the long *i*-vowels, whether original (a
in *write, ride, wine*) or unrounded from Anglo-Saxo
ü (as in *hide, bride, mice, defile*), became diphthong
ized to *ei* (i.e., *e* of *met* + short *i*). Shakespeare pro
nounced *mice* as *meis* (almost the same as the presen
Cockney pronunciation of *mace*).

8. About the same time the long *u*-vowels wer
diphthongized to *ou* (i.e., *o* of present Scotch *not* + :
of *full*). The Chaucerian *mus: mis* now appears as th
Shakespearean *mous: meis*. This change may hav
manifested itself somewhat later than 7; all Englisl
dialects have diphthongized old Germanic long *i*,[8] bu
the long undiphthongized *u* is still preserved in Low
land Scotch, in which *house* and *mouse* rhyme witl
our *loose*. 7 and 8 are analogous developments, a
were 5 and 6; 8 apparently lags behind 7 as 6, cen
turies earlier, lagged behind 7.

9. Some time before 1550 the long *e* of *fet* (writter
feet) took the position that had been vacated by the
old long *i*, now diphthongized (see 7), i.e., *e* took the
higher tongue position of *i*. Our (and Shakespeare's
"long *e*" is, then, phonetically the same as the old
long *i*. *Feet* now rhymed with the old *write* and the
present *beat*.

10. About the same time the long *o* of *fot* (writter
foot) took the position that had been vacated by the
old long *u*, now diphthongized (see 8), i.e., *o* took the
higher tongue position of *u*. Our (and Shakespeare's)
"long *oo*" is phonetically the same as the old long *u*.
Foot now rhymed with the old *out* and the present
boot. To summarize 7 to 10, Shakespeare pronounced

[8] As have most Dutch and German dialects.

neis, mous, fit, fut, of which *meis* and *mous* would
affect our ears as a rather "mincing" rendering of our
present *mice* and *mouse, fit* would sound practically
identical with (but probably a bit more "drawled"
than) our present *feet,* while *foot,* rhyming with *boot,*
would now be set down as "broad Scotch."

11. Gradually the first vowel of the diphthong in
nice (see 7) was retracted and lowered in position.
The resulting diphthong now varies in different English dialects, but *ai* (i.e., *a* of *father,* but shorter, +
short *i*) may be taken as a fairly accurate rendering of
its average quality.[9] What we now call the "long *i*"
of words like *ride, bite, mice*) is, of course, an *ai*-diph-
thong. *Mice* is now pronounced *mais.*

12. Analogously to 11, the first vowel of the diphthong in *mouse* (see 8) was unrounded and lowered
in position. The resulting diphthong may be phonetically rendered *au,* though it too varies considerably according to dialect. *Mouse,* then, is now pronounced *maus.*

13. The vowel of *foot* (see 10) became "open" in
quality and shorter in quantity, i.e., it fell together
with the old short *u*-vowel of words like *full, wolf,
wool.* This change has taken place in a number of
words with an originally long *u* (Chaucerian long close
ǫ), such as *forsook, hook, book, look, rook, shook,* all
of which formerly had the vowel of *boot.* The older
vowel, however, is still preserved in most words of
this class, such as *fool, moon, spool, stoop.* It is highly
significant of the nature of the slow spread of a "phonetic law" that there is local vacillation at present in
several words. One hears *roof, soot,* and *hoop,* for
instance, both with the "long" vowel of *boot* and the
"short" of *foot.* It is impossible now, in other words,
to state in a definitive manner what is the "phonetic
law" that regulated the change of the older *foot*
(rhyming with *boot*) to the present *foot.* We know

[9] At least in America.

that there is a strong drift towards the short, open vowel of *foot*, but whether or not all the old "long *oo*" words will eventually be affected we cannot presume to say. If they all, or practically all, are taken by the drift, phonetic law 13 will be as "regular," as sweeping, as most of the twelve that have preceded it. If not, it may eventually be possible, if past experience is a safe guide, to show that the modified words form a natural phonetic group, that is, that the "law" will have operated under certain definable limiting conditions, e.g., that all words ending in a voiceless consonant (such as *p*, *t*, *k*, *f*) were affected (e.g., *hoof, foot, look, roof*), but that all words ending in the *oo*-vowel or in a voiced consonant remained unaffected (e.g., *do, food, move, fool*). Whatever the upshot, we may be reasonably certain that when the "phonetic law" has run its course, the distribution of "long" and "short" vowels in the old *oo*-words will not seem quite as erratic as at the present transitional moment.[10] We learn, incidentally, the fundamental fact that phonetic laws do not work with spontaneous automatism, that they are simply a formula for a consummated drift that sets in at a psychologically exposed point and gradually worms its way through a gamut of phonetically analogous forms.

It will be instructive to set down a table of form sequences, a kind of gross history of the words *foot*, *feet, mouse, mice* for the last 1500 years:[11]

I. *fot: foti; mus: musi* (West Germanic)
II. *fot: föti; mus: müsi*
III. *fot: föte; mus: müse*
IV. *fot: föt; mus: müs*
V. *fot: fet; mus: müs* (Anglo-Saxon)

[10] It is possible that other than purely phonetic factors are also at work in the history of these vowels.

[11] The orthography is roughly phonetic. Pronounce all accented vowels long except where otherwise indicated, unaccented vowels short; give continental values to vowels, not present English ones.

VI.   *fot: fet; mus: mis* (Chaucer)
VII.   *fot: fet; mous: meis*
III.   *fut* (rhymes with *boot*): *fit; mous: meis* (Shakespeare)
IX.   *fut: fit; maus: mais*
X.   *fut* (rhymes with *put*): *fit; maus: mais* (English of 1900)

It will not be necessary to list the phonetic laws that gradually differentiated the modern German equivalents of the original West Germanic forms from their English cognates. The following table gives a rough idea of the form sequences in German:[12]

I.   *fot: foti; mus: musi* (West Germanic)
II.   *foss:*[13] *fossi; mus: musi*
III.   *fuoss: fuossi; mus: musi* (Old High German)
IV.   *fuoss: füessi; mus: müsi*
V.   *fuoss: füesse; mus: müse* (Middle High German)
VI.   *fuoss: füesse; mus: müze*[14]
VII.   *fuos: füese; mus: müze*
VIII.   *fuos: füese; mous: möüze*
IX.   *fus: füse; mous: möüze* (Luther)
X.   *fus: füse; maus: moize* (German of 1900)

We cannot even begin to ferret out and discuss all the psychological problems that are concealed behind

[12] After I. the numbers are not meant to correspond chronologically to those of the English table. The orthography is again roughly phonetic.

[13] I use *ss* to indicate a peculiar long, voiceless *s*-sound that was etymologically and phonetically distinct from the old Germanic *s*. It always goes back to an old *t*. In the old sources it is generally written as a variant of *z*, though it is not to be confused with the modern German *z* (= *ts*). It was probably a dental (lisped) *s*.

[14] Z is to be understood as French or English *z*, not in its German use. Strictly speaking, this "z" (intervocalic -*s*-) was not voiced but was a soft voiceless sound, a sibilant intermediate between our *s* and *z*. In modern North German it has become voiced to *z*. It is important not to confound this *s* — *z* with the voiceless intervocalic *s* that soon arose from the older lisped *ss*. In Modern German (aside from certain dialects), old *s* and *ss* are not now differentiated when final (*Maus* and *Fuss* have identical sibilants), but can still be distinguished as voiced and voiceless *s* between vowels (*Mäusse* and *Füsse*).

these bland tables. Their general parallelism is obvious. Indeed we might say that to-day the English and German forms resemble each other more than does either set the West Germanic prototypes from which each is independently derived. Each table illustrates the tendency to reduction of unaccented syllables, the vocalic modification of the radical element under the influence of the following vowel, the rise in tongue position of the long middle vowels (English *o* to *u*, *e* to *i*; German *o* to *uo* to *u*, *üe* to *ü*), the diphthongizing of the old high vowels (English *i* to *ei* to *ai*; English and German *u* to *ou* to *au*; German *ü* to *öü* to *oi*). These dialectic parallels cannot be accidental. They are rooted in a common, pre-dialectic drift.

Phonetic changes are "regular." All but one (English table, X.), and that as yet uncompleted, of the particular phonetic laws represented in our tables affect all examples of the sound in question or, if the phonetic change is conditional, all examples of the same sound that are analogously circumstanced.[15] An example of the first type of change is the passage in English of all old long *i*-vowels to diphthongal *ai* via *ei*. The passage could hardly have been sudden or automatic, but it was rapid enough to prevent an irregularity of development due to cross drifts. The second type of change is illustrated in the development of Anglo-Saxon long *o* to long *e*, via *ö*, under the influence of a following *i*. In the first case we may say that *au* mechanically replaced long *u*, in the second that the old long *o* "split" into two sounds— long *o*, eventually *u*, and long *e*, eventually *i*. The

---

[15] In practice phonetic laws have their exceptions, but more intensive study almost invariably shows that these exceptions are more apparent than real. They are generally due to the disturbing influence of morphological groupings or to special psychological reasons which inhibit the normal progress of the phonetic drift. It is remarkable with how few exceptions one need operate in linguistic history, aside from "analogical leveling" (morphological replacement).

former type of change did no violence to the old phonetic pattern, the formal distribution of sounds into groups; the latter type rearranged the pattern somewhat. If neither of the two sounds into which an old one "splits" is a new sound, it means that there has been a phonetic leveling, that two groups of words, each with a distinct sound or sound combination, have fallen together into one group. This kind of leveling is quite frequent in the history of language. In English, for instance, we have seen that all the old long *ü*-vowels, after they had become unrounded, were indistinguishable from the mass of long *i*-vowels. This meant that the long *i*-vowel became a more heavily weighted point of the phonetic pattern than before. It is curious to observe how often languages have striven to drive originally distinct sounds into certain favorite positions, regardless of resulting confusions.[16] In Modern Greek, for instance, the vowel *i* is the historical resultant of no less than ten etymologically distinct vowels (long and short) and diphthongs of the classical speech of Athens. There is, then, good evidence to show that there are general phonetic drifts toward particular sounds.

More often the phonetic drift is of a more general character. It is not so much a movement toward a particular set of sounds as toward particular types of articulation. The vowels tend to become higher or lower, the diphthongs tend to coalesce into monophthongs, the voiceless consonants tend to become voiced, stops tend to become spirants. As a matter of fact, practically all the phonetic laws enumerated in the two tables are but specific instances of such far-reaching phonetic drifts. The raising of English long *o* to *u* and of long *e* to *i,* for instance, was part of a general tendency to raise the position of the long

---

[16] These confusions are more theoretical than real, however. A language has countless methods of avoiding practical ambiguities.

vowels, just as the change of *t* to *ss* in Old High German was part of a general tendency to make voiceless spirants of the old voiceless stopped consonants. A single sound change, even if there is no phonetic leveling, generally threatens to upset the old phonetic pattern because it brings about a disharmony in the grouping of sounds. To reëstablish the old pattern without going back on the drift the only possible method is to have the other sounds of the series shift in analogous fashion. If, for some reason or other, *p* becomes shifted to its voiced correspondent *b*, the old series *p, t, k* appears in the unsymmetrical form *b, t, k*. Such a series is, in phonetic effect, not the equivalent of the old series, however it may answer to it in etymology. The general phonetic pattern is impaired to that extent. But if *t* and *k* are also shifted to their voiced correspondents *d* and *g*, the old series is reëstablished in a new form: *b, d, g*. The pattern as such is preserved, or restored. *Provided that* the new series *b, d, g* does not become confused with an old series *b, d, g* of distinct historical antecedents. If there is no such older series, the creation of a *b, d, g* series causes no difficulties. If there is, the old patterning of sounds can be kept intact only by shifting the old *b, d, g* sounds in some way. They may become aspirated to *bh, dh, gh* or spirantized or nasalized or they may develop any other peculiarity that keeps them intact as a series and serves to differentiate them from other series. And this sort of shifting about without loss of pattern, or with a minimum loss of it, is probably the most important tendency in the history of speech sounds. Phonetic leveling and "splitting" counteract it to some extent but, on the whole, it remains the central unconscious regulator of the course and speed of sound changes.

The desire to hold on to a pattern, the tendency to "correct" a disturbance by an elaborate chain of supplementary changes, often spread over centuries or

n millennia—these psychic undercurrents of lan-
age are exceedingly difficult to understand in terms
individual psychology, though there can be no de-
l of their historical reality. What is the primary
se of the unsettling of a phonetic pattern and what
the cumulative force that selects these or those par-
ular variations of the individual on which to float
pattern readjustments we hardly know. Many
guistic students have made the fatal error of think-
g of sound change as a quasi-physiological instead
as a strictly psychological phenomenon, or they
ve tried to dispose of the problem by bandying such
chwords as "the tendency to increased ease of ar-
ulation" or "the cumulative result of faulty per-
tion" (on the part of children, say, in learning to
ak). These easy explanations will not do. "Ease
articulation" may enter in as a factor, but it is a
her subjective concept at best. Indians find hope-
sly difficult sounds and sound combinations that
simple to us; one language encourages a phonetic
ft that another does everything to fight. "Faulty
ception" does not explain that impressive drift in
ech sounds which I have insisted upon. It is much
ter to admit that we do not yet understand the pri-
ry cause or causes of the slow drift in phonetics,
ough we can frequently point to contributing fac-
s. It is likely that we shall not advance seriously
til we study the intuitional bases of speech. How
n we understand the nature of the drift that frays
d reforms phonetic patterns when we have never
ought of studying sound patterning as such and the
eights" and psychic relations of the single elements
e individual sounds) in these patterns?
Every linguist knows that phonetic change is fre-
ently followed by morphological rearrangements,
t he is apt to assume that morphology exercises
tle or no influence on the course of phonetic his-
ry. I am inclined to believe that our present tend-

ency to isolate phonetics and grammar as mutual
irrelevant linguistic provinces is unfortunate. The
are likely to be fundamental relations between the
and their respective histories that we do not yet ful
grasp. After all, if speech sounds exist merely becau
they are the symbolic carriers of significant concep
and groupings of concepts, why may not a strong dr
or a permanent feature in the conceptual sphere exe
cise a furthering or retarding influence on the ph
netic drift? I believe that such influences may
demonstrated and that they deserve far more caref
study than they have received.

This brings us back to our unanswered questio
How is it that both English and German develope
the curious alternation of unmodified vowel in t
singular (*foot*, *Fuss*) and modified vowel in the plur
(*feet*, *Füsse*)? Was the pre-Anglo-Saxon alternation
fot and *föti* an absolutely mechanical matter, witho
other than incidental morphological interest? It
always so represented, and, indeed, all the extern
facts support such a view. The change from *o* to
later *e,* is by no means peculiar to the plural. It
found also in the dative singular (*fet*), for it too go
back to an older *foti*. Moreover, *fet* of the plural a
plies only to the nominative and accusative; the ge
tive has *fota,* the dative *fotum*. Only centuries lat
was the alternation of *o* and *e* reinterpreted as a mea
of distinguishing number; *o* was generalized for t
singular, *e* for the plural. Only when this reassortme
of forms took place[17] was the modern symbolic val
of the *foot: feet* alternation clearly established. Agai
we must not forget that *o* was modified to *ö* (*e*) in
manner of other grammatical and derivative form
tions. Thus, a pre-Anglo-Saxon *hohan* (later *hon*) "
hang" corresponded to a *höhith, hehith* (later *heht*
"hangs"; to *dom* "doom," *blod* "blood," and *f*

---

[17] A type of adjustment generally referred to as "analogi
leveling."

'food" corresponded the verbal derivatives *dömian* (later *deman*) "to deem," *blödian* (later *bledan*) "to bleed," and *födian* (later *fedan*) "to feed." All this seems to point to the purely mechanical nature of the modification of *o* to *ö* to *e*. So many unrelated functions were ultimately served by the vocalic change that we cannot believe that it was motivated by any one of them.

The German facts are entirely analogous. Only later in the history of the language was the vocalic alternation made significant for number. And yet consider the following facts. The change of *foti* to *föti* antedated that of *föti* to *föte, föt*. This may be looked upon as a "lucky accident," for if *foti* had become *fote, fot* before the *-i* had had the chance to exert a retroactive influence on the *o*, there would have been no difference between the singular and the plural. This would have been anomalous in Anglo-Saxon for a masculine noun. But was the sequence of phonetic changes an "accident"? Consider two further facts. All the Germanic languages were familiar with vocalic change as possessed of functional significance. Alternations like *sing, sang, sung* (Anglo-Saxon *singan, sang, sungen*) were ingrained in the linguistic consciousness. Further, the tendency toward the weakening of final syllables was very strong even then and had been manifesting itself in one way and another for centuries. I believe that these further facts help us to understand the actual sequence of phonetic changes. We may go so far as to say that the *o* (and *u*) could afford to stay the change to *ö* (and *ü*) until the destructive drift had advanced to the point where failure to modify the vowel would soon result in morphological embarrassment. At a certain moment the *-i* ending of the plural (and analogous endings with *i* in other formations) was felt to be too weak to quite bear its functional burden. The unconscious Anglo-Saxon mind, if I may be allowed a somewhat summary way of putting the complex facts, was glad of the opportunity afforded by certain individual variations, until then automatically canceled out, to have some share of the burden thrown on them. These particular variations won through because they so beautifully allowed the general phonetic drift to take its course without unsettling the morphological contours of the language. And the presence of symbolic variation (*sing, sang, sung*) acted as an attracting force on the rise of a new variation of similar character. All these factors were equally true of the German vocalic shift. Owing to the fact that the destructive phonetic drift was proceeding at a slower rate in German than in English, the preservative change of *uo* to *üe* (*u* to *ü*) did not need to set in until 300 years or more after the analogous English change. Nor did it. And this is to my mind a highly significant fact. Phonetic changes may sometimes be unconsciously encouraged in order to keep intact the psychological spaces between words and word forms. The general drift seizes upon those individual sound variations that help to preserve the morphological balance or to lead to the new balance that the language is striving for.

I would suggest, then, that phonetic change is compacted of at least three basic strands: (1) A general drift in one direction, concerning the nature of which we know almost nothing but which may be suspected to be of prevailingly dynamic character (tendencies, e.g., to greater or less stress, greater or less voicing of elements); (2) A readjusting tendency which aims to preserve or restore the fundamental phonetic pattern of the language; (3) A preservative tendency which sets in when a too serious morphological unsettlement is threatened by the main drift. I do not imagine for a moment that it is always possible to separate these strands or that this purely schematic statement does justice to the complex forces that guide the phonetic drift. The phonetic pattern of a language is not invariable, but it changes far less readily than the sounds that compose it. Every phonetic element that it possesses may change radically and yet the pattern remain unaffected. It would be absurd to claim that our present English pattern is identical with the old Indo-European one, yet it is impressive to note that even at this late day the English series of initial consonants:

$$p \quad t \quad k$$
$$b \quad d \quad g$$
$$f \quad th \quad h$$

corresponds point for point to the Sanskrit series:

$$b \quad d \quad g$$
$$bh \quad dh \quad gh$$
$$p \quad t \quad k$$

The relation between phonetic pattern and individual sound is roughly parallel to that which obtains between the morphologic type of a language and one of its specific morphological features. Both phonetic pattern and fundamental type are exceedingly conservative, all superficial appearances to the contrary notwithstanding. Which is more so we cannot say. I suspect that they hang together in a way that we cannot at present quite understand.

If all the phonetic changes brought about by the phonetic drift were allowed to stand, it is probable that most languages would present such irregularities of morphological contour as to lose touch with their formal ground-plan. Sound changes work mechanically. Hence they are likely to affect a whole morphological group here—this does not matter—, only part of a morphological group there—and this may be disturbing. Thus, the old Anglo-Saxon paradigm:

	Sing.	Plur.
N. Ac.	*fot*	*fet* (older *foti*)
G.	*fotes*	*fota*
D.	*fet* (older *foti*)	*fotum*

could not long stand unmodified. The *o—e* alternation was welcome in so far as it roughly distinguished the singular from the plural. The dative singular *fet*, however, though justified historically, was soon felt to be an intrusive feature. The analogy of simpler and more numerously represented paradigms created the form *fote* (compare, e.g., *fisc* "fish," dative singular *fisce*). *Fet* as a dative becomes obsolete. The singular now had *o* throughout. But this very fact made the genitive and dative *o*-forms of the plural seem out of place. The nominative and accusative *fet* was naturally far more frequently in use than were the corresponding forms of the genitive and dative. These, in the end, could not but follow the analogy of *fet*. At the very beginning of the Middle English period, therefore, we find that the old paradigm has yielded to a more regular one:

	Sing.	Plur.
N. Ac.	*fot	*fet
G.	*fotes	fete
D.	fote	feten

The starred forms are the old nucleus around which the new paradigm is built. The unstarred forms are not genealogical kin of their formal prototypes. They are analogical replacements.

The history of the English language teems with such levelings or extensions. *Elder* and *eldest* were at one time the only possible comparative and superlative forms of *old* (compare German *alt, älter, der älteste;* the vowel following the *old-, alt-* was originally an *i*, which modified the quality of the stem vowel). The general analogy of the vast majority of English adjectives, however, has caused the replacement of the forms *elder* and *eldest* by the forms with unmodified vowel, *older* and *oldest*. *Elder* and *eldest* survive only as somewhat archaic terms for the older and oldest brother or sister. This illustrates the tendency for words that are psychologically disconnected from their etymological or formal group to preserve traces of phonetic laws that have otherwise left no recognizable trace or to preserve a vestige of a morphological process that has long lost its vitality. A careful study of these survivals or atrophied forms is not without value for the reconstruction of the earlier history of a language or for suggestive hints as to its remoter affiliations.

Analogy may not only refashion forms within the confines of a related cluster of forms (a "paradigm") but may extend its influence far beyond. Of a number of functionally equivalent elements, for instance, only one may survive, the rest yielding to its constantly widening influence. This is what happened with the English -*s* plural. Originally confined to a particular class of masculines, though an important class, the -*s* plural was gradually generalized for all nouns but a mere handful that still illustrate plural types now all but extinct (*foot: feet, goose: geese, tooth: teeth, mouse: mice, louse: lice; ox: oxen; child: children; sheep: sheep, deer: deer*). Thus analogy not only regularizes irregularities that have come in the wake of phonetic processes but introduces disturbances, generally in favor of greater simplicity or regularity, in a long established system of forms. These analogical adjustments are practically always symptoms of the general morphological drift of the language.

A morphological feature that appears as the incidental consequence of a phonetic process, like the English plural with modified vowel, may spread by analogy no less readily than old features that owe their origin to other than phonetic causes. Once the *e*-vowel of Middle English *fet* had become confined to the plural, there was no theoretical reason why alternations of the type *fot: fet* and *mus: mis* might not have become established as a productive type of number distinction in the noun. As a matter of fact, it did not so become established. The *fot: fet* type of plural secured but a momentary foothold. It was swept into being by one of the surface drifts of the language, to be swept aside in the Middle English period by the more powerful drift toward the use of simple distinctive forms. It was too late in the day for our language to be seriously interested in such pretty symbolisms as *foot: feet*. What examples of the type arose legitimately, in other words *via* purely phonetic processes, were tolerated for a time, but the type as such never had a serious future.

It was different in German. The whole series of phonetic changes comprised under the term "umlaut," of which *u: ü* and *au: oi* (written *äu*) are but specific examples, struck the German language at a time when the general drift to morphological simplification was not so strong but that the resulting formal types (e.g., *Fuss: Füsse; fallen* "to fall": *fällen* "to fell"; *Horn* "horn": *Gehörne* "group of horns"; *Haus* "house": *Häuslein* "little house") could keep themselves intact and even extend to forms that did not legitimately come within their sphere of influence. "Umlaut" is still a very live symbolic process in German, possibly more alive to-day than in medieval times. Such analogical plurals as *Baum* "tree": *Bäume* (contrast Middle High German *boum: boume*) and derivatives as *lachen* "to laugh": *Gelächter* "laughter" (contrast Middle High German *gelach*) show that vocalic mutation has won through to the status of a productive morphologic process. Some of the dialects have even gone further than standard German, at least in certain respects. In Yiddish,[18] for instance, "umlaut" plurals have been formed where there are no Middle High German prototypes or modern literary

[18] Isolated from other German dialects in the late fifteenth and early sixteenth centuries. It is therefore a good test for gauging the strength of the tendency to "umlaut," particularly as it has developed a strong drift towards analytic methods.

parallels, e.g., *tog* "day": *teg* "days" (but German *Tag: Tage*) on the analogy of *gast* "guest": *gest* "guests" (German *Gast: Gäste*), *shuch*[19] "shoe": *shich* "shoes" (but German *Schuh: Schuhe*) on the analogy of *fus* "foot": *fis* "feet." It is possible that "umlaut" will run its course and cease to operate as a live functional process in German, but that time is still distant. Meanwhile all consciousness of the merely phonetic nature of "umlaut" vanished centuries ago. It is now a strictly morphological process, not in the least a mechanical phonetic adjustment. We have in it a splendid example of how a simple phonetic law, meaningless in itself, may eventually color or transform large reaches of the morphology of a language.

[19] *Ch* as in German *Buch.*

CHAPTER IX

How Languages Influence Each Other

○

Languages, like cultures, are rarely sufficient unto themselves. The necessities of intercourse bring the speakers of one language into direct or indirect contact with those of neighboring or culturally dominant languages. The intercourse may be friendly or hostile. It may move on the humdrum plane of business and trade relations or it may consist of a borrowing or interchange of spiritual goods—art, science, religion. It would be difficult to point to a completely isolated language or dialect, least of all among the primitive peoples. The tribe is often so small that intermarriages with alien tribes that speak other dialects or even totally unrelated languages are not uncommon. It may even be doubted whether intermarriage, intertribal trade, and general cultural interchanges are not of greater relative significance on primitive levels than on our own. Whatever the degree or nature of contact between neighboring peoples, it is generally sufficient to lead to some kind of linguistic interinfluencing. Frequently the influence runs heavily in one direction. The language of a people that is looked upon as a center of culture is naturally far more likely to exert an appreciable influence on other languages spoken in its vicinity than to be influenced by them. Chinese has flooded the vocabularies of Korean, Japanese, and

Annamite for centuries, but has received nothing in return. In the western Europe of medieval and modern times French has exercised a similar, though probably a less overwhelming, influence. English borrowed an immense number of words from the French of the Norman invaders, later also from the court French of Isle de France, appropriated a certain number of affixed elements of derivational value (e.g., *-ess* of *princess, -ard* of *drunkard, -ty* of *royalty*), may have been somewhat stimulated in its general analytic drift by contact with French,[1] and even allowed French to modify its phonetic pattern slightly (e.g., initial *v* and *j* in words like *veal* and *judge;* in words of Anglo-Saxon origin *v* and *j* can only occur after vowels, e.g., *over, hedge*). But English has exerted practically no influence on French.

The simplest kind of influence that one language may exert on another is the "borrowing" of words. When there is cultural borrowing there is always the likelihood that the associated words may be borrowed too. When the early Germanic peoples of northern Europe first learned of wine-culture and of paved streets from their commercial or warlike contact with the Romans, it was only natural that they should adopt the Latin words for the strange beverage (*vinum,* English *wine,* German *Wein*) and the unfamiliar type of road (*strata* [*via*], English *street,* German *Strasse*). Later, when Christianity was introduced into England, a number of associated words, such as *bishop* and *angel,* found their way into English. And so the process has continued uninterruptedly down to the present day, each cultural wave bringing to the language a new deposit of loan-words. The careful study of such loan-words constitutes an interesting commentary on the history of culture. One can almost

[1] The earlier students of English, however, grossly exaggerated the general "disintegrating" effect of French on Middle English. English was moving fast toward a more analytic structure long before the French influence set in.

estimate the rôle which various peoples have played in the development and spread of cultural ideas by taking note of the extent to which their vocabularies have filtered into those of other peoples. When we realize that an educated Japanese can hardly frame a single literary sentence without the use of Chinese resources, that to this day Siamese and Burmese and Cambodgian bear the unmistakable imprint of the Sanskrit and Pali that came in with Hindu Buddhism centuries ago, or that whether we argue for or against the teaching of Latin and Greek our argument is sure to be studded with words that have come to us from Rome and Athens, we get some inkling of what early Chinese culture and Buddhism and classical Mediterranean civilization have meant in the world's history. There are just five languages that have had an overwhelming significance as carriers of culture. They are classical Chinese, Sanskrit, Arabic, Greek, and Latin. In comparison with these even such culturally important languages as Hebrew and French sink into a secondary position. It is a little disappointing to learn that the general cultural influence of English has so far been all but negligible. The English language itself is spreading because the English have colonized immense territories. But there is nothing to show that it is anywhere entering into the lexical heart of other languages as French has colored the English complexion or as Arabic has permeated Persian and Turkish. This fact alone is significant of the power of nationalism, cultural as well as political, during the last century. There are now psychological resistances to borrowing, or rather to new sources of borrowing,[2] that were not greatly alive in the Middle Ages or during the Renaissance.

Are there resistances of a more intimate nature to the borrowing of words? It is generally assumed that

[2] For we still name our new scientific instruments and patent medicines from Greek and Latin.

the nature and extent of borrowing depend entirely on the historical facts of culture relation; that if German, for instance, has borrowed less copiously than English from Latin and French it is only because Germany has had less intimate relations than England with the culture spheres of classical Rome and France. This is true to a considerable extent, but it is not the whole truth. We must not exaggerate the physical importance of the Norman invasion nor underrate the significance of the fact that Germany's central geographical position made it peculiarly sensitive to French influences all through the Middle Ages, to humanistic influences in the latter fifteenth and early sixteenth centuries, and again to the powerful French influences of the seventeenth and eighteenth centuries. It seems very probable that the psychological attitude of the borrowing language itself towards linguistic material has much to do with its receptivity to foreign words. English has long been striving for the completely unified, unanalyzed word, regardless of whether it is monosyllabic or polysyllabic. Such words as *credible, certitude, intangible* are entirely welcome in English because each represents a unitary, well-nuanced idea and because their formal analysis (*cred-ible, cert-itude, in-tang-ible*) is not a necessary act of the unconscious mind (*cred-, cert-,* and *tang-* have no real existence in English comparable to that of *good-* in *goodness*). A word like *intangible,* once it is acclimated, is nearly as simple a psychological entity as any radical monosyllable (say *vague, thin, grasp*). In German, however, polysyllabic words strive to analyze themselves into significant elements. Hence vast numbers of French and Latin words, borrowed at the height of certain cultural influences, could not maintain themselves in the language. Latin-German words like *kredibel* "credible" and French-German words like *reussieren* "to succeed" offered nothing that the unconscious mind could assimilate to its customary method of feeling and handling words. It is as though this unconscious mind said: "I am perfectly willing to accept *kredibel* if you will just tell me what you mean by *kred-*." Hence German has generally found it easier to create new words out of its own resources, as the necessity for them arose.

The psychological contrast between English and German as regards the treatment of foreign material is a contrast that may be studied in all parts of the world. The Athabaskan languages of America are spoken by peoples that have had astonishingly varied cultural contacts, yet nowhere do we find that an Athabaskan dialect has borrowed at all freely[3] from a neighboring language. These languages have always found it easier to create new words by compounding afresh elements ready to hand. They have for this reason been highly resistant to receiving the linguistic impress of the external cultural experiences of their speakers. Cambodgian and Tibetan offer a highly instructive contrast in their reaction to Sanskrit influence. Both are analytic languages, each totally different from the highly wrought, inflective language of India. Cambodgian is isolating, but, unlike Chinese, it contains many polysyllabic words whose etymological analysis does not matter. Like English, therefore, in its relation to French and Latin, it welcomed immense numbers of Sanskrit loan-words, many of which are in common use to-day. There was no psychological resistance to them. Classical Tibetan literature was a slavish adaptation of Hindu Buddhist literature and nowhere has Buddhism implanted itself more firmly than in Tibet, yet it is strange how few Sanskrit words have found their way into the language. Tibetan was highly resistant to the polysyllabic words of Sanskrit because they could not automatically fall into significant syllables, as they should have in order

[3] One might all but say, "has borrowed at all."

to satisfy the Tibetan feeling for form. Tibetan was therefore driven to translating the great majority of these Sanskrit words into native equivalents. The Tibetan craving for form was satisfied, though the literally translated foreign terms must often have done violence to genuine Tibetan idiom. Even the proper names of the Sanskrit originals were carefully translated, element for element, into Tibetan; e.g., *Surya-garbha* "Sun-bosomed" was carefully Tibetanized into *Nyi-mai snying-po* "Sun-of heart-the, the heart (or essence) of the sun." The study of how a language reacts to the presence of foreign words—rejecting them, translating them, or freely accepting them— may throw much valuable light on its innate formal tendencies.

The borrowing of foreign words always entails their phonetic modification. There are sure to be foreign sounds or accentual peculiarities that do not fit the native phonetic habits. They are then so changed as to do as little violence as possible to these habits. Frequently we have phonetic compromises. Such an English word as the recently introduced *camouflage,* as now ordinarily pronounced, corresponds to the typical phonetic usage of neither English nor French. The aspirated *k,* the obscure vowel of the second syllable, the precise quality of the *l* and of the last *a,* and, above all, the strong accent on the first syllable, are all the results of unconscious assimilation to our English habits of pronunciation. They differentiate our *camouflage* clearly from the same word as pronounced by the French. On the other hand, the long, heavy vowel in the third syllable and the final position of the "zh" sound (like *z* in *azure*) are distinctly un-English, just as, in Middle English, the initial *j* and v^4 must have been felt at first as not strictly in accord with English usage, though the strangeness has worn off by now. In all four of these cases—initial *j,* initial

[4] See page 193.

v, final "zh," and unaccented *a* of *father*—English has not taken on a new sound but has merely extended the use of an old one.

Occasionally a new sound is introduced, but it is likely to melt away before long. In Chaucer's day the old Anglo-Saxon *ü* (written *y*) had long become unrounded to *i*, but a new set of *ü*-vowels had come in from the French (in such words as *due, value, nature*). The new *ü* did not long hold its own; it became diphthongized to *iu* and was amalgamated with the native *iw* of words like *new* and *slew*. Eventually this diphthong appears as *yu*, with change of stress—*dew* (from Anglo-Saxon *deaw*) like *due* (Chaucerian *dü*). Facts like these show how stubbornly a language resists radical tampering with its phonetic pattern.

Nevertheless, we know that languages do influence each other in phonetic respects, and that quite aside from the taking over of foreign sounds with borrowed words. One of the most curious facts that linguistics has to note is the occurrence of striking phonetic parallels in totally unrelated or very remotely related languages of a restricted geographical area. These parallels become especially impressive when they are seen contrastively from a wide phonetic perspective. Here are a few examples. The Germanic languages as a whole have not developed nasalized vowels. Certain Upper German (Suabian) dialects, however, have now nasalized vowels in lieu of the older vowel + nasal consonant (*n*). Is it only accidental that these dialects are spoken in proximity to French, which makes abundant use of nasalized vowels? Again, there are certain general phonetic features that mark off Dutch and Flemish in contrast, say, to North German and Scandinavian dialects. One of these is the presence of unaspirated voiceless stops (*p, t, k*), which have a precise, metallic quality reminiscent of the corresponding French sounds, but which contrast with the stronger, aspirated stops of English, North German, and Danish. Even if we assume that the unaspirated stops are more archaic, that they are the unmodified descendants of the old Germanic consonants, is it not perhaps a significant historical fact that the Dutch dialects, neighbors of French, were inhibited from modifying these consonants in accordance with what seems to have been a general Germanic phonetic drift? Even more striking than these instances is the peculiar resemblance, in certain special phonetic respects, of Russian and other Slavic languages to the unrelated Ural-Altaic languages[5] of the Volga region. The peculiar, dull vowel, for instance, known in Russian as "yeri" [6] has Ural-Altaic analogues, but is entirely wanting in Germanic, Greek, Armenian, and Indo-Iranian, the nearest Indo-European congeners of Slavic. We may at least suspect that the Slavic vowel is not historically unconnected with its Ural-Altaic parallels. One of the most puzzling cases of phonetic parallelism is afforded by a large number of American Indian languages spoken west of the Rockies. Even at the most radical estimate there are at least four totally unrelated linguistic stocks represented in the region from southern Alaska to central California. Nevertheless all, or practically all, the languages of this immense area have some important phonetic features in common. Chief of these is the presence of a "glottalized" series of stopped consonants of very distinctive formation and of quite unusual acoustic effect.[7] In the northern part of the area all the languages, whether related or not, also possess various voiceless *l*-sounds and a series of "velar" (back-guttural) stopped consonants which are etymologically distinct from the ordinary *k*-series. It is difficult to believe that three

---

[5] Ugro-Finnic and Turkish (Tartar).

[6] Probably, in Sweet's terminology, high-back (or, better, between back and "mixed" positions)-narrow-unrounded. It generally corresponds to an Indo-European long *u*.

[7] There seem to be analogous or partly analogous sounds in certain languages of the Caucasus.

such peculiar phonetic features as I have mentioned could have evolved independently in neighboring groups of languages.

How are we to explain these and hundreds of similar phonetic convergences? In particular cases we may really be dealing with archaic similarities due to a genetic relationship that it is beyond our present power to demonstrate. But this interpretation will not get us far. It must be ruled entirely out of court, for instance, in two of the three European examples I have instanced; both nasalized vowels and the Slavic "yeri" are demonstrably of secondary origin in Indo-European. However we envisage the process in detail, we cannot avoid the inference that there is a tendency for speech sounds or certain distinctive manners of articulation to spread over a continuous area in somewhat the same way that elements of culture ray out from a geographical center. We may suppose that individual variations arising at linguistic borderlands —whether by the unconscious suggestive influence of foreign speech habits or by the actual transfer of foreign sounds into the speech of bilingual individuals—have gradually been incorporated into the phonetic drift of a language. So long as its main phonetic concern is the preservation of its sound patterning, not of its sounds as such, there is really no reason why a language may not unconsciously assimilate foreign sounds that have succeeded in worming their way into its gamut of individual variations, provided always that these new variations (or reinforced old variations) are in the direction of the native drift.

A simple illustration will throw light on this conception. Let us suppose that two neighboring and unrelated languages, A and B, each possess voiceless *l*-sounds (compare Welsh *ll*). We surmise that this is not an accident. Perhaps comparative study reveals the fact that in language A the voiceless *l*-sounds correspond to a sibilant series in other related languages.

that an old alternation *s:sh* has been shifted to the
new alternation *l* (voiceless): *s*.[8] Does it follow that
the voiceless *l* of language B has had the same history? Not in the least. Perhaps B has a strong tendency toward audible breath release at the end of a
word, so that the final *l*, like a final vowel, was originally followed by a marked aspiration. Individuals
perhaps tended to anticipate a little the voiceless release and to "unvoice" the latter part of the final
l-sound (very much as the *l* of English words like *felt*
tends to be partly voiceless in anticipation of the
voicelessness of the *t*). Yet this final *l* with its latent
tendency to unvoicing might never have actually developed into a fully voiceless *l* had not the presence
of voiceless *l*-sounds in A acted as an unconscious
stimulus or suggestive push toward a more radical
change in the line of B's own drift. Once the final
voiceless *l* emerged, its alternation in related words
with medial voiced *l* is very likely to have led to its
analogical spread. The result would be that both A
and B have an important phonetic trait in common.
Eventually their phonetic systems, judged as mere
assemblages of sounds, might even become completely
assimilated to each other, though this is an extreme
case hardly ever realized in practice. The highly significant thing about such phonetic interinfluencings
is the strong tendency of each language to keep its
phonetic pattern intact. So long as the respective
alignments of the similar sounds is different, so long
as they have differing "values" and "weights" in the
unrelated languages, these languages cannot be said
to have diverged materially from the line of their
inherent drift. In phonetics, as in vocabulary, we must
be careful not to exaggerate the importance of inter-
linguistic influences.

I have already pointed out in passing that English
has taken over a certain number of morphological

---

[8] This can actually be demonstrated for one of the Athabaskan
dialects of the Yukon.

elements from French. English also uses a number of affixes that are derived from Latin and Greek. Some of these foreign elements, like the *-ize* of *materialize* or the *-able* of *breakable,* are even productive to-day. Such examples as these are hardly true evidences of a morphological influence exerted by one language on another. Setting aside the fact that they belong to the sphere of derivational concepts and do not touch the central morphological problem of the expression of relational ideas, they have added nothing to the structural peculiarities of our language. English was already prepared for the relation of *pity* to *piteous* by such a native pair as *luck* and *lucky; material* and *materialize* merely swelled the ranks of a form pattern familiar from such instances as *wide* and *widen.* In other words, the morphological influence exerted by foreign languages on English, if it is to be gauged by such examples as I have cited, is hardly different in kind from the mere borrowing of words. The introduction of the suffix *-ize* made hardly more difference to the essential build of the language than did the mere fact that it incorporated a given number of words. Had English evolved a new future on the model of the synthetic future in French or had it borrowed from Latin and Greek their employment or reduplication as a functional device (Latin *tango: tetigi;* Greek *leipo: leloipa*), we should have the right to speak of true morphological influence. But such far-reaching influences are not demonstrable. Within the whole course of the history of the English language we can hardly point to one important morphological change that was not determined by the native drift, though here and there we may surmise that this drift was hastened a little by the suggestive influence of French forms.[9]

[9] In the sphere of syntax one may point to certain French and Latin influences, but it is doubtful if they ever reached deeper than the written language. Much of this type of influence belongs rather to literary style than to morphology proper.

It is important to realize the continuous, self-contained morphological development of English and the very modest extent to which its fundamental build has been affected by influences from without. The history of the English language has sometimes been represented as though it relapsed into a kind of chaos on the arrival of the Normans, who proceeded to play nine-pins with the Anglo-Saxon tradition. Students are more conservative to-day. That a far-reaching analytic development may take place without such external foreign influence as English was subjected to is clear from the history of Danish, which has gone even further than English in certain leveling tendencies. English may be conveniently used as an *a fortiori* test. It was flooded with French loan-words during the later Middle Ages, at a time when its drift toward the analytic type was especially strong. It was therefore changing rapidly both within and on the surface. The wonder, then, is not that it took on a number of external morphological features, mere accretions on its concrete inventory, but that, exposed as it was to remolding influences, it remained so true to its own type and historic drift. The experience gained from the study of the English language is strengthened by all that we know of documented linguistic history. Nowhere do we find any but superficial morphological interinfluencings. We may infer one of several things from this:—That a really serious morphological influence is not, perhaps, impossible, but that its operation is so slow that it has hardly ever had the chance to incorporate itself in the relatively small portion of linguistic history that lies open to inspection; or that there are certain favorable conditions that make for profound morphological disturbances from without, say a peculiar instability of linguistic type or an unusual degree of cultural contact, conditions that do not happen to be realized in our documentary material; or, finally, that we have not the right to assume that a language may easily exert a remolding morphological influence on another.

Meanwhile we are confronted by the baffling fact that important traits of morphology are frequently found distributed among widely differing languages within a large area, so widely differing, indeed, that it is customary to consider them genetically unrelated. Sometimes we may suspect that the resemblance is due to a mere convergence, that a similar morphological feature has grown up independently in unrelated languages. Yet certain morphological distributions are too specific in character to be so lightly dismissed. There must be some historical factor to account for them. Now it should be remembered that the concept of a "linguistic stock" is never definitive[10] in an exclusive sense. We can only say, with reasonable certainty, that such and such languages are descended from a common source, but we cannot say that such and such other languages are not genetically related. All we can do is to say that the evidence for relationship is not cumulative enough to make the inference of common origin absolutely necessary. May it not be, then, that many instances of morphological similarity between divergent languages of a restricted area are merely the last vestiges of a community of type and phonetic substance that the destructive work of diverging drifts has now made unrecognizable? There is probably still enough lexical and morphological resemblance between modern English and Irish to enable us to make out a fairly conclusive case for their genetic relationship on the basis of the present-day descriptive evidence alone. It is true that the case would seem weak in comparison to the case that we can actually make with the help of the historical and the comparative data that we possess. It would not be a bad case nevertheless. In another two or three millennia, however, the points of resemblance are likely

[10] See page 153.

to have become so obliterated that English and Irish, in the absence of all but their own descriptive evidence, will have to be set down as "unrelated" languages. They will still have in common certain fundamental morphological features, but it will be difficult to know how to evaluate them. Only in the light of the contrastive perspective afforded by still more divergent languages, such as Basque and Finnish, will these vestigial resemblances receive their true historic value.

I cannot but suspect that many of the more significant distributions of morphological similarities are to be explained as just such vestiges. The theory of "borrowing" seems totally inadequate to explain those fundamental features of structure, hidden away in the very core of the linguistic complex, that have been pointed out as common, say, to Semitic and Hamitic, to the various Soudanese languages, to Malayo-Polynesian and Mon-Khmer[11] and Munda,[12] to Athabaskan and Tlingit and Haida. We must not allow ourselves to be frightened away by the timidity of the specialists, who are often notably lacking in the sense of what I have called "contrastive perspective."

Attempts have sometimes been made to explain the distribution of these fundamental structural features by the theory of diffusion. We know that myths, religious ideas, types of social organization, industrial devices, and other features of culture may spread from point to point, gradually making themselves at home in cultures to which they were at one time alien. We also know that words may be diffused no less freely than cultural elements, that sounds also may be "borrowed," and that even morphological elements may be taken over. We may go further and recognize that

---

[11] A group of languages spoken in southeastern Asia, of which Khmer (Cambodian) is the best known representative.
[12] A group of languages spoken in northeastern India.

certain languages have, in all probability, taken on
structural features owing to the suggestive influence
of neighboring languages. An examination of such
cases,[13] however, almost invariably reveals the signifi
cant fact that they are but superficial additions on
the morphological kernel of the language. So long a
such direct historical testimony as we have gives u
no really convincing examples of profound morpho
logical influence by diffusion, we shall do well not to
put too much reliance in diffusion theories. On the
whole, therefore, we shall ascribe the major con
cordances and divergences in linguistic form—pho
netic pattern and morphology—to the autonomous
drift of language, not to the complicating effect of
single, diffused features that cluster now this way
now that. Language is probably the most self-con
tained, the most massively resistant of all social
phenomena. It is easier to kill it off than to disinte
grate its individual form.

[13] I have in mind, e.g., the presence of postpositions in Upper
Chinook, a feature that is clearly due to the influence of neigh
boring Sahaptin languages; or the use by Takelma of instrumen
tal prefixes, which are likely to have been suggested by neigh
boring "Hokan" languages (Shasta, Karok).

CHAPTER X

Language, Race and Culture

○

Language has a setting. The people that speak it belong to a race (or a number of races), that is, to a group which is set off by physical characteristics from other groups. Again, language does not exist apart from culture, that is, from the socially inherited assemblage of practices and beliefs that determines the texture of our lives. Anthropologists have been in the habit of studying man under the three rubrics of race, language, and culture. One of the first things they do with a natural area like Africa or the South Seas is to map it out from this threefold point of view. These maps answer the questions: What and where are the major divisions of the human animal, biologically considered (e.g., Congo Negro, Egyptian White; Australian Black, Polynesian)? What are the most inclusive linguistic groupings, the "linguistic stocks," and what is the distribution of each (e.g., the Hamitic languages of northern Africa, the Bantu languages of the south; the Malayo-Polynesian languages of Indonesia, Melanesia, Micronesia, and Polynesia)? How do the peoples of the given area divide themselves as cultural beings? what the outstanding "cultural areas" and what are the dominant ideas in each (e.g., the Mohammedan north of Africa; the primitive hunting, non-agricultural culture of the Bushmen in the south;

the culture of the Australian natives, poor in physical
respects but richly developed in ceremonialism; the
more advanced and highly specialized culture of Polynesia)?

The man in the street does not stop to analyze his
position in the general scheme of humanity. He feels
that he is the representative of some strongly integrated portion of humanity—now thought of as a
"nationality," now as a "race"—and that everything
that pertains to him as a typical representative of this
large group somehow belongs together. If he is an
Englishman, he feels himself to be a member of the
"Anglo-Saxon" race, the "genius" of which race has
fashioned the English language and the "Anglo-
Saxon" culture of which the language is the expression. Science is colder. It inquires if these three types
of classification—racial, linguistic, and cultural—are
congruent, if their association is an inherently necessary one or is merely a matter of external history. The
answer to the inquiry is not encouraging to "race"
sentimentalists. Historians and anthropologists find
that races, languages, and cultures are not distributed
in parallel fashion, that their areas of distribution
intercross in the most bewildering fashion, and that
the history of each is apt to follow a distinctive course.
Races intermingle in a way that languages do not. On
the other hand, languages may spread far beyond
their original home, invading the territory of new
races and of new culture spheres. A language may
even die out in its primary area and live on among
peoples violently hostile to the persons of its original
speakers. Further, the accidents of history are constantly rearranging the borders of culture areas without necessarily effacing the existing linguistic cleav-
ages. If we can once thoroughly convince ourselves
that race, in its only intelligible, that is biological,
sense, is supremely indifferent to the history of languages and cultures, that these are no more directly
explainable on the score of race than on that of the

aws of physics and chemistry, we shall have gained
viewpoint that allows a certain interest to such
nystic slogans as Slavophilism, Anglo-Saxondom, Teu-
onism, and the Latin genius but that quite refuses
o be taken in by any of them. A careful study of
inguistic distributions and of the history of such
listributions is one of the driest of commentaries on
hese sentimental creeds.

That a group of languages need not in the least cor-
espond to a racial group or a culture area is easily
lemonstrated. We may even show how a single lan-
ruage intercrosses with race and culture lines. The
nglish language is not spoken by a unified race. In
he United States there are several millions of negroes
who know no other language. It is their mother-
ongue, the formal vesture of their inmost thoughts
nd sentiments. It is as much their property, as inal-
enably "theirs," as the King of England's. Nor do the
nglish-speaking whites of America constitute a defi-
ite race except by way of contrast to the negroes. Of
he three fundamental white races in Europe generally
ecognized by physical anthropologists—the Baltic or
North European, the Alpine, and the Mediterranean
—each has numerous English-speaking representatives
n America. But does not the historical core of Eng-
ish-speaking peoples, those relatively "unmixed" populations that still reside in England and its colonies,
epresent a race, pure and single? I cannot see that
the evidence points that way. The English people are
an amalgam of many distinct strains. Besides the old
'Anglo-Saxon," in other words North German, element which is conventionally represented as the basic
strain, the English blood comprises Norman French,[1]
Scandinavian, "Celtic," [2] and pre-Celtic elements. If

---

[1] Itself an amalgam of North "French" and Scandinavian elements.

[2] The "Celtic" blood of what is now England and Wales is by
no means confined to the Celtic-speaking regions—Wales and,
until recently, Cornwall. There is every reason to believe that
the invading Germanic tribes (Angles, Saxons, Jutes) did not

by "English" we mean also Scotch and Irish,[3] then the term "Celtic" is loosely used for at least two quite distinct racial elements—the short, dark-complexioned type of Wales and the taller, lighter, often ruddy-haired type of the Highlands and parts of Ireland. Even if we confine ourselves to the Saxon element, which, needless to say, nowhere appears "pure," we are not at the end of our troubles. We may roughly identify this strain with the racial type now predominant in southern Denmark and adjoining parts of northern Germany. If so, we must content ourselves with the reflection that while the English language is historically most closely affiliated with Frisian, in second degree with the other West Germanic dialects (Low Saxon or "Plattdeutsch," Dutch, High German), only in third degree with Scandinavian, the specific "Saxon" racial type that overran England in the fifth and sixth centuries was largely the same as that now represented by the Danes, who speak a Scandinavian language, while the High German-speaking population of central and southern Germany[4] is markedly distinct.

But what if we ignore these finer distinctions and simply assume that the "Teutonic" or Baltic or North European racial type coincided in its distribution with that of the Germanic languages? Are we not on safe

exterminate the Brythonic Celts of England nor yet drive them altogether into Wales and Cornwall (there has been far too much "driving" of conquered peoples into mountain fastnesses and land's ends in our histories), but simply intermingled with them and imposed their rule and language upon them.

[3] In practice these three peoples can hardly be kept altogether distinct. The terms have rather a local-sentimental than a clearly racial value. Intermarriage has gone on steadily for centuries and it is only in certain outlying regions that we get relatively pure types, e.g., the Highland Scotch of the Hebrides. In America, English, Scotch, and Irish strands have become inextricably interwoven.

[4] The High German now spoken in northern Germany is not of great age, but is due to the spread of standardized German, based on Upper Saxon, a High German dialect, at the expense of "Plattdeutsch."

ground then? No, we are now in hotter water than ever. First of all, the mass of the German-speaking population (central and southern Germany, German Switzerland, German Austria) do not belong to the tall, blond-haired, long-headed [5] "Teutonic" race at all, but to the shorter, darker-complexioned, short-headed [6] Alpine race, of which the central population of France, the French Swiss, and many of the western and northern Slavs (e.g., Bohemians and Poles) are equally good representatives. The distribution of these "Alpine" populations corresponds in part to that of the old continental "Celts," whose language has everywhere given way to Italic, Germanic, and Slavic pressure. We shall do well to avoid speaking of a "Celtic race," but if we were driven to give the term a content, it would probably be more appropriate to apply it to, roughly, the western portion of the Alpine peoples than to the two island types that I referred to before. These latter were certainly "Celticized," in speech and, partly, in blood, precisely as, centuries later, most of England and part of Scotland was "Teutonized" by the Angles and Saxons. Linguistically speaking, the "Celts" of to-day (Irish Gaelic, Manx, Scotch Gaelic, Welsh, Breton) are Celtic and most of the Germans of to-day are Germanic precisely as the American Negro, Americanized Jew, Minnesota Swede, and German-American are "English." But, secondly, the Baltic race was, and is, by no means an exclusively Germanic-speaking people. The northernmost "Celts," such as the Highland Scotch, are in all probability a specialized offshoot of this race. What these people spoke before they were Celticized nobody knows, but there is nothing whatever to indicate that they spoke a Germanic language. Their language may quite well have been as remote from any known Indo-European idiom as are Basque and Turkish to-day. Again, to the

[5] "Dolichocephalic."
[6] "Brachycephalic."

east of the Scandinavians are non-Germanic members of the race—the Finns and related peoples, speaking languages that are not definitely known to be related to Indo-European at all.

We cannot stop here. The geographical position of the Germanic languages is such[7] as to make it highly probable that they represent but an outlying transfer of an Indo-European dialect (possibly a Celto-Italic prototype) to a Baltic people speaking a language or a group of languages that was alien to Indo-European.[8] Not only, then, is English not spoken by a unified race at present but its prototype, more likely than not, was originally a foreign language to the race with which English is more particularly associated. We need not seriously entertain the idea that English or the group of languages to which it belongs is in any intelligible sense the expression of race, that there are embedded in it qualities that reflect the temperament or "genius" of a particular breed of human beings.

Many other, and more striking, examples of the lack of correspondence between race and language could be given if space permitted. One instance will do for many. The Malayo-Polynesian languages form a well-defined group that takes in the southern end of the Malay Peninsula and the tremendous island world to the south and east (except Australia and the greater part of New Guinea). In this vast region we find represented no less than three distinct races—the Negro-

---

[7] By working back from such data as we possess we can make it probable that these languages were originally confined to a comparatively small area in northern Germany and Scandinavia. This area is clearly marginal to the total area of distribution of the Indo-European-speaking peoples. Their center of gravity, say 1000 B.C., seems to have lain in southern Russia.

[8] While this is only a theory, the technical evidence for it is stronger than one might suppose. There are a surprising number of common and characteristic Germanic words which cannot be connected with known Indo-European radical elements and which may well be survivals of the hypothetical pre-Germanic language; such are *house, stone, sea, wife* (German *Haus, Stein, See, Weib*).

like Papuans of New Guinea and Melanesia, the Malay race of Indonesia, and the Polynesians of the outer islands. The Polynesians and Malays *all* speak languages of the Malayo-Polynesian group, while the languages of the Papuans belong partly to this group (Melanesian), partly to the unrelated languages ("Papuan") of New Guinea.[9] In spite of the fact that the greatest race cleavage in this region lies between the Papuans and the Polynesians, the major linguistic division is of Malayan on the one side, Melanesian and Polynesian on the other.

As with race, so with culture. Particularly in more primitive levels, where the secondarily unifying power of the "national" [10] ideal does not arise to disturb the flow of what we might call natural distributions, is it easy to show that language and culture are not intrinsically associated. Totally unrelated languages share in one culture, closely related languages—even a single language—belong to distinct culture spheres. There are many excellent examples in aboriginal America. The Athabaskan languages form as clearly unified, as structurally specialized, a group as any that I know of.[11] The speakers of these languages belong to four distinct culture areas—the simple hunting culture of western Canada and the interior of Alaska (Loucheux, Chipewyan), the buffalo culture of the Plains (Sarcee),

[9] Only the easternmost part of this island is occupied by Melanesian-speaking Papuans.

[10] A "nationality" is a major, sentimentally unified, group. The historical factors that lead to the feeling of national unity are various—political, cultural, linguistic, geographic, sometimes specifically religious. True racial factors also may enter in, though the accent on "race" has generally a psychological rather than a strictly biological value. In an area dominated by the national sentiment there is a tendency for language and culture to become uniform and specific, so that linguistic and cultural boundaries at least tend to coincide. Even at best, however, the linguistic unification is never absolute, while the cultural unity is apt to be superficial, of a quasi-political nature, rather than deep and far-reaching.

[11] The Semitic languages, idiosyncratic as they are, are no more definitely earmarked.

the highly ritualized culture of the southwest (Navaho), and the peculiarly specialized culture of north-
western California (Hupa). The cultural adaptability
of the Athabaskan-speaking peoples is in the strangest
contrast to the inaccessibility to foreign influences of
the languages themselves.[12] The Hupa Indians are
very typical of the culture area to which they belong.
Culturally identical with them are the neighboring
Yurok and Karok. There is the liveliest intertribal
intercourse between the Hupa, Yurok, and Karok, so
much so that all three generally attend an important
religious ceremony given by any one of them. It is difficult to say what elements in their combined culture
belong in origin to this tribe or that, so much at one
are they in communal action, feeling, and thought.
But their languages are not merely alien to each other;
they belong to three of the major American linguistic
groups, each with an immense distribution on the
northern continent. Hupa, as we have seen, is Athabaskan and, as such, is also distantly related to Haida
(Queen Charlotte Islands) and Tlingit (southern
Alaska); Yurok is one of the two isolated Californian
languages of the Algonkin stock, the center of gravity
of which lies in the region of the Great Lakes; Karok
is the northernmost member of the Hokan group,
which stretches far to the south beyond the confines
of California and has remoter relatives along the Gulf
of Mexico.

Returning to English, most of us would readily
admit, I believe, that the community of language between Great Britain and the United States is far from
arguing a like community of culture. It is customary
to say that they possess a common "Anglo-Saxon" cultural heritage, but are not many significant differences
in life and feeling obscured by the tendency of the
"cultured" to take this common heritage too much for
granted? In so far as America is still specifically "English," it is only colonially or vestigially so; its prevail-

[12] See page 196.

ing cultural drift is partly towards autonomous and distinctive developments, partly towards immersion in the larger European culture of which that of England is only a particular facet. We cannot deny that the possession of a common language is still and will long continue to be a smoother of the way to a mutual cultural understanding between England and America, but it is very clear that other factors, some of them rapidly cumulative, are working powerfully to counteract this leveling influence. A common language cannot indefinitely set the seal on a common culture when the geographical, political, and economic determinants of the culture are no longer the same throughout its area.

Language, race, and culture are not necessarily correlated. This does not mean that they never are. There is some tendency, as a matter of fact, for racial and cultural lines of cleavage to correspond to linguistic ones, though in any given case the latter may not be of the same degree of importance as the others. Thus, there is a fairly definite line of cleavage between the Polynesian languages, race, and culture on the one hand and those of the Melanesians on the other, in spite of a considerable amount of overlapping.[13] The racial and cultural division, however, particularly the former, are of major importance, while the linguistic division is of quite minor significance, the Polynesian languages constituting hardly more than a special dialectic subdivision of the combined Melanesian-Polynesian group. Still clearer-cut coincidences of cleavage may be found. The language, race, and culture of the Eskimo are markedly distinct from those of their neighbors;[14] in southern Africa the language, race, and

---

[13] The Fijians, for instance, while of Papuan (negroid) race, are Polynesian rather than Melanesian in their cultural and linguistic affinities.

[14] Though even here there is some significant overlapping. The southernmost Eskimo of Alaska were assimilated in culture to their Tlingit neighbors. In northeastern Siberia, too, there is no sharp cultural line between the Eskimo and the Chukchi.

culture of the Bushmen offer an even stronger contrast to those of their Bantu neighbors. Coincidences of this sort are of the greatest significance, of course, but this significance is not one of inherent psychological relation between the three factors of race, language, and culture. The coincidences of cleavage point merely to a readily intelligible historical association. If the Bantu and Bushmen are so sharply differentiated in all respects, the reason is simply that the former are relatively recent arrivals in southern Africa. The two peoples developed in complete isolation from each other; their present propinquity is too recent for the slow process of cultural and racial assimilation to have set in very powerfully. As we go back in time, we shall have to assume that relatively scanty populations occupied large territories for untold generations and that contact with other masses of population was not as insistent and prolonged as it later became. The geographical and historical isolation that brought about race differentiations was naturally favorable also to far-reaching variations in language and culture. The very fact that races and cultures which are brought into historical contact tend to assimilate in the long run, while neighboring languages assimilate each other only casually and in superficial respects,[15] indicates that there is no profound causal relation between the development of language and the specific development of race and of culture.

But surely, the wary reader will object, there must be some relation between language and culture, and between language and at least that intangible aspect of race that we call "temperament." Is it not inconceivable that the particular collective qualities of mind that have fashioned a culture are not precisely the same as were responsible for the growth of a particular linguistic morphology? This question takes us

[15] The supersession of one language by another is of course not truly a matter of linguistic assimilation.

into the heart of the most difficult problems of social psychology. It is doubtful if any one has yet attained to sufficient clarity on the nature of the historical process and on the ultimate psychological factors involved in linguistic and cultural drifts to answer it intelligently. I can only very briefly set forth my own views, or rather my general attitude. It would be very difficult to prove that "temperament," the general emotional disposition of a people,[16] is basically responsible for the slant and drift of a culture, however much it may manifest itself in an individual's handling of the elements of that culture. But granted that temperament has a certain value for the shaping of culture, difficult though it be to say just how, it does not follow that it has the same value for the shaping of language. It is impossible to show that the form of a language has the slightest connection with national temperament. Its line of variation, its drift, runs inexorably in the channel ordained for it by its historic antecedents; it is as regardless of the feelings and sentiments of its speakers as is the course of a river of the atmospheric humors of the landscape. I am convinced that it is futile to look in linguistic structure for differences corresponding to the temperamental variations which are supposed to be correlated with race. In this connection it is well to remember that the emotional aspect of our psychic life is but meagerly expressed in the build of language.[17]

Language and our thought-grooves are inextricably

[16] "Temperament" is a difficult term to work with. A great deal of what is loosely charged to national "temperament" is really nothing but customary behavior, the effect of traditional ideals of conduct. In a culture, for instance, that does not look kindly upon demonstrativeness, the natural tendency to the display of emotion becomes more than normally inhibited. It would be quite misleading to argue from the customary inhibition, a cultural fact, to the native temperament. But ordinarily we can get at human conduct only as it is culturally modified. Temperament in the raw is a highly elusive thing.

[17] See pages 38, 39.

interrelated, are, in a sense, one and the same. As there is nothing to show that there are significant racial differences in the fundamental conformation of thought, it follows that the infinite variability of linguistic form, another name for the infinite variability of the actual process of thought, cannot be an index of such significant racial differences. This is only apparently a paradox. The latent content of all languages is the same—the intuitive *science* of experience. It is the manifest form that is never twice the same, for this form, which we call linguistic morphology, is nothing more nor less than a collective *art* of thought, an art denuded of the irrelevancies of individual sentiment. At last analysis, then, language can no more flow from race as such than can the sonnet form.

Nor can I believe that culture and language are in any true sense causally related. Culture may be defined as *what* a society does and thinks. Language is a particular *how* of thought. It is difficult to see what particular causal relations may be expected to subsist between a selected inventory of experience (culture, a significant selection made by society) and the particular manner in which the society expresses all experience. The drift of culture, another way of saying history, is a complex series of changes in society's selected inventory—additions, losses, changes of emphasis and relation. The drift of language is not properly concerned with changes of content at all, merely with changes in formal expression. It is possible, in thought, to change every sound, word, and concrete concept of a language without changing its inner actuality in the least, just as one can pour into a fixed mold water or plaster or molten gold. If it can be shown that culture has an innate form, a series of contours, quite apart from subject-matter of any description whatsoever, we have a something in culture that may serve as a term of comparison with and possibly a means of relating it to language. But until such purely formal patterns of culture are discovered and laid bare, we shall do well to hold the drifts of language and of culture to be non-comparable and unrelated processes. From this it follows that all attempts to connect particular types of linguistic morphology with certain correlated stages of cultural development are vain. Rightly understood, such correlations are rubbish. The merest *coup d'œil* verifies our theoretical argument on this point. Both simple and complex types of language of an indefinite number of varieties may be found spoken at any desired level of cultural advance. When it comes to linguistic form, Plato walks with the Macedonian swineherd, Confucius with the head-hunting savage of Assam.

It goes without saying that the mere content of language is intimately related to culture. A society that has no knowledge of theosophy need have no name for it; aborigines that had never seen or heard of a horse were compelled to invent or borrow a word for the animal when they made his acquaintance. In the sense that the vocabulary of a language more or less faithfully reflects the culture whose purposes it serves it is perfectly true that the history of language and the history of culture move along parallel lines. But this superficial and extraneous kind of parallelism is of no real interest to the linguist except in so far as the growth or borrowing of new words incidentally throws light on the formal trends of the language. The linguistic student should never make the mistake of identifying a language with its dictionary.

If both this and the preceding chapter have been largely negative in their contentions, I believe that they have been healthily so. There is perhaps no better way to learn the essential nature of speech than to realize what it is not and what it does not do. Its superficial connections with other historic processes are so close that it needs to be shaken free of them if we are to see it in its own right. Everything that we have so far seen to be true of language points to the fact that it is the most significant and colossal work that the human spirit has evolved—nothing short of a finished form of expression for all communicable experience. This form may be endlessly varied by the individual without thereby losing its distinctive contours; and it is constantly reshaping itself as is all art. Language is the most massive and inclusive art we know, a mountainous and anonymous work of unconscious generations.

CHAPTER XI

Language and Literature

o

Languages are more to us than systems of thought-transference. They are invisible garments that drape themselves about our spirit and give a predetermined form to all its symbolic expression. When the expression is of unusual significance, we call it literature.[1] Art is so personal an expression that we do not like to feel that it is bound to predetermined form of any sort. The possibilities of individual expression are infinite, language in particular is the most fluid of mediums. Yet some limitation there must be to this freedom, some resistance of the medium. In great art there is the illusion of absolute freedom. The formal restraints imposed by the material—paint, black and white, marble, piano tones, or whatever it may be—are not perceived; it is as though there were a limitless margin of elbow-room between the artist's fullest utilization of form and the most that the material is innately capable of. The artist has intuitively surrendered to the inescapable tyranny of the material, made its brute nature fuse easily with his conception.[2] The

[1] I can hardly stop to define just what kind of expression is "significant" enough to be called art or literature. Besides, I do not exactly know. We shall have to take literature for granted.

[2] This "intuitive surrender" has nothing to do with subservience to artistic convention. More than one revolt in modern art has been dominated by the desire to get out of the material just

material "disappears" precisely because there is nothing in the artist's conception to indicate that any other material exists. For the time being, he, and we with him, move in the artistic medium as a fish moves in the water, oblivious of the existence of an alien atmosphere. No sooner, however, does the artist transgress the law of his medium than we realize with a start that there is a medium to obey.

Language is the medium of literature as marble or bronze or clay are the materials of the sculptor. Since every language has its distinctive peculiarities, the innate formal limitations—and possibilities—of one literature are never quite the same as those of another. The literature fashioned out of the form and substance of a language has the color and the texture of its matrix. The literary artist may never be conscious of just how he is hindered or helped or otherwise guided by the matrix, but when it is a question of translating his work into another language, the nature of the original matrix manifests itself at once. All his effects have been calculated, or intuitively felt, with reference to the formal "genius" of his own language; they cannot be carried over without loss or modification. Croce[3] is therefore perfectly right in saying that a work of literary art can never be translated. Nevertheless literature does get itself translated, sometimes with astonishing adequacy. This brings up the question whether in the art of literature there are not intertwined two distinct kinds or levels of art—a generalized, non-linguistic art, which can be transferred without loss into an alien linguistic medium, and a

what it is really capable of. The impressionist wants light and color because paint can give him just these; "literature" in painting, the sentimental suggestion of a "story," is offensive to him because he does not want the virtue of his particular form to be dimmed by shadows from another medium. Similarly, the poet, as never before, insists that words mean just what they really mean.

[3] See Benedetto Croce, *Aesthetic*.

specifically linguistic art that is not transferable.[4] I
believe the distinction is entirely valid, though we
never get the two levels pure in practice. Literature
moves in language as a medium, but that medium
comprises two layers, the latent content of language
—our intuitive record of experience—and the particular conformation of a given language—the specific
how of our record of experience. Literature that draws
its sustenance mainly—never entirely—from the lower
level, say a play of Shakespeare's, is translatable without too great a loss of character. If it moves in the
upper rather than in the lower level—a fair example
is a lyric of Swinburne's—it is as good as untranslat-
able. Both types of literary expression may be great or
mediocre.

There is really no mystery in the distinction. It can
be clarified a little by comparing literature with science. A scientific truth is impersonal, in its essence it
is untinctured by the particular linguistic medium in
which it finds expression. It can as readily deliver its
message in Chinese[5] as in English. Nevertheless it must
have some expression, and that expression must needs
be a linguistic one. Indeed the apprehension of the
scientific truth is itself a linguistic process, for thought
is nothing but language denuded of its outward garb.
The proper medium of scientific expression is there-

[4] The question of the transferability of art productions seems
to me to be of genuine theoretic interest. For all that we speak
of the sacrosanct uniqueness of a given art work, we know very
well, though we do not always admit it, that not all productions
are equally intractable to transference. A Chopin étude is in-
violate; it moves altogether in the world of piano tone. A Bach
fugue is transferable into another set of musical timbres without serious loss of esthetic significance. Chopin plays with the
language of the piano as though no other language existed (the
medium "disappears"); Bach speaks the language of the piano
as a handy means of giving outward expression to a conception
wrought in the generalized language of tone.

[5] Provided, of course, Chinese is careful to provide itself with
the necessary scientific vocabulary. Like any other language, it
can do so without serious difficulty if the need arises.

fore a generalized language that may be defined as a
symbolic algebra of which all known languages are
translations. One can adequately translate scientific
literature because the original scientific expression is
itself a translation. Literary expression is personal and
concrete, but this does not mean that its significance
is altogether bound up with the accidental qualities of
the medium. A truly deep symbolism, for instance,
does not depend on the verbal associations of a particular language but rests securely on an intuitive basis
that underlies all linguistic expression. The artist's
"intuition," to use Croce's term, is immediately fashioned out of a generalized human experience—
thought and feeling—of which his own individual experience is a highly personalized selection. The thought
relations in this deeper level have no specific linguistic
vesture; the rhythms are free, not bound, in the first
instance, to the traditional rhythms of the artist's language. Certain artists whose spirit moves largely in the
non-linguistic (better, in the generalized linguistic)
layer even find a certain difficulty in getting themselves expressed in the rigidly set terms of their accepted idiom. One feels that they are unconsciously
striving for a generalized art language, a literary algebra, that is related to the sum of all known languages
as a perfect mathematical symbolism is related to all
the roundabout reports of mathematical relations that
normal speech is capable of conveying. Their art expression is frequently strained, it sounds at times like
a translation from an unknown original—which, indeed, is precisely what it is. These artists—Whitmans
and Brownings—impress us rather by the greatness of
their spirit than the felicity of their art. Their relative
failure is of the greatest diagnostic value as an index
of the pervasive presence in literature of a larger,
more intuitive linguistic medium than any particular
language.

Nevertheless, human expression being what it is, the

greatest—or shall we say the most satisfying—literary artists, the Shakespeares and Heines, are those who have known subconsciously to fit or trim the deeper intuition to the provincial accents of their daily speech. In them there is no effect of strain. Their personal "intuition" appears as a completed synthesis of the absolute art of intuition and the innate, specialized art of the linguistic medium. With Heine, for instance, one is under the illusion that the universe speaks German. The material "disappears."

Every language is itself a collective art of expression. There is concealed in it a particular set of esthetic factors—phonetic, rhythmic, symbolic, morphological —which it does not completely share with any other language. These factors may either merge their potencies with those of that unknown, absolute language to which I have referred—this is the method of Shakespeare and Heine—or they may weave a private, technical art fabric of their own, the innate art of the language intensified or sublimated. The latter type, the more technically "literary" art of Swinburne and of hosts of delicate "minor" poets, is too fragile for endurance. It is built out of spiritualized material, not out of spirit. The successes of the Swinburnes are as valuable for diagnostic purposes as the semi-failures of the Brownings. They show to what extent literary art may lean on the collective art of the language itself. The more extreme technical practitioners may so over-individualized this collective art as to make it almost unendurable. One is not always thankful to have one's flesh and blood frozen to ivory.

An artist must utilize the native esthetic resources of his speech. He may be thankful if the given palette of colors is rich, if the springboard is light. But he deserves no special credit for felicities that are the language's own. We must take for granted this language with all its qualities of flexibility or rigidity and see the artist's work in relation to it. A cathedral on the lowlands is higher than a stick on Mont Blanc. In other words, we must not commit the folly of admiring a French sonnet because the vowels are more sonorous than our own or of condemning Nietzche's prose because it harbors in its texture combinations of consonants that would affright on English soil. To so judge literature would be tantamount to loving "Tristan und Isolde" because one is fond of the timbre of horns. There are certain things that one language can do supremely well which it would be almost vain for another to attempt. Generally there are compensations. The vocalism of English is an inherently drabber thing than the vowel scale of French, yet English compensates for this drawback by its greater rhythmical alertness. It is even doubtful if the innate sonority of a phonetic system counts for as much, as esthetic determinant, as the relations between the sounds, the total gamut of their similarities and contrasts. As long as the artist has the wherewithal to lay out his sequences and rhythms, it matters little what are the sensuous qualities of the elements of his material.

The phonetic groundwork of a language, however, is only one of the features that give its literature a certain direction. Far more important are its morphological peculiarities. It makes a great deal of difference for the development of style if the language can or cannot create compound words, if its structure is synthetic or analytic, if the words of its sentences have considerable freedom of position or are compelled to fall into a rigidly determined sequence. The major characteristics of style, in so far as style is a technical matter of the building and placing of words, are given by the language itself, quite as inescapably, indeed, as the general acoustic effect of verse is given by the sounds and natural accents of the language. These necessary fundamentals of style are hardly felt by the artist to constrain his individuality of expression. They rather point the way to those stylistic developments that most suit the natural bent of the language.

It is not in the least likely that a truly great style can seriously oppose itself to the basic form patterns of the language. It not only incorporates them, it builds on them. The merit of such a style as W. H. Hudson's or George Moore's[6] is that it does with ease and economy what the language is always trying to do. Carlylese, though individual and vigorous, is yet not style; it is a Teutonic mannerism. Nor is the prose of Milton and his contemporaries strictly English; it is semi-Latin done into magnificent English words.

It is strange how long it has taken the European literatures to learn that style is not an absolute, a something that is to be imposed on the language from Greek or Latin models, but merely the language itself, running in its natural grooves, and with enough of an individual accent to allow the artist's personality to be felt as a presence, not as an acrobat. We understand more clearly now that what is effective and beautiful in one language is a vice in another. Latin and Eskimo, with their highly inflected forms, lend themselves to an elaborately periodic structure that would be boring in English. English allows, even demands, a looseness that would be insipid in Chinese. And Chinese, with its unmodified words and rigid sequences, has a compactness of phrase, a terse parallelism, and a silent suggestiveness that would be too tart, too mathematical, for the English genius. While we cannot assimilate the luxurious period of Latin nor the pointilliste style of the Chinese classics, we can enter sympathetically into the spirit of these alien techniques.

I believe that any English poet of to-day would be thankful for the concision that a Chinese poetaster attains without effort. Here is an example:[7]

---

[6] Aside from individual peculiarities of diction, the selection and evaluation of particular words as such.

[7] Not by any means a great poem, merely a bit of occasional verse written by a young Chinese friend of mine when he left Shanghai for Canada.

Wu-river[8] stream mouth evening sun sink,
North look Liao-Tung,[9] not see home.
Steam whistle several noise, sky-earth boundless,
Float float one reed out Middle-Kingdom.

These twenty-eight syllables may be clumsily interpreted: "At the mouth of the Yangtsze River, as the
sun is about to sink, I look north toward Liao-Tung
but do not see my home. The steam-whistle shrills
several times on the boundless expanse where meet
sky and earth. The steamer, floating gently like a hollow reed, sails out of the Middle Kingdom." [10] But
we must not envy Chinese its terseness unduly. Our
more sprawling mode of expression is capable of its
own beauties, and the more compact luxuriance of
Latin style has its loveliness too. There are almost as
many natural ideals of literary style as there are languages. Most of these are merely potential, awaiting
the hand of artists who will never come. And yet in
the recorded texts of primitive tradition and song
there are many passages of unique vigor and beauty.
The structure of the language often forces an assemblage of concepts that impresses us as a stylistic discovery. Single Algonkin words are like tiny imagist
poems. We must be careful not to exaggerate a fresh-
ness of content that is at least half due to our fresh-
ness of approach, but the possibility is indicated none
the less of utterly alien literary styles, each distinctive
with its disclosure of the search of the human spirit
for beautiful form.

Probably nothing better illustrates the formal de-
pendence of literature on language than the prosodic
aspect of poetry. Quantitative verse was entirely natural to the Greeks, not merely because poetry grew

[8] The old name of the country about the mouth of the Yangtsze.
[9] A province of Manchuria.
[10] I.e., China.

up in connection with the chant and the dance,[11] but because alternations of long and short syllables were keenly live facts in the daily economy of the language. The tonal accents, which were only secondarily stress phenomena, helped to give the syllable its quantitative individuality. When the Greek meters were carried over into Latin verse, there was comparatively little strain, for Latin too was characterized by an acute awareness of quantitative distinctions. However, the Latin accent was more markedly stressed than that of Greek. Probably, therefore, the purely quantitative meters modeled after the Greek were felt as a shade more artificial than in the language of their origin. The attempt to cast English verse into Latin and Greek molds has never been successful. The dynamic basis of English is not quantity,[12] but stress, the alternation of accented and unaccented syllables. This fact gives English verse an entirely different slant and has determined the development of its poetic forms, is still responsible for the evolution of new forms. Neither stress nor syllabic weight is a very keen psychologic factor in the dynamics of French. The syllable has great inherent sonority and does not fluctuate significantly as to quantity and stress. Quantitative or accentual metrics would be as artificial in French as stress metrics in classical Greek or quantitative or purely syllabic metrics in English. French prosody was compelled to develop on the basis of unit syllable-groups. Assonance, later rhyme, could not but prove a welcome, an all but necessary, means of articulating or sectioning the somewhat spineless movement of sonorous syllables. English was hospitable to the French

[11] Poetry everywhere is inseparable in its origins from the singing voice and the measure of the dance. Yet accentual and syllabic types of verse, rather than quantitative verse, seem to be the prevailing norms.

[12] Quantitative distinctions exist as an objective fact. They have not the same inner, psychological value that they had in Greek.

suggestion of rhyme, but did not seriously need it in its rhythmic economy. Hence rhyme has always been strictly subordinated to stress as a somewhat decorative feature and has been frequently dispensed with. It is no psychologic accident that rhyme came later into English than in French and is leaving it sooner.[13] Chinese verse has developed along very much the same lines as French verse. The syllable is an even more integral and sonorous unit than in French, while quantity and stress are too uncertain to form the basis of a metric system. Syllable-groups—so and so many syllables per rhythmic unit—and rhyme are therefore two of the controlling factors in Chinese prosody. The third factor, the alternation of syllables with level tone and syllables with inflected (rising or falling) tone, is peculiar to Chinese.

To summarize, Latin and Greek verse depends on the principle of contrasting weights; English verse, on the principle of contrasting stresses; French verse, on the principles of number and echo; Chinese verse, on the principles of number, echo, and contrasting pitches. Each of these rhythmic systems proceeds from the unconscious dynamic habit of the language, falling from the lips of the folk. Study carefully the phonetic system of a language, above all its dynamic features, and you can tell what kind of a verse it has developed—or, if history has played pranks with its psychology, what kind of verse it should have developed and some day will.

Whatever be the sounds, accents, and forms of a language, however these lay hands on the shape of its literature, there is a subtle law of compensations that gives the artist space. If he is squeezed a bit here, he can swing a free arm there. And generally he has rope

[13] Verhaeren was no slave to the Alexandrine, yet he remarked to Symons, à propos of the translation of Les Aubes, that while he approved of the use of rhymeless verse in the English version, he found it "meaningless" in French.

enough to hang himself with, if he must. It is not strange that this should be so. Language is itself the collective art of expression, a summary of thousands upon thousands of individual intuitions. The individual goes lost in the collective creation, but his personal expression has left some trace in a certain give and flexibility that are inherent in all collective works of the human spirit. The language is ready, or can be quickly made ready, to define the artist's individuality. If no literary artist appears, it is not essentially because the language is too weak an instrument, it is because the culture of the people is not favorable to the growth of such personality as seeks a truly individual verbal expression.

INDEX

Glottal cords, 47; action of, 47–9

Glottal stop, 48

Gothic, 78, 164, 172

Grammar, 38

Grammatical element, 26–32

Grammatical concepts. See *Concepts, grammatical.*

Grammatical processes, classified by, languages, 126–8; particular, development by each language of, 60–1; types of, 61–2; variety, use in one language of, 59–60

Greek, dialectic history of, 151–2

Greek, classical: affixing, 137; compounds, 65; concord, 114–15; infixing, 72; influence, 194, 202; pitch accent, 79; plurality, 95; reduplicated perfects, 78, 202; stress, 79; structure, 131, 141, 143; synthetic character, 129; verse, 228–9, 230

Greek, modern, 129, 153, 181, 199

Haida (British Columbia), 55, 142, 205, 214

Hamitic languages (N. Africa), 73–4, 205, 207

Hausa (Soudan), 78

Hebrew, 59–60, 70, 73, 143, 194

Heine, 225

Hesitation, 161–2, 171

History, linguistic, 144–6, 147–191

Hokan languages (N. Amer.), 206, 214

Hottentot (S. Africa), 53, 68, 77

Hudson, W. H., 227

Humming, 49

Hupa (N. California), 68, 69, 70, 214

Hupa Indians, 214

Icelandic, Old, 164

India, languages of, 52

Indians, American, languages of, 33–5, 48, 50, 55, 56, 80–1, 99, 123, 199–200. See also *Algonkin; Athabaskan; Chimariko; Chinook; Eskimo; Fox; Haida; Hokan; Hupa; Iroquois; Karok; Kwakiutl; Nahuatl; Nass; Navaho; Nootka; Ojibwa; Paiute; Sahaptin; Salinan; Shasta; Siouan; Sioux; Takelma; Tlingit; Tsimshian; Washo; Yana; Yokuts; Yurok.*

Indo-Chinese languages, 146, 154

Indo-European, 24, 72, 78, 153–4, 163–4, 171, 174, 187, 199, 200, 212

Indo-Iranian languages, 163, 199

Infixes, 26, 61, 72–3

Inflection. See *Inflective languages.*

Inflective languages, 123, 129–33, 135–6, 137–8, 145–6

Influence, cultural, reflected in language, 192–7; morphological, of alien language, 202–04, 206; phonetic, of alien language, 197–201

Inspiratory sounds, 53

Interjections, 5–7

Irish, 210, 211

Irish, 75, 153, 204–05

Iroquois (N. Amer.), 66, 67

Isolating languages, 123, 126, 139, 142

Italian, 52, 53, 129, 153

"Its," history of, 156, 165

Japanese, 192–3, 194

Jutes, 209

Juxtaposing. See *Agglutination.*

Karok (N. California), 206, 214; K. Indians, 214

Khmer. See *Cambodian.*

Knowledge, source of: as grammatical category, 109

Koine, 151, 152

HARVEST BOOKS